Palgrave Studies i

Serie
Thoma
Clark Unive.

Deborah Mayersen
University of Wollongong, Australia

Tom Lawson
Northumbria University, UK

Genocide has shaped human experience throughout history and is one of the greatest challenges of the twenty-first century. Palgrave Studies in the History of Genocide is dedicated to the study of this phenomenon across its entire geographic, chronological and thematic range. The series acts as a forum to debate and discuss the nature, the variety, and the concepts of genocide. In addition to histories of the causes, course, and perpetration of genocide, the series devotes attention to genocide's victims, its aftermaths and consequences, its representation and memorialization, and to genocide prevention. Palgrave Studies in the History of Genocide encompasses both comparative work, which considers genocide across time and space, and specific case studies.

More information about this series at
http://www.palgrave.com/gp/series/14582

Taner Akçam

Killing Orders

Talat Pasha's Telegrams and
the Armenian Genocide

Taner Akçam
Clark University
Worcester, MA, USA

Palgrave Studies in the History of Genocide
ISBN 978-3-319-69786-4   ISBN 978-3-319-69787-1   (eBook)
https://doi.org/10.1007/978-3-319-69787-1

Library of Congress Control Number: 2017961007

Cover illustration: The Ottoman Archives of the Prime Minister's Office (the Ottoman archives): BOA.A.}d, Ministry Registries, 01520.001

Printed on acid-free paper

This Palgrave Macmillan imprint is published by Springer Nature
The registered company is Springer International Publishing AG
The registered company address is: Gewerbestrasse 11, 6330 Cham, Switzerland

To my dear friend Hrant Dink, who dreamt of bringing the Armenians and people of Turkey together on the basis of Truth and Justice.
His assassination in 2007 did not kill this dream, but instead inspired hundreds of thousands of individuals to follow in his footsteps.
And to my daughter Helin, who gives me hope in the next generation's ability to carry on Hrant's dream for a better future.

ABOUT THE BOOK

This book presents new evidence and arguments that prove the killing orders for the Armenian Genocide issued by Talat Pasha are authentic. For decades it has been claimed that these incriminating documents and the memoirs of the Ottoman bureaucrat Naim Efendi, in which they are preserved, were forgeries.

A NOTE ON TRANSLITERATION

We have strived for consistency in the spelling of names, even when the same name is spelled differently within the same document. Armenian names are rendered as they are spelled in Naim's text, followed in square brackets by how they are commonly known in modern English in the west.

Ottoman Turkish names are rendered generally as they are spelled in modern Turkish, with a few exceptions. Characters with a circumflex, such as "â," are rendered without the circumflex. The capital letter "İ" is rendered as "I." The names of individuals well-known in the English language are rendered in anglicized form, e.g., "Talat" instead of "Talaat" or "Talât," the title "Pasha" instead of "Paşa." The names of cities well-known in the English language are rendered in anglicized form, e.g., "Aleppo" instead of "Halep," "Beirut" instead of "Beyrut," "Diyarbekir", instead of "Diyarbakır," "Marash" instead of "Maraş." Turkish language publications referenced in the footnotes, however, are reproduced in their full, Modern Turkish form.

Key to Transcription and Pronunciation of Ottoman-Turkish Words and Names

Turkish Special Characters and Their Pronunciation

c *j* as in *just*
ç *ch* as in *chair*
ğ *gh* as in *though*, or *w* as in *sowing*
ı *u* as in *just*
j *zh* as in *gendarme, azure,* or *garage*
ö *oe* as in *Goethe* or, *i*, as in *girl*; French *eu* as in *seul*; German *ö* as in *Öl* or *öffentlich*
ş *sh* as in *sugar, shut,* or *she*
ü high *u* as in *blue*; French *u* as in *du*; German *ü* as in *Lüge*

Major Abbreviations in the Book

AMMU	General Directorate of Tribal and Immigrant Settlement (*Aşair ve Muhacirin Müdiriyeti Umumiyesi*)
BOA.A.}d	Ministry Registries (*Sadaret Defteri*)
BOA.BEO.	Grand Vezier's Chancery Office (*Babıali Evrak Odası Evrakı*)

BOA.DH.EUM.	Interior Ministry Public Security Directorate (*Dahiliye Nezareti Emniyet-i Umumiye Müdürlüğü*)
BOA.DH.EUM. 2.	Şube: Second Department of Public Security of the Interior Ministry (*Dahiliye Nezareti Emniyet-i Umumiye İkinci Şube*)
BOA.DH.EUM.LVZ.	Provisioning Office of the Interior Ministry's General Security (*Dahiliye Nezareti Emniyeti Umumiye Levazım Kalemi*)
BOA.DH.EUM.MH.	Record Office of Officials of the Interior Ministry's General Security (*Dahiliye Nezareti Emniyeti Umumiye Memurin Kalem Evrakı*)
BOA.DH.EUM.VRK.	The Records Office of the Interior Ministry's General Security [Office] Registry (*Dahiliye Nezareti Emniyeti Umumiye Evrak Odası Kalemi Evrakı*)
BOA.DH.KMS.	Record Office of the Interior Ministry's Private Secretariat (*Dahiliye Nezareti Dahiliye Kalemi Mahsus Evrakı*)
BOA.DH.ŞFR.	Cipher Office of the Interior Ministry (*Dahiliye Nezareti Şifre Kalemi*)
BOA.İ.MMS.	Directorate of Personnel and Service Registers (*İrada Meclisi Mahsus*)
BOA.MF.MKT.	The Correspondence Office of the Education Ministry (*Maarif Nezareti Mektubi Kalemi*)
BOA.ŞD.	Papers of the Council of State (*Şuray-ı Devlet Evrakı*)
CUP	Ittihad ve Terakki (Committee of Union and Progress; members are Unionists)
DE/PA-AA	German Foreign Ministry Political Archive (*Politisches Archiv des Auswärtigen Amts*)
IAMM	Interior Ministry's Office of Tribal and Immigrant Settlement (*Dahiliye Nezareti İskan-ı Aşair ve Muhacir'in Müdüriyeti*)
SO	Teşkilatı Mahsusa (Special Organization)
TV	*Takvimi Vekayi* ("Calendar of Events"—Official Gazette of the Ottoman Government)

THE OTTOMAN PROVINCIAL HIERARCHY OF GOVERNORS

Rank in Turkish	Rank in English	Jurisdiction in Turkish	Jurisdiction in English
Vali	Governor-General	Vilayet	Province
Mutasarrif	District Governor	Sancak, liva	Provincial district
		Mutasarrıflık	Provincial district government
Kaymakam (Kadı)	County Executive [Head]	Kaza	County
Müdir	Administrator	Nahiye	Township
Muhtar	Headman	Karye	Village

CONTENTS

LIST OF FIGURES

Subjects and Events Mentioned by Naim Efendi Corroborated in Ottoman Documents

Preface

FACTS, TRUTHS, AND DENIAL

There is a story, according to which French Premier Clemenceau, shortly before his death in 1929, was engaged in a friendly chat with a representative of the Weimar Republic on the question of guilt for the outbreak of the First World War. "What, in your opinion," Clemenceau was asked, "will future historians think of this troublesome and controversial issue?" He replied "This I don't know. But I know for certain that they will not say Belgium invaded Germany."[1]

The relationship between facts and truth remains a hotly contested topic in the social sciences. As a rule, facts, opinions, and interpretations are considered as different things, separate from one another. The "truth" rests upon established facts, over which there is a consensus; as such, they are not the same thing as opinion or interpretation; to deny the truth is to deny established facts. So we would like to believe. Yet, as Hannah Arendt once mused,

> But do facts, independent of opinion and interpretation, exist at all? Have not generations of historians and philosophers of history demonstrated the impossibility of ascertaining facts without interpretation, since they must first be picked out of a chaos of sheer happenings (and the principles of choice are surely not factual data) and then be fitted into a story that can be told only in a certain perspective, which has nothing to do with the original occurrence? No doubt these and a great many more perplexities inherent in

© The Author(s) 2018
T. Akçam, *Killing Orders*, Palgrave Studies in the History of Genocide,
https://doi.org/10.1007/978-3-319-69787-1_1

the historical sciences are real, but they are no argument against the existence of factual matter, nor can they serve as a justification for blurring the dividing lines between fact, opinion, and interpretation, or as an excuse for the historian to manipulate facts as he pleases.[2]

Continuing with Arendt's thoughts, we can argue that each generation has the right to write its own history and *interpret* facts in accordance with its own perspective, but not to *alter* them. The honest effort must be made to differentiate between that which is claimed to have happened and what the evidence indicates actually *did* happen. One does not have the right to manipulate the factual matter itself.[3]

In this context, the practice of "denialism" in regard to mass atrocities is usually thought of as a simple denial of the facts, but this is not true. Rather, it is in that nebulous territory between facts and truth where such denialism germinates. Denialism marshals its own facts and it has its own truth. Ultimately, the debates over denialism do not revolve around the acceptance or rejection of a group of accepted facts, or a truth derived therefrom. Rather, they are a struggle for power between *different* sets of facts and truths, driven by ulterior motives.

Such a struggle for power can be witnessed in regard to the reality of the Armenian Genocide, which, between the years 1915–1918, resulted in the death and/or murder of more than one million individuals. Over the century since its occurrence, consecutive Turkish governments have succeeded in creating their own version of "official history" and "holding history hostage" with their own documentary evidence and truths. In doing so, they have succeeded, at the very least, in broadly publicizing their own "historical viewpoint," thereby raising it to the level of reasonable historical possibility. Turkish denialism in regard to the events of the First World War is perhaps the most successful example of how the well-organized, deliberate, and systematic spreading of falsehoods can play an important role in the field of public debate, employing factual statements to construct a false "truth." Those who abide by the dictum, "everyone is entitled to his own opinion, but not to his own facts,"[4] have followed with amazement the public and historical debates over the Armenian Genocide over the past decades, whereby fact-based truths have been discredited and relegated to the status of mere opinion.[5] Keeping the truth hidden and condemning it to silence has been one important aspect of this strategy.

The book you now hold in your hands aims to serve as a major clarification in the debate and confusion created over the relationship between facts and truth regarding the Armenian Genocide. It will serve as a detailed case study and show precisely how those who hid these truths, dismembered them, and felt themselves successful in this regard, are mistaken.

*   *   *

The following passage from Michel-Rolph Trouillot is directly relevant to the issue: "Silences enter the process of historical production at four crucial moments," he wrote: "(1) the moment of fact creation (the making of *sources*); (2) the moment of fact assembly (the making of *archives*); (3) the moment of fact retrieval (the making of *narratives*); and (4) the moment of retrospective significance (the making of *history* in the final instance)."[6] To these, I would add a fifth: (5) the moment of destroying or attempting to disprove the authenticity of critical documents.

If every case of genocide can be understood as possessing its own unique character, then the Armenian case is unique among genocides in the long-standing efforts to deny its historicity, and to thereby hide the truths surrounding it. Another characteristic of this century of denialism is that it has been an inherent component of the genocide, since the beginning of the events themselves. In other words, the denial of the Armenian Genocide began not in the wake of the massacres but was an intrinsic part of the plan itself. The deporting of the Armenians from their homeland to the Syrian deserts and their elimination, both on the route and at their final destinations, were performed under the guise of a decision to resettle them. The entire process was, in fact, organized and carried out in an effort to present this image.

Even though we cannot discuss it in detail here, the most pressing question in this context is the roots of this particular policy. The weakness of the Ottoman state at that juncture seems the most important reason for such a policy. The Ottoman authorities had to organize the entire deportation and extermination process especially under the scrutiny of Germany and the United States. The Ottomans depended on German military and financial support, and wanted that the Americans should be kept as a neutral power; they could not ignore these two powers and felt compelled to justify their actions. Denial and deception were important ways to ease the American and German pressure. The lack of an ideological mass-movement to provide popular support within Ottoman society for a genocidal policy seems to be another reason.[7] This also explains the high amount of bribery among Ottoman bureaucrats, which played an important role (especially in Syria), which is one of the subjects of this book, and the government's incitement of the populace to plunder the vulnerable Armenians as an incentive for supporting the genocidal policy.

The official documentation that presents the entire deportation and extermination as a legitimate resettlement began to be produced from the very first days of the deportations. In other words, what Trouillot has described as "the moment of fact creation (the making of sources)" began, if not earlier, on 25 April 1915, which serves as the symbolic date marking the beginning of the Armenian Genocide.

On the aforementioned date, some 200 Armenian intellectuals and community leaders in Istanbul were arrested. They were sent to Ayaş [Ayash] and Çankırı (either in prison or compulsory residence), both close to the city of Ankara, and, in the following months, more intellectuals were sent to both places. A majority of these individuals would subsequently be re-deported to their final destinations and killed on their way. The Ottoman archives are full of documents reporting that such persons perished from heart attacks and other natural causes, or, alternatively, that they fled or were released at some point. In an article written by Yusuf Sarınay, who served long years as Director-General of the Ottoman archives, based on these documents and dedicated to this topic, it is claimed that of 155 intellectuals in Çankırı, only 29 were kept in prison there, 35 were found innocent and returned to Istanbul, 31 were pardoned by the government and allowed to go to any city they wanted, 57 were deported to Deyr-i Zor, and three foreigners were exiled from the country. It was claimed that none of these intellectuals was the subject of murder.[8]

We would like to provide three striking examples that illuminate this process of "fact creation" and developing a historical narrative. The prominent Armenian parliamentary deputy for Istanbul, Krikor Zohrab, was arrested in Istanbul on 2 June 1915.[9] He was sent off to the southeast Anatolian city of Diyarbekir on the pretext of standing trial for charges filed at a military tribunal there, but was murdered en route near Urfa on July 19, his head being bashed in with a rock.[10] At the moment that Zohrab was being killed, official documents were already being prepared reporting his demise from a heart attack. According to a report dated 20 July 1915, signed by the Urfa municipality physician, Zohrab experienced chest pains while in Urfa and underwent treatment there as a result. After being treated, Zohrab was once again sent on his way to Diyarbekir, but was later reported to have died en route. The doctor traveled to the place of the incident and determined the cause of death to be cardiac arrest.[11]

Another report on the incident was ordered by the priest, Hayrabet, the son of Kürçü Vanis, a member of the clergy of the Armenian church in Urfa. In this report, which bears his own signature, the priest claims that Zohrab "died as the result of a heart ailment" and was buried "in accordance with [his] religious traditions." At the bottom of the report, there is a note certifying that it was "the personal signature of Hayrabet, son of Vanis, of the priests of the Urfa Armenian Church," along with the official seal of the Ottoman authorities.[12] We have a third official document in hand that also indicates that Zohrab was not murdered but died as a result of an accident. According to an Interior Ministry cable sent to Aleppo on 17 October 1915, it was confirmed through the investigation document "number 516, dated 25 September 1915, that [Zohrab] perished as the result of a mishap en route."[13]

As has been seen, the official "facts and truth" of Zohrab's death are that he died of a heart attack, and there is sufficient documentation of this. Later on, this was no longer employed as a significant part of the denialist narrative, since Zohrab's actual killers, Çerkez Ahmet and his accomplices, well-known members of the Unionist Special Organization, were arrested, charged, sentenced to death, and executed. Ali Fuat Erden, the aide to Cemal Pasha—one of the triumvirate of the ruling Committee of Union and Progress party (henceforth CUP) who played a central role in the hanging of the killers, wrote the following about the CUP's treatment of the assailants: "the means used for 'dirty business' (defecation) were necessary during the time of need and use; but after being used they were no longer important and had to be disposed of (like toilet paper)."[14] Ahmet and his associates were probably used in the killing of other Armenian intellectuals too, and therefore had posed a risk for the Unionist leadership.

The relevant information on this incident appeared not only in some of the memoirs of the period, but also found its way into the parliamentary minutes of the Ottoman Chamber of Deputies in November 1916.[15] On 12 November 1916, the question was raised in the Chamber as to the fate of Zohrab and another deputy, Vartkes Serengülyan, who was killed with him. Sixteen days later, on November 28, Grand Vizier Sait Halim Pasha responded to the question, stating that "During their journey to Diyarbekir, where they had been summoned to stand trial in the Court-Martial, Erzurum Deputy Vartkes Serengülyan and Istanbul Deputy Krikor Zohrab were murdered by a gang under the leadership of Çerkez Ahmet. The killers were tried and executed in Diyarbekir."[16]

The second example that we shall provide concerns Agnuni (Khachatur Malumyan), one of the leaders of the Dashnaktsutiun organization.[17] He was arrested, on 24 April 1915, taken into custody and held in the Ayaş Prison in Central Anatolia near Ankara. On June 2, Agnuni, along with five friends, was also dispatched to Diyarbekir to stand trial at the military court there.[18] The group, which reached Aleppo before Krikor Zohrab, was then sent further to Diyarbekir in accordance with an order given on 24 June 1915.[19] In all probability, these men were killed in a similar fashion to that of Zohrab—probably by Zohrab's assailants—only a few days earlier, at the beginning of July.[20] However, certain Ottoman documents in our possession state that Agnuni and his companions were not killed but instead managed to escape while on the road to Diyarbekir and flee to Russia. A note sent by Talat Pasha to Foreign Minister Halil Menteşe on 19 July 1916 stated: "it has been understood that, without a doubt, while being sent to the military court in Diyarbekir," Agnuni and his friends "deceived their guards and fled to Russia."[21]

The final example is that of Diran Kelekyan, the editor-in-chief of the daily *Sabah*. Kelekyan, who was known to be close to the Unionists, was also among those arrested on 24 April 1915. He was released on May 8 on the understanding that he would "resettle himself and his family in an area of his choice within a province where there were no other Armenians, and on the condition that he would not return to Istanbul." However, Kelekyan remained in Çankırı, where he had been previously deported.[22] On July 18, he submitted a request to be allowed to return to Istanbul, but the official reply, which was sent back eleven days later, reiterated the previous conditions: he could settle where he wanted on the condition that he not return to Istanbul.[23] Like Zohrab and Agnuni before him, Diran Kelekyan was eventually dispatched to Diyarbekir for the alleged purpose of standing trial, but was murdered en route by armed gangs on 2 November 1915.[24] Yusuf Sarınay, the author of the article mentioned above, cited a note that Diran Kelekyan "is excused by Ministry of Interior order dated 4 August 1915 and will go to the center of Izmir."[25]

The Ottoman archives themselves are, as Trouillot described in his second point, a monument to "the moment of fact assembly (the making of archives)." Apart from the aforementioned documents dealing with the arrested Armenian intelligentsia, they are replete with documents bearing government orders that present the deportations and massacres as run-of-the-mill, legal relocation efforts. Prime examples of this are the government decree of 30 May 1915 and list of regulations (44 articles' worth)

issued on 10 June 1915. According to the latter, the property and possessions left by Armenian deportees were to be recorded, and the owners
would be reimbursed the value of the goods in their new places of settlement. The following instructions come from the May decree: "properties
and land will be distributed to them [the Armenians in their newly resettled areas] in proportion to their previous financial and economic situations. The state will construct houses for the needy, distribute seeds to
farmers, [and] distribute tools and implements to those with professions
who need them. The things and goods which remain in the places they left
or their equivalent values will be given to them in the same form."[26] Later,
with the 26 September 1915 law and the Regulation of 8 November
1915, the points described above were more developed and laid down the
process of transfering the revenues from Armenian properties to the
Armenians in their new settlement areas.[27]

Another important document is a new set of regulations, or
Talimatname, issued on 7 October 1915. These regulations, consisting
of 55 separate articles, were written to arrange the orderly dispersal of
those Armenians who arrived in Syria and accumulated in great number
in the environs of Aleppo. According to them, the names of the
Armenians to be dispatched to the new areas of resettlement were to be
recorded in the deportation registries; they, themselves, were to be sent
off in 1000-person groups; each convoy was to be given 150 donkeys,
mules, and camels. They were also to be assured at least four days' worth
of food and water; flour depots were to be set up along the route, and
ovens built to bake bread. Additionally, there would be areas for rest and
repose along the routes, and health and sanitation officials would be
posted there; those who were unable to continue their journey would be
able to receive treatment there. Finally, the Armenian deportees would
be resettled on fertile lands, and each family would be given sufficient
land to survive.[28]

As these documents show, throughout the genocidal process, a parallel
process was underway of constructing a "truth" on the foundations of a
fabricated body of facts whose authenticity was indisputable…. The inevitable result of this, of course, was that an alternative account was created,
thereby paving the way for a historical debate—a power struggle, in some
sense—over whose truth was more accurate. These "facts," produced
throughout the genocide process, laid the groundwork for the process
wherein "truth" could be transformed into nothing more than "one opinion among many."

Despite all efforts in the contrary, every mass atrocity leaves inevitable traces. This was the case in the Armenian Genocide; there are, indeed, enough materials showing the genocidal intent of the Ottoman-Turkish government. Because of this, the silencing and taking hostage of history could not be simply limited to fabricating facts. The existing incriminatory materials had to be either made to vanish or declared invalid. This is what we were referring to in our addition to Trouillot's list as point (5): "the moment of destroying and/or proving the falsity of critical documents." Turkish denialism has long been characterized by the erasure of the material foundations of "true reality."

We now possess detailed evidence that vital official Ottoman documents regarding the Armenian Genocide were intentionally destroyed. Chief among these is the information provided in the indictment filed against the Unionist leaders in the main post-war trial in Istanbul in 1919. In the indictment, the prosecutor's office claimed that the Unionist government, facing imminent defeat in the First World War, performed a "cleansing" of its archives. Among those documents destroyed were a significant part of the Interior Ministry's papers, the papers of the Union and Progress Party, and those of the Special Organization, which played a central role in the annihilation of the Armenians. Additionally, a circular was sent to all of the regional administrative centers instructing that all of the orders sent in regard to the Armenians be burned.[29]

Chief among the documents of which no trace remains were the case dossiers and associated documents from the trials against the Union and Progress leaders that took place between the years 1919 and 1922. These include the papers of the commission of inquiry established in November 1918, the papers from the investigations carried out by the courts-martial themselves, the case files for the approximately 63 cases filed at these courts, the minutes of the court sessions, the testimonies of both the witnesses and defendants, and the investigation papers regarding dozens of persons and events that did not make it to trial. All of this—all of it—has disappeared without a trace and without a clue as to its fate or whereabouts.[30]

During the investigations that were performed before the cases were filed, as well as during the subsequent trials, hundreds of official documents were produced showing how the genocide was organized. Some of these were telegraphic orders. For instance, there were 42 telegrams from the Province of Ankara alone. There were also the oral and written testimonies of a number of high-level Ottoman civilian and military officials, who confirm that the massacres were planned and systematic, and carried out under the aegis of the Union and Progress Party. Today, this enormous compendium of information has disappeared completely. If we consider what the Nuremberg Trials might have been like had all the existing evidence been lost, we can begin to better understand the meaning and magnitude of this loss.

Apart from the 13 indictments and final judgments found in the Ottoman Gazette (*Takvim-i Vekayi*), all that remains of the historical record of these events is the reports on the trials found in the daily newspapers. In the end, by concealment and destruction of documentary evidence, the genocide, a well-documented, robust historical truth, was transformed into a thin sheet of ice, a fragile hypothesis, very easily breakable.

After concealment and destruction, there was one more thing needed: to prove that every remaining incriminating document was fabricated or somehow inauthentic. The most striking example of this is the telegraphic cables of Talat Pasha ordering the annihilation of the Armenians, which are the subject of this book. The original telegrams, and/or handwritten copies of them, were sold to the Armenian journalist and intellectual, Aram Andonian, in November 1918 by an Ottoman bureaucrat by the name of Naim Efendi, who worked in the Aleppo Deportation Office.[31] Naim not only copied ca. 52 telegrams in his own hand, but also sold ca. 24 original documents and wrote his recollections related these specific telegrams in the form of small notes. This is the reason Aram Andonian would later call these recollections, "Naim Bey's Memoirs."[32]

Andonian would subsequently organize these invaluable cables, which show that the Ottoman Armenians were eliminated by direct government order, along with Naim's notes, and publish them in three different languages between the years 1920–1921.[33] In 1983, the Turkish Historical Society published the work, *Ermenilerce Talat Paşa'ya Atfedilen Telgrafların Gerçek Yüzü*, by Şinasi Orel and Süreyya Yuca, which was translated into English in 1986 with the title, *The Talat Pasha Telegrams, Historical Fact or Armenian Fiction?*[34] The book claimed that both the memoirs and cables published by Andonian were forgeries, and that the telegrams were produced by Armenians, most likely by Andonian himself.

In the years following the appearance of Orel and Yuca's book, their view of the inauthenticity of both Naim's memoirs and the accompanying cables became widely accepted, the latter even being known and referred to as "the fake telegrams attributed to Talat Pasha." Orel and Yuca's work appeared to have "closed the book" on the topic. Critical scholars tended to avoid the subject altogether until now. This book that you now hold in your hands can be said to "turn a new page" in this saga.

*   *   *

Regarding Trouillot's third and fourth steps in silencing the past and taking history hostage, "the moment of fact retrieval (the making of narratives)," and "the moment of retrospective significance (the making of history in the final instance)," essentially, this task has fallen to the field of history and its practitioners. A great many historians, who claim to aspire to the pursuit of objective history in accordance with scientific principles, have nevertheless joined the chorus of those who embrace this "document-based narrative." They have invited those who claim the existence of an Armenian Genocide to engage in a discussion on the basis of documents. Such discussions often end with the call to "show us the originals." The well-known Islamic and Middle Eastern scholar, Bernard Lewis, was himself a prominent spokesman for this chorus of voices, at one point declaring that "there exists no serious proof of a decision and a plan by the Ottoman government aimed at exterminating the Armenian nation."[35]

Guenter Lewy is another prime example of this chorus of voices.[36] The central thesis of his 2004 book is that "no authentic documentary evidence exists to prove the culpability of the central government of Turkey for the massacre of 1915–6... it is safe to say that no such evidence exists for the events of 1915–6."[37] According to Lewy, the materials-documentation that were published in either the Ottoman Gazette (*Takvim-i Vekayi*) or daily papers during the post-war war crimes trials of the Unionist leaders cannot be accepted as reliable sources because "the loss of all of the original documentation leaves the findings of the military tribunals of 1919–20 unsupported by credible evidence... the reproductions can hardly be considered a valid substitute for the original documentation."[38] He even went so far as to refer to these materials as "alleged documents."[39]

Lewy rejected the telegrams given to Andonian by Naim as invalid and unreliable. Repeating Orel and Yuca's view that they are "crude forgeries," he claimed that "Orel and Yuca's painstaking analysis of these documents has raised enough questions about their genuineness [so as to] make any use of them in a serious scholarly work unacceptable."[40]

This is a peculiar alliance indeed. On one hand, there are successive Turkish governments that have destroyed any and all evidence that would show the events of 1915 to have been a systematic program of annihilation; this has included all of the case files from the post-war trials of the Unionists (1919–1921), all of the Talat Pasha telegrams and other incriminating documents, as well as any trace of their ultimate fate. On the other hand, there is the chorus of historians who reiterate the line that, in the absence of solid, reliable documentary evidence—in other words, "smoking guns" from the Ottoman archives or elsewhere—proving otherwise, there can be no objective claim of a government-sponsored genocide against the Armenians. In light of this odd coalition, the awarding to Lewy of the "Turkish Grand National Assembly Medal" by parliamentary speaker Bülent Arınç on 22 November 2005 should come as no surprise.[41]

A final brushstroke is needed to complete the picture of denial: to discredit the accounts of the genocide given by Armenian survivors and classify them as "unreliable sources." Official Ottoman documents were referred to as the only fully reliable source, and held pride of place in the "hierarchy of sources." The British "Blue Book," prepared during the war by Arnold Toynbee and Viscount Bryce, detailing Ottoman atrocities, was rejected out of hand as "war propaganda," since much of the information contained within it was obtained from Armenians.[42] In the words of Marc Nichanian, "[the Armenians] had to provide the proof of their own death."[43] The events themselves, in the sense of their very nature as events, have been invalidated from the outset. In this way, the factuality of genocide, its reality as an historical fact, has already been, if not called into question, nevertheless reduced to an opinion with no substantive evidence.

What should have been done was very simple: treat survivors' accounts as important as the Ottoman documents and pose a simple question to the Turkish regime: What *did* happen to those files that came to the light during the 1919–1922 trials? If the government did hide or destroy them, it can only be because they were unwilling to allow the information contained within them to become widely known, something that unambiguously points to its incriminating nature. The ferreting away or willful destruction of trial documents and case files should be enough to raise the serious suspicions of those historians who demand solid, reliable documentary evidence, and claim that the absence of directly incriminating documents does not allow them to pass judgment.

In this situation, it has fallen to us, as historians, to bring to light the information that we managed to uncover in documents long lost or hidden away, and to show, in the face of opposition from the denialist school, their authenticity. The time has come for the reigning narrative, one based on their version of truth and carefully constructed from their own selected facts, to be done away with. This is my aim with this work: to give voice to information heretofore condemned to silence, and to show that a verifiable set of facts regarding the events of 1915 can indeed be extracted from the muddled swirl of "opinion" and "interpretation."

*   *   *

We owe a great debt to one person, Armenian Catholic Priest Krikor Guerguerian, who has enabled us to accomplish the challenge described above. The majority of the materials that build the foundation of this work was found in his private archive. The private archive was preserved by the priest's nephew, Edmund Guerguerian, and in 2015, he gave us permission to see the archive and use the materials. Before introducing anything from this archive, it is important to give the basic information about Father Krikor Guerguerian and the creation of his archive.

Krikor Guerguerian and His Archive

Krikor Guerguerian (12 May 1911–7 May 1988) was born in the district of Gürün, which is in the province of Sivas. He was the youngest of 16 siblings, eight boys and eight girls,[44] only six of whom survived the Deportations. The other ten were killed, along with their parents. Krikor personally witnessed the killing of his parents. Together with one of his older brothers, he succeeded in reaching Beirut in 1916, where he was taken into an orphanage, and it is there that he spent his childhood years. In 1925 he enrolled in the Zımmar (Bzemmar) Catholic Monastery-School, and, after graduating from Beirut's St. Joseph University in the early 1930s, he went to Rome, to the Levonian Academy, with the intention of continuing his theological education and becoming a monk, an ambition that was fulfilled in 1937, when he earned the right to become a Catholic monk. During the same year, Father Krikor decided to pursue a doctorate on the subject of the Armenian Genocide, but he would never complete it, despite working on it for the rest of his life. The archive is actually the product of his life's work.

Before the genocide, Krikor's eldest brother, Bedros, had gone to Cairo and settled there. After he became a monk, Krikor settled there himself. There, while continuing his research, he met Kürt ["Kurdish"] Mustafa Pasha around 1952. The latter, who was also known as Nemrut Mustafa Pasha, had been one of the presiding judges in Istanbul's First Military Tribunal/Court-Martial (*Divan-i Harb-i Örfi*) that heard the cases against the Union and Progress officials between the years 1919 and 1921. While serving in this capacity, Mustafa Pasha had been arrested in October 1920 on the charge of having intentionally forged documents in one of the trials, that of the Bayburt County Executive (*kaymakam*) Nusret, so as to be able to sentence him to death. Mustafa Pasha was convicted but later pardoned by the Sultan. Fearing that he might be rearrested when Istanbul was captured by the Turkish Nationalist Forces in 1922, he fled to Cairo.[45]

Father Krikor's meeting with the former Ottoman judge would become a turning point in the life of the monk. In a brief note, he wrote that he and Mustafa met numerous times and held lengthy discussions and debates. For his part, Mustafa provided important information to the young Guerguerian. According to Mustafa's account, the Armenian Patriarchate of Istanbul was an intervenor in the trials of the former Unionist officials and, in this capacity, it had (and exercised) the right to have a copy made of the papers contained in the various case files. When the Turkish Nationalist forces took control of Istanbul, the patriarchate decided to send all of the documents in its possession to Marseilles, France, for safe-keeping. One of the reasons for sending them to Marseilles was the presence there of Father Grigoris Balakian. Later on, these documents would be sent to Manchester, eventually making their way to the final destination, the Armenian Patriarchate of Jerusalem.[46] Krikor Guerguerian would thus make his way to the Jerusalem Armenian Patriarchate. Years later, he would tell his nephew, Dr. Edmund Guerguerian, that "[he] photographed everything [he] saw there."

An important part of the documents that Guerguerian found in Jerusalem is the documents of the case files of the Istanbul Union and Prosecution proceedings, which we have mentioned above, which are still hidden by the Turkish Government. The telegrams of the Armenian extermination orders, captured during the investigations; the statements of the military and civilian officials; oral and written testimonies of both suspects and witnesses given during both the trial and the pre-trial interrogations, constitute an important part of these documents. We utilize only two of the documents in this introduction to illustrate the priceless value of these materials.

Guerguerian did not collect only documents from the Jerusalem Patriarchate archives; he also traveled to the Boghos Nubar Library in Paris in 1950, at a time when Aram Andonian was serving as its director. While he was there, Guerguerian saw both the Naim Efendi memoirs and the related Talat Pasha telegrams and photographed them both, which are the main subject of this work.

When we consider that the archives of the Armenian Patriarchate in Jerusalem are closed to researchers,[47] and that key documents in the Boghos Nubar Pasha Library have disappeared, the value of the Guerguerian archive for Armenian Genocide research quickly becomes apparent. For this reason, it is of the utmost importance that the documents stored in this collection be made known not merely to a limited number of experts, but to everyone. Within Clark University, we have begun the "*Krikor Guerguerian Archival Project*" with this very purpose in mind. We placed the entire archival collection on the university's website by the end of 2017. Through a detailed index, the online reader will have the opportunity to easily access the entire archive.

* * *

The denialist argument of successive Turkish governments rests on two main pillars: the first can be termed the "produce the originals" argument; the second is the dismissal of Naim's memoirs and Talat Pasha's telegrams, which point towards an Armenian Genocide, as forgeries. The latter is the subject of this book. For the former, we introduce here only two telegrams from the Guerguerian archive. Both telegrams were mentioned in the indictment for the trial against the Union and Progress government leaders, begun in Istanbul on 28 April 1919, and were published in the Ottoman Gazette, *Takvim-i Veyaki*.[48] (see Image 1). Both telegrams belong to the category of materials that document the genocidal intent of the Ottoman Government. Since the originals were either concealed or destroyed by Turkish authorities, however, denialists like Lewy consider them untrustworthy sources.

The first is an order from Third Army Commander Mahmut Kamil Pasha, dated 24 July 1915 (see Image 2). The Third Army was both politicaly and militarily responsible for control of the area known as Historic Armenia, where the majority of the Armenian population lived and were subjected to deportation. The second telegram is from Unionist Central Committee member and Special Organization head Bahaettin

Image 1 Pages from 1919–1921 Military Tribunal Main Indictment published in Takvim-i Vekayi 3540—quotes underlined in red

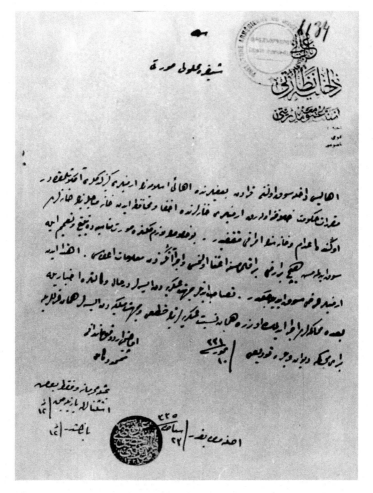

Image 2   Third Army Commander Mahmut Kamil Pasha's order, 24 July 1915

Şakir, dated 4 July 1915, and concerns the coordination of the efforts to annihilate the Armenians.

The first telegram reads as follows:

> It has been learned that Muslims in some of the towns and villages from which the [Armenian] population has been deported have been hiding Armenians. It is necessary that those homeowners who have hidden and

protected Armenians in violation of government decisions be executed in front of their residences and their houses burned. [Please] inform all of the concerned parties of this in an appropriate manner and take special care that not a single Armenian who has not [yet] been deported be left behind. Armenians who have converted to Islam will also be deported. If those protecting [the Armenians] are members of the armed forces, the relevant ministries should first be informed [of their actions], and, after they are convicted, their ties with the military are to be severed immediately; administrative functionaries are to be summarily dismissed and they are [all] to be given over to the martial law courts for trial.

The classification reference given for this document in the indictment is "Dossier 13; Document 1" (*tertîb 13 vesîka 1*). The document itself has the letterhead of the Interior Ministry Public Security Directorate, and on the bottom of the document is the stamp of the Interior Ministry dated 23 February 1919 and that reads: "confirms the original." There is no question of the authenticity of this document.

In the Guerguerian archive, there is also a second telegram from Mahmut Kamil Pasha on the subject. It can be understood that the order contained in the July 24 cable produced some confusion among his subordinates, and the purpose of this telegram, dated 1 August 1915, was to issue a second set of orders that would clear up any confusion caused by the earlier one. In it, Kamil Pasha states that "executions were reported of those hiding Armenians who are [slated] to be deported to the interior," and clarifies that this penalty does not apply to "those who shelter or protect women and children...who have been officially distributed by the government to Muslim houses." Rather, such a punishment is reserved for "those, who, regardless of their sex or religion, hide Armenians in their houses without the knowledge of the government." Such persons "will be punished as ordered previously." This cable appears to reveal that a great many Muslims in the various villages and towns were hiding Armenians, and the government was intent on preventing this, even if it meant going to such extreme lengths as execution and house razing.

The other telegram was written by Committee of Union and Progress Central Committee member and Special Organization head Bahaettin Şakir and sent from the city of Erzurum to Sabit Bey, the Governor of the province of Mamuretülaziz (Elazığ-Harput), with instructions for it to be forwarded to the Unionist Party secretary Nazım in the same city. In it, Bahaettin Şakir wrote: "Have Armenians who were deported from there been eliminated? Have those harmful elements who were distanced [from there] through deportation been liquidated or simply deported? Please be frank and open in your report [on the matter], my brother." (see Image 3).

The mark of the official letterhead of the Civil Administration Inspectorate of the Interior Ministry is found at the top right of the telegram, leaving no room for doubt as to the authenticity of this document. As can be seen from the image, the lower part of the document contains a set of Arabic numbers in the form of four-digit groups, which is the ciphered form of the original text. The word or suffix equivalent of each of these four-digit groups is written on top of each number group.

In order to fully understand the importance of this cable, a certain amount of background will first be necessary. Even before the Ottoman Empire officially entered the First World War in October 1914, Bahaettin Şakir had been sent to Erzurum in August in order to direct the activities of the Unionist paramilitary entity known as the Special Organization (*Teşkilat-ı Mahsusa*). He had previously been entrusted with organizing an uprising among the Muslim populations of the Caucasus. There are a great number of easily accessed Ottoman archival documents showing Şakir as the person in charge of coordinating the Special Organization's actions in the region, some of which even bear his signature as "Bahaettin Şakir, head of the Special Organization in Erzurum."[49] According to the indictment in the main trial against Unionist leaders, which was published in issue no. 3540 of the Ottoman Gazette *Takvim-i Vekayi*, before Şakir set out for Erzurum, the leadership of the Special Organization in Istanbul supplied him with a large sum of money, explosives, and an automobile. In addition, Şakir was in possession of a special encryption key to be used for communicating both with Istanbul and with the various provinces.[50]

Bahaettin Şakir was a defendant in two of the post-war trials in Istanbul: the main trial against the Unionist leadership, and the Mamuretülaziz (Elazığ-Harput) trial, where he was tried in absentia. Both his activities and his character were frequently mentioned in both indictments. Indeed, one of the most important pieces of evidence for the prosecution in both trials is the telegram from him dated 4 July 1915. In the Mamuretülaziz trial, it is referred to both in the indictment as well as in the judges' decision to convict. In the main trial indictment, it is reproduced in full by the prosecution and referred to as the "cipher cable." It states that a "photograph" of the document is to be found among the court papers within "Dossier 9."[51]

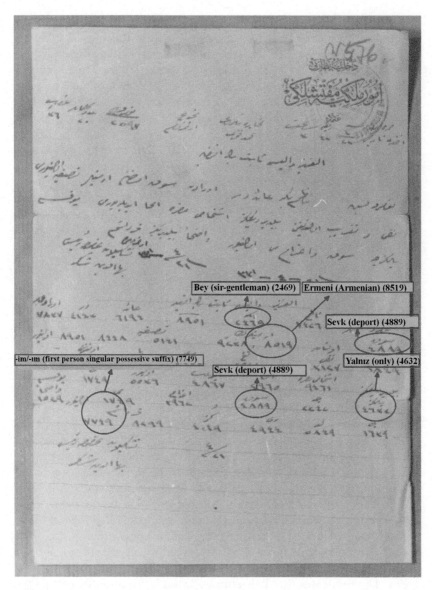

Image 3   Bahaettin Shakir's telegram 4 July 1915 with decoded numbers

Erzurum Governor Tahsin Bey would later report that one of the encryption keys given to Bahaettin Şakir was from the Interior Ministry and that he (Şakir) would dispatch cables here and there signing them "Special Organization Head." Tahsin, who testified in the Mamuretülaziz Trial, claimed during the session of 2 August 1919 that "Bahaettin Şakir Bey had an encryption [key]. He corresponded with both the Sublime Porte and the Ministry of War. During the deportations he was also in communication with the army."[52]

During this trial as well (10 January 1920), the aforementioned cable of 4 July 1915 was read as evidence.[53] Let us repeat, the existence or contents of this document were not unknown, but scholars like Lewy claimed that, since the original was lacking, only the quotation in the indictment could be accepted as a trustworthy source. Needless to add, the letterhead on the document alone leaves no doubt as to its authenticity, but we have also other, very important information testifying to it being the original.

THE ENCRYPTION METHOD IN THE DOCUMENT MATCHES OTHER DOCUMENTS IN THE ARCHIVES

As we can see in the photograph of Bahaettin Şakir's telegram, it contains a set of Arabic numbers in the form of four-digit groups. The word or suffix equivalent of each of these four-digit groups is written on top of each number group. Here, some of the words or suffixes can be identified very easily: Ermeni (Armenian) (8519); Sevk (deport) [4889]; yalnız (only) [4632]; Bey (sir, gentleman) [2469]; -leri (plural suffix) [9338]; -im/-ım (first person singular possessive suffix) [7749].

There are a great number of encrypted documents from the interior ministry in the Ottoman archive available to researchers. These are primarily telegraphic cables sent to Istanbul from the provinces. A significant portion of the cables dating from the war years also contain the four-digit groups like Şakir's telegram. We compared the four digit groups of the Şakir documents with those from the same months (June–July 1915) in the Ottoman archive. It is actually a very simple operation to do so, since the archival documents themselves have already been deciphered, and the equivalent words and suffixes are already written above the numerical codes. The result was that Bahaettin Şakir did indeed use the encryption key used by the Ottoman Interior Ministry. In the 25 different telegrams we reviewed, we identified 34 times in which the words and suffixes used were identical with ones in the Şakir telgram (see Image 4).

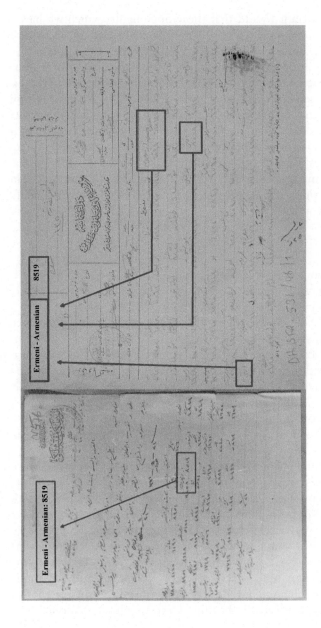

Image 4   DH.ŞFR., 531/46-1 Coded Cable from Elazig, 7 September 1916

It is important to add that these documents, which we have discovered in the Ottoman archives, were only made available to researchers in the present decade (2010s). In other words, the existence of these ciphers was not even generally known until then, and thus there was no chance of actually using them for comparison. But now, the existence and confirmed authenticity of these telegrams of Mahmut Kamil Pasha and Bahaettin Şakir bring us back to our topic of the relationship between fact and truth. As we discussed, one of the strategies of the successive Turkish governments' denialist policy was based on the concealment or destruction of original historic documents. The revelation of these documents strikes a powerful blow against this strategy. This leads us to the topic of this book, the question of authenticity of the Talat Pasha telegrams.

*   *   *

The book you are now reading contains, in addition to a number of related documents, the memoirs of an Ottoman bureaucrat by the name of Naim Efendi, who worked in the Deportation Office in Aleppo (*Halep Sevkiyat Müdürlüğü*) during the years 1915–1916, and which we discovered in the private archive of the Catholic Priest Krikor Guerguerian.[54] The memoirs contain the cables sent by Ottoman Interior Minister Talat Pasha ordering the annihilation of the Armenians, as well as the aforementioned Naim Efendi's personal observations from that period. As mentioned above, in 1918, Naim sold both his memoirs and the telegrams to an Armenian intellectual by the name of Aram Andonian, who, in turn, published the documents and a portion of the memoirs in Armenian, English, and French translation in 1920–1921.

The documents published in this work as appendices will be presented to the English reader for the first time (in translation). We present the original, unpublished sections of Naim Efendi's memoirs alongside those related sections originally appearing in Andonian's Armenian translation, thereby giving the reader access to the entirety of these recollections. Other documents in the appendices include original letters by Andonian, in which he mentions and provides further information regarding Naim, and a letter to Andonian from a doctor by the name of Avedis Nakkashian. These letters offer the reader detailed information regarding Naim Efendi. Finally, a report about Andonian's book is reproduced here that was written by Walter Rössler (Rößler), the German consul in Aleppo during the war years.

* * *

Every book has a page for acknowledgements. With the full awareness that it will require a lengthier list of persons and institutions, I will not limit the acknowledgments simply to those who have assisted with the book itself, but wish to also recognize and thank all of those who have helped me to make the Krikor Guerguerian Archive available electronically. First and foremost, I wish to express my gratitude to Krikor Guerguerian's nephew, Dr. Edmund Guerguerian, both for his meticulous preservation of his uncle's archive after the latter's death in 1988, and for showing great flexibility and indulgence over the process of transferring the archive to the digital medium. A special thanks also goes to Berc Panossian, who has scanned and digitalized the entire archive. Berc did not approach this project simply as a professional and as a businessman, but he did so also with the emotional investment of one putting his whole heart into the work. Indeed, it was through his expertise that some of the fragile or unreadable documents are now, in digital form, more accessible *and* readable than their originals.

Apart from the need to thoroughly go through the archive, which is currently in a rather disorganized state, the Guerguerian holdings had to be subjected to a detailed indexing in order to be of service to future researchers. The materials in the archive are in a variety of languages, including English, French, Italian, Armenian, Turkish, Ottoman, and Turkish written in the Armenian script. It was therefore necessary to employ a number of persons with broad language skills in order to translate and index this 100,000-page+ collection of documents. Such an endeavor would have been doomed to failure without the support of a reliable group of individuals and institutions to see it through. Among those whose unflagging support was crucial to its success were Mr. and Mrs. Nazar & Artemis Nazarian, Mr. & Mrs Harry and Suzanne Toufayan, Mr. & Mrs Sarkis & Ruth Bedevian, Mr. & Mrs Hagop & Silva Bagdadlian, Saro & Hilda Hartounian, Antranig Baghdassarian, Anoush Mathevosian, and a certain friend in New York who wishes to remain anonymous. Other individuals and agencies who helped to see the project through to completion were the Calouste Gulbenkian Foundation, and especially Dr. Razmik Panossian, who has given a whole new face to the foundation's Armenian

Communities Division; the Dadourian Foundation; the Jirair Nishanian Foundation; the Armenian General Benevolent Union (AGBU); Knights & Daughters of Vartan; and the National Association for Armenian Studies and Research (NAASR).

I wish to convey a personal thank you to those who helped in the preparation of this book, over the course of which I have received much help from a great number of persons. Chief among these is Ömer Türkoğlu. Ömer not only transliterated the Ottoman documents in this book—including the memoirs of Naim Efendi—with the utmost care, he also undertook to closely edit things that he did not translate and made a number of constructive suggestions regarding the book's contents. If not for his contribution, this book would not have achieved its present form. Ani Değirmencioğlu, Sevan Deirmendjian, Nazlı Temir Beylerian, and Tabita Toparlak translated the Armenian texts in this work into Turkish to allow me to understand the content of those materials. The translation of these Armenian materials into English was done by Aram Arkun. My doctoral students, Anna Aleksanyan, Emre Can Dağlıoğlu, Burçin Gerçek, and Ümit Kurt (now Dr. Kurt), not only worked on the indexing of the archive, but also closely read the entire work for errors and made a number of constructive suggestions. To this list I would like to add Rober Koptaş, who closely read over the text of this work for errors and made constructive suggestions in the process, and Marc Mamigonian, the Director of Academic Affairs at NAASR, with whom I carried on a constant discussion regarding problems and questions related to this work. Among those to whom I owe a debt of gratitude, I must include my long-time friend and collaborator, Paul Bessemer, who has translated all of my books and many of my articles. It is thanks to his masterful translation that you now hold this work. Belinda Cooper and Jennifer Manoukian are two other translators who helped me to render original texts in the appendix into English. To each one of these persons I owe a special debt of gratitude. George Shrinian took upon himself the arduous task of editing the entire text and preparing it for publication.

As a final expression of gratitude, I would like to thank those who work in the Turkish Republican Archives in Ankara. By means of modern technology, this collection is electronically linked to the Ottoman Archives in Istanbul. It was for this reason that I was able to access and use the Istanbul Ottoman archives from Ankara. The archival employees in Ankara were very helpful in all matters; apart from providing a pleasant and conducive work environment, they also greatly facilitated my accessing the documents I sought. When I asked them their names in order to mention them in my work, they replied, "the names come and go, professor; thank the institution instead," a symbol and abiding reminder for me of the graciousness with which they always operate.

It goes without saying that the responsibility for any oversights and errors contained in this work are mine alone.

NOTES

1. The story is taken from Hannah Arendt, *Between Past and Future: Eight Exercises in Political Thought* (New York: Penguin Books, 2006), 536.
2. Ibid., 535.
3. Ibid.
4. This famous quote is attributed to the U.S. senator, Daniel Patrick Moynihan (1927–2003), https://en.wikipedia.org/wiki/Daniel_Patrick_Moynihan, and may be an echo of American statesman Bernard Baruch (1870–1965), "I have always maintained that every man has a right to be wrong in his opinions. But no man has a right to be wrong in his facts." *Baruch: The Public Years* (New York: Holt, Rinehart and Winston, 1960), 376.
5. For a work that demonstrates how fact-based realities have been successfully transformed into just "one opinion among others" regarding the Armenian Genocide, see Marc Mamigonian, "Academic Denial of the Armenian Genocide in American Scholarship: Denialism as Manufactured Controversy," *Genocide Studies International*, 9, no. 1 (Spring 2015): 61–82. For some of the recent debates on denialism of Armenian Genocide see, Jennifer M. Dixon, "Rhetorical Adaptation and Resistance to International Norms," *Perspectives on Politics*, 15, no. 1 (2017): 83–99; Richard G. Hovannisian, "Denial of the Armenian Genocide 100 Years Later: The New Practitioners and Their Trade," *Genocide Studies International*, 9, no. 2 (2015): 228–247; and Taner Akçam, *The Young Turks' Crime Against Humanity* (Princeton, NJ: Princeton University Press, 2012), 273–449.
6. Michel-Rolph Trouillot, *Silencing the Past: Power and the Production of History* (Boston: Beacon Press, 1995), 26. The enumeration of the four moments was added by this author.
7. As Mahmut Kamil Pasha's telegram below shows, there was considerable popular disagreement with the government's treatment of the Armenians. On this topic see George N. Shirinian, "Turks Who Saved Armenians: Righteous Muslims during the Armenian Genocide," *Genocide Studies International*, 9, no. 2 (2015): 208–227; and Burçin Gerçek, *Akıntıya Karşı: Ermeni Soykırımında Emirlere karşı Gelenler, Kurtaranlar, Direnenler* (Istanbul: Iletişim, 2016).

8. Yusuf Sarınay, "What Happened on April 24, 1915, the Circular of April 24, 1915 and the Arrest of Armenian Committee Members in Istanbul," *International Journal of Turkish Studies*, 14, nos. 1&2 (Fall 2008): 75–101, 80. For a critical review of this article see, Ara Sarafian, "What Happened on 24 April 1915? The Ayash Prisoners," URL: http://www.gomidas.org/submissions/show/5 (Accessed 22 April 2013).

9. Krikor Zohrab (1861–1915) was a mercurial figure and a leading Armenian intellectual: attorney, engineer, architect, and author, he was also elected as a representative for Istanbul in the Ottoman Chamber of Deputies in 1908, 1912, and 1914. For more on his life and death, see: Nesim Ovadya Izrail, *1915 Bir Ölüm Yolculuğu Krikor Zohrab* (Istanbul: Pencere Yayınları, 2013).

10. Zohrab's murder was revealed by his assailant, who admitted to bashing his skull in with a rock. Ahmet Refik Altınay, *Iki Komite Iki Kıtal* (Istanbul: Bedir Yayınları, 1999), 51–52.

11. Krikor Guerguerian Archive, Ottoman Documents, 13-Krikor Zohrab, Document 03. [Author's Note: The archival identification numbers that are given in this work are temporary and will eventually be changed. We suggest that researchers employ the online-index that we have prepared for finding articles and other documents.]

12. Ibid., Document 04.

13. Ibid., Document 02.

14. Ali Fuat Erden, *Birinci Dünya Savaşı'nda Suriye Hatıraları* (Istanbul: TIŞ Bankası Kültür Yayınları, 2006), 226.

15. For more from the various memoirs dealing with the murder of Zohrab and the capture, trial, and execution of his assailants, see Nesim Ovadya Izrail, *1915 Bir Ölüm Yolculuğu*, 355–384.

16. Ibid., 363–364.

17. Dashnaktsutiun is the Armenian name for the Armenian Revolutionary Federation, one of the most important Armenian political organizations, established in 1890 in Tiflis. It formed the first government of the Armenian Republic in 1918.

18. BOA.DH.ŞFR., 53/211, Cipher cable from Interior Minister Talat to the Province of Ankara, 3 June 1915.

19. BOA.DH.ŞFR., 54/132, Cipher cable from Interior Minister Talat to the Province of Aleppo, 24 June 1915.

20. Rössler, the German consul in Aleppo, reported in a cable dated 29 June 1915 that Agnuni and his companions were still in Aleppo. (DE/PA-AA/BoKon/169). Raymond Kévorkian claims that the killing was performed by the Haci Tellal gang. R. Kévorkian, *Armenian Genocide A Complete History* (London: I.B. Tauris, 2011), 524.

21. BOA.DH.EUM., 5. ŞB. 26/23 Confidential note from Interior Minister Talat Bey to Foreign Minister Halil Bey, 19 July 1915.

PREFACE 27

22. BOA.DH.ŞFR., 52/266, Cipher cable from Interior Minister Talat to the Province of Kastamonu, 8 May 1915.
23. BOA.DH.ŞFR., 54-A/183, Cipher cable from Interior Minister Talat to the Province of Kastamonu, 29 July 1915.
24. Grigoris Balakian, *Armenian Golgotha* (New York: Alfred A. Knopf, 2009), 301–304.
25. Yusuf Sarınay, "What Happened on April 24, 1915," 97.
26. Genelkurmay Başkanlığı, *Arşiv Belgeleriyle Ermeni Faaliyetleri, 1914–1918*, Vol. 1 (Ankara: Genelkurmay Basımevi, 2005), 131.
27. For more on the law of 26 September and Regulation of 8 November 1915, see Taner Akçam and Umit Kurt, *Spirit of the Laws: The Plunder of Wealth in the Armenian Genocide*, translated by Aram Arkun (New York: Berghahn Books, 2015), 24–29.
28. BOA.DH.EUM.VRK., 15/71-2, Muamele-i Umumiye-i Sevkiye Hakkında Talimatname (Regulatory Decree regarding the General Conduct of the Deportations).
29. For detailed information on the Ottoman archives and the destruction of documents, see Taner Akçam, *The Young Turks' Crime Against Humanity*, 9–20.
30. For detailed information on the post-war trials of the Unionists, see Vahakn N. Dadrian and Taner Akçam, *Judgment at Istanbul: The Armenian Genocide Trials* (New York: Berghahn Books, 2011).
31. Journalist-author Aram Andonian (1875–1952) was one of the leading members of Istanbul's Armenian intelligentsia. He was arrested on 24 April 1915, along with other members of the Armenian intelligentsia, and only escaped their fate by virtue of having broken his leg on the deportation route. He thus passed the deportation years in the concentration camp of Meskene and in the city of Aleppo, where he met Naim Efendi. Beginning in 1928 and until his death in 1952, he served as director at the Boghos Nubar Library in Paris. For more information on Andonian, see Rita Soulahian Kuyumjian (ed.), *Exile, Trauma and Death: On the Road to Chankiri with Komitas Vartabed* (London: Gomidas Institute and Tekeyan Cultural Association, 2010).
32. Efendi or Bey are Ottoman titles like Mister or Sir and defined the rank of the individual in society. Efendi is a lower rank compared to Bey, and Naim is reffered to as Efendi in Ottoman documents.
33. Aràm Andonian, *Documents officiels concernant les massacres Arméniens* (Paris: Imprimerie H. Turabian 227, Boulevard Raspail, 1920); Andonian, *The Memoirs of Naim Bey, Turkish Official Documents relating to the Deportations and Massacres of Armenians*, compiled by Aram Andonian with an introduction by Viscount Gladstone (London: Hodder and Stoughton, 1920); Aram Andonian, *Medz Vojirě*, [The Great Crime]

(Boston: Bahag Printing House, 1921). The English edition is quite problematic and should not be used as as source, while the French one, although a faithful translation of the Armenian original, leaves out several chapters. In this work, reference is made only to the Armenian text.

34. Şinasi Orel ve Süreyya Yuca, *Ermenilerce Talat Paşa'ya Atfedilen Telgrafların Gerçek Yüzü* (Ankara: Türk Tarih Kurumu, 1983); Şinasi Orel and Süreyya Yuca, *The Talat Pasha Telegrams, Historical Fact or Armenian Fiction?* (Nicosia: K. Rustem & Brother, 1986).
35. "Les explications de Bernard Lewis," *Le Monde*, 1 January 1994.
36. Guenter Lewy, *The Armenian Massacres in Ottoman Turkey: A Disputed Genocide* (Salt Lake City: University of Utah Press, 2004).
37. Ibid., 206.
38. Ibid.
39. Ibid., 73, 206.
40. Ibid., 65.
41. https://www.tbmm.gov.tr/develop/owa/tbmm_basin_aciklamalari_sd.aciklama?p1=30684 (Accessed 14 April 2017). Needless to add, the emphasis here is not on the point that the Turkish Government gave a prize (they give so many prizes for so many purposes), but the reason for the prize.
42. Arnold Toynbee and James Bryce, *The Treatment of Armenians in the Ottoman Empire, Documents presented to Viscount Grey of Fallodon, Secretary of State for Foreign Affairs By Viscount Bryce*. Uncensored edition (Princeton and London: Gomidas Institute, 2005). For more on the "hierarchy syndrome," which has been internalized by a number of critical historians, see Taner Akçam, "The Relationship between Historians and Archival Records: A Critique of Single Source Scholarship on the Armenian Genocide," *Journal of the Society for Armenian Studies*, 19, no. 2 (2010): 43–92.
43. Marc Nichanian, "The Truth of the Facts About the New Revisionism," in *Remembrance and Denial: The Case of the Armenian Genocide*, edited by Richard G. Hovannisian (Detroit: Wayne State University Press, 1999), 257.
44. All of the information regarding Father Krikor Guerguerian's life we received from Dr. Edmund Guerguerian.
45. Nusret had been convicted, sentenced to death, and executed in August 1920. For more on the Kürt Mustafa Pasha trial, see Vahakn N. Dadrian and Taner Akçam, *Judgment at Istanbul*, 305–306.
46. For a brief note by Krikor Guerguerian on the transfer of his documents, see Krikor Guerguerian Archive, 03 "19—Zaven Yeghiayan."
47. The author of these lines has made numerous efforts to be allowed to work in these archives over the years, all of which were unsuccessful. Our wish to compare the original materials in the Guerguerian archive with those found in Jerusalem has thus far been met with no response.

48. *Takvim-i Vekayi*, no. 3540, 5 May 1919. For full text of the indictment, see Vahakn N. Dadrian and Taner Akçam, *Judgment at Istanbul*, 179–190.
49. For more detailed information on the activities of both Bahaettin Şakir and the Special Organization, see Taner Akçam, *A Shameful Act: The Armenian Genocide and the Question of Turkish Responsibility* (New York: Metropolitan, 2006), 149–205. A couple of the cables in question are: BOA.DH.ŞFR., 441/80; 442/31, and 498/67.
50. Vahakn N. Dadrian and Taner Akçam, *Judgment at Istanbul*, 180–181.
51. For the testimony in the main Unionist trial, see ibid., 184; for the judges' decision in the Mamuretülaziz case, see ibid., 207–212.
52. *Yeni Gazete*, 3 August 1919.
53. *Alemdar*, 11 January 1920.
54. We call the text that we discovered in the archive, following A. Andonian's definition *Hatırat* [Memoirs], all references given from this Turkish text is *Hatırat* henceforth.

Introduction

When Dickran H. Boyajian published one of the earliest studies of the Armenian Genocide, he subtitled his book, "The Case for a Forgotten Genocide."[1] Since then decades have passed, and hundreds of publications in a variety of languages have been printed on the subject. It can now be said that the Armenian Genocide has taken its rightfully important place within the field of Genocide Studies. It is no longer a "forgotten genocide."

Recent publications in the field have successfully demonstrated, despite the resilient denialism of Turkish governments, that the Armenians on their historic homeland were subjected to a systematic destruction carried out by Ottoman-Turkish governments. As one of the oldest Christian peoples of the region, Armenians lived for nearly two millennia as a Christian minority, surrounded by a Muslim environment, and were deprived the basic social, economic and political rights within an empire that was ruled according to Islamic law. The Armenian quest for more social justice and political equality started in the second half of the nineteenth century, but was met with increasing repression by successive Ottoman governments.

Symbolically, the 1878 Congress of Berlin is accepted as the beginning of a long process of destruction, which ended, again symbolically, with the establishment of Soviet Armenia in 1921 and the Republic of Turkey in 1923. The period 1878–1923 can be called one of an ongoing genocidal process and was marked by three big mass-atrocities against the Armenian

© The Author(s) 2018
T. Akçam, *Killing Orders*, Palgrave Studies in the History of Genocide,
https://doi.org/10.1007/978-3-319-69787-1_2

population. The wide-scale massacres committed especially during 1894–1896 in the reign of Sultan Abdul Hamid (known as the Hamidian Massacres) cost, as a conservative estimate, around 100,000 human lives.[2] The 1909 Adana massacres ended with the destruction of a city and the death of ca. 20,000 Armenians. Then came the Genocide of 1915–1918, in which the entire Armenian population was uprooted from its historic homeland. From ca. 2 million Armenians in Anatolia in 1914, today there is only a very small minority left (40–60 thousand) in Istanbul.

The Genocide not only cost the Armenians their existence but also forced them with the burden of proof of their own destruction because of the consistent denial of Turkish governments. As we explained in the preface, the telegrams of Talat Pasha play a crucial role in providing this "proof." These telegrams, which were published by Aram Andonian as part of the memoirs of the Ottoman bureaucrat, Naim, contained the extermination orders of Armenian people. To show the authenticity of these telegrams and Naim's memoirs means nothing but to remove the last brick from denialist wall.

NAIM EFENDI AND HIS MEMOIRS

Naim worked as the office secretary in the Deportation Office (*Sevkiyat Müdürlüğü*) of the Aleppo Branch of the Interior Ministry's Directorate for Tribal and Immigrant Settlement (*İskan-ı Aşair ve Muhacirin Müdüriyeti*).[3] The text that is referred to here as "memoirs" is not a book of recollections in the classic sense; it is a collection of handwritten copies of some 52 Ottoman documents,[4] along with supplementary notes explaining them, all written out by Naim himself. Most of the documents within this collection are attributed to the Unionist Triumvir and Interior Minister Talat Pasha, and some contain his orders regarding the liquidation of the Armenian population. Additionally, Naim relates what he himself knew about the subjects and events mentioned in the telegraphic cables. However, an important part of these "memoirs" has never been published and is only now seeing the light of day (see Appendix A.1).

The person to first bring these recollections to the public was the Armenian journalist and intellectual, Aram Andonian, who, along with the other leading members of Istanbul's Armenian community, was arrested on 24 April 1915 and only by a curious circumstance managed to escape arrest (and the grisly fate of many others).[5] After Aleppo fell to the English in November 1918, Andonian, who was there at the time, purchased the original work from Naim himself, who did not abandon the city when the British entered it. But Andonian did not simply purchase the handwritten copies of the documents (what are referred to here as the "memoirs"), but also ca. 24 original Ottoman documents.[6]

Here is a general overview of those 24 original documents. We have handwritten copies of 16 of them included in Naim's memoirs. Six of 24 were related to Armenian deputy Krikor Zohrab and not mentioned in the memoirs at all. Another two of the 24 documents, which are not mentioned in the memoirs also, are letters written by Union and Progress Party Central Committee Member Bahaettin Şakir. Andonian reproduced photographs of 14 of the 24 documents in his book in the Armenian language including Şakir's letters.[7] Seven of the 24 documents were encrypted telegrams using two- and three-digit encryption techniques. In his book, Andonian provided five images of these seven ciphered cables. Twelve of the total 24 are telegrams bearing the signature of the Governor of Aleppo, Mustafa Abdülhalik. Andonian provided photographs of seven of these in the book.

In a note that he kept private, Andonian recounts the specific days on which he met with Naim and those on which he purchased the documents. According to his account, he met with Naim in Aleppo's well-known Baron Hotel (owned by the Mazlumyan brothers) on the 6th, 10th and 14th of November 1918, and it was there that he purchased and received the memoirs and documents in separate batches. The November 14 visit was one in which Naim came to express his gratitude for the payment, and he told Andonian at this encounter that he could provide him with even more copies of documents. Andonian refused, instead informing the former Ottoman bureaucrat that he could receive more money only if he provided the original documents themselves.

> Naim came to the hotel personally in order to thank [me]. He again wanted me to mediate [for him] with B [i.e., Onnik Mazlumyan, owner of the Baron Hotel—author's note] for the documents that he had promised to bring. I told him that I wouldn't do it [i.e., make any more payments] if they were just [handwritten] copies. If he brought the originals [that would be] different... (see Image 1)

In the end, Naim would indeed bring more original documents.

On the basis of Naim's recollections and the documents he brought, Andonian would write a book in Armenian in 1919, which was published

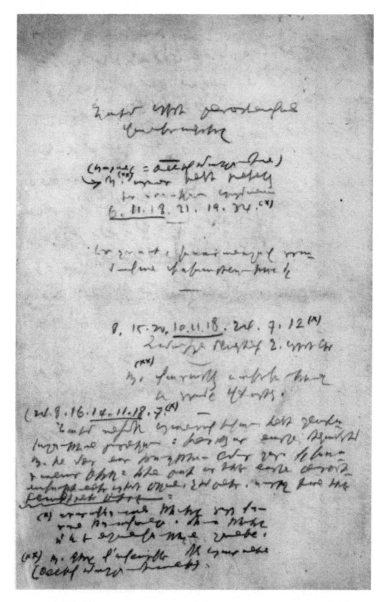

Image 1   Andonian' handwritten notes on his meetings with Naim Efendi

only after the English and French editions.[8] The work's greatest importance is in its containing cables said to have been sent by Talat Pasha. In these, the Ottoman Interior Minister gave orders dealing with the annihilation of the Armenians. To give but a few examples, in a message dated 22 September 1915, Talat Pasha gave the order "that all of the Armenians' rights on Turkish soil, such as the rights to live and work, have been eliminated, and not one is to be left—not even the infant in the cradle; the government accepts all responsibility for this [situation]," and states that "effective measures" in line with this order "have already been seen in some provinces."[9]

In another cable, sent to the Provincial Governor of Aleppo on 29 September 1915, it states,

It had previously been communicated that the government, by order of the Cemiyet (the Committee of the Ittihad), had decided to completely annihilate all Armenians living in Turkey. Those who oppose this command and decision cannot remain part of the official structure of the state. Without paying attention to woman, child, [and] incompetent, no matter how tragic the methods of annihilation might be, without listening to feelings of conscience, their existence must be ended.[10]

In a similar vein, another cable, this one undated, claims that

Although the intent has long existed to eliminate the [empire's] Armenian subjects, who have for centuries longed to undermine the sound foundations of the state and posed a serious threat for the government, the [suitable] conditions [to do so] did not exist, and it was therefore not possible to realize this sacred aim. Since all obstacles [to this course of action] have now been removed, and the time has come to rescue the homeland from this dangerous element, it is necessary to work, both consciously and with full commitment, and without giving in to feelings of mercy and compassion, to blot out the name "Armenian" in Turkey by putting a complete end to their existence.[11]

Another cable, dated 16 October 1915, states, "Since the general crimes and misdeeds carried out by the [local] population against certain known [deported] individuals en route will ensure that the aims pursued by the government are achieved,[12] there is no need to pursue legal investigations in this regard. The necessary message has been communicated to the Provincial Districts of [Deyr-i] Zor and Urfa."[13] Another message to the administration in Aleppo, dated 14 December 1915, states that "the most important persons whose extermination should be attempted are the religious clergy. It would be an utmost mistake to give them permission to travel and settle into the hazardous areas like Syria and Jerusalem. The best place of settlement for these individuals, whose character is prone to conspire maliciously against the government, is the place in which they will be exterminated..."[14]

It goes without saying that a book containing these and similar documents pose a serious problem for the official version of Turkish history espoused by the Republic of Turkey. This was the main reason for the 1983 publication of the Turkish Historical Society authored by Şinasi Orel and Süreyya Yuca. The authors questioned the very existence of an Ottoman bureaucrat by the name of Naim and claimed that both his alleged memoirs and the attached documents had actually been produced by Andonian himself.[15]

The authors based their claims on three main arguments: (1) It was unlikely that there was an individual by the name of Naim Efendi; (2) a non-existent person cannot write a memoir, and such memoir cannot therefore exist; (3) the telegraphic cables attributed to Talat Pasha were falsified. They thus concluded that both the memoirs and the documents are forgeries perpetrated by Armenians, most likely by Andonian himself.

Since the book's publication, it has become customary to refer to the documents in these memoirs as "the falsified cables attributed to Talat Pasha." However, as we will show, Orel and Yuca are wrong on all counts. There was indeed an Ottoman bureaucrat by the name of Naim Efendi, and there is an original memoir written by Naim himself, that we have in our possession. We can also show that the stories told by Naim in his memoir are authentic and can be confirmed with relevant documents from the Ottoman archives. We can also demonstrate that all arguments brought by Orel and Yuca regarding the authenticity of Talat Pasha cables are either false or entirely speculative, and ultimately wrong.

Notes

1. Dickran H. Boyajian, *Armenia: The Case for a Forgotten Genocide* (Westwood, NJ: Educational Book Crafters, 1972).
2. There were ongoing massacres during Abdul Hamid reign. For an extensive bibliograpy on the topic, see George N. Shirinian, "The Armenian Massacres of 1894–1897: A Bibliography," *Armenian Review*, 47, nos. 1–2 (2001): 113–164.

3. Throughout the text, different terms are used for the same Office: "Office of Deportation," "Director of Tribal and Immigrant Settlement Affairs," "Director-General of Immigrant Affairs," etc., because different people refer to the agency in different ways. The main office was in Istanbul and it also had a branch in Aleppo.

4. The number 52 was given by Krikor Guerguerian himself, who, in 1965, published an article on the subject in Armenian under his nom de plume, "Krieger," "Aram Andoniani Hradaragadz Turk Bashdonagan Vaverakreru Vaveraganutyunı" [The Truth About the Official Turkish [sic] Documents published by Aram Andonian], Zartonk Gazetesi (publ.), *1915-1965 Hushamadyan Medz Yegherni* [Album of the Great Disaster], (Beirut: Atlas, 1965), 238–239. In 1986, Vahakn Dadrian edited and corrected several errors in Guerguerian's list and prepared a new annotated list of 52 documents. Vahakn N. Dadrian, "The Naim-Andonian Documents on the World War I Destruction of Ottoman Armenians: The Anatomy of a Genocide," *International Journal of Middle Eastern Studies*, 18, no. 3 (August 1986): 311–360, 316–317. In fact, whether or not certain quotations of Naim should or should not be counted as "documents" should be the subject of debate. Some of the descriptions that both Guerguerian and Dadrian consider "documents" consist more of Naim's recounting of information and his recollections of events than of copies of actual documents. Without belaboring the issue further here, we use the figure 52.

5. Aram Andonian wrote memoirs about his arrest on 24 April 1915 and on his subsequent odyssey over the years of deportation and war. See Rita Soulahian Kuyumjian (ed.), *Exile, Trauma and Death*.

6. We do not know the exact number of the documents that Naim sold to Andonian. Guerguerian claimed that Naim actually delivered three separate original cables dealing with the murder of the Armenian parliamentary deputy Krikor Zohrab, which would make 21 documents all together. Krieger, "Aram Andoniani Hradaragadz Turk Başdonagan Vaverakreru," 236. However, the number of documents related to Zohrab in the Guerguerian archive is in total six. How many of these documents were given by Naim, or how many of them came through other channels, we do not know. We use the number 24 because it is more accurate.

7. In this work, we do not discuss the authenticity of Şakir's two letters because they are not relevant for Naim's memoirs. However, these letters are authentic, not only because the content of the letters is corroborated by information that is accumulated in Armenian Genocide research, but also because Şakir's signature under the letters is original. Şakir was also a columnist in one of the Unionist newspapers, *Şurayı Ümmet* (1902–1910), and used his signature under his columns. We compared Şakir's signature in the letters with those in the newspaper. They are the same, leaving no room for doubt.

8. See note 33 in chapter "Preface."
9. Naim Efendi, *Hatırat* [Memoir], [15]. The page numbers are on the original document and can be seen in the text published here.
10. Aram Andonian, *Medz Vojirě*, 208, 210. There is a photographic image of this document and it contains only numbers (p. 217). A deciphered version was published by Andonian in Naim's Memoirs. Unfortunately, in the version in our possession, this part of the text is missing.
11. *Hatırat* [20].
12. The term *eşhası malume* is used in official Ottoman telegrams to refer to Armenians.
13. *Hatırat* [07].
14. *Hatırat* [14].
15. Şinasi Orel ve Süreyya Yuca, *Ermenilerce Talat Paşa'ya Atfedilen Telgrafların Gerçek Yüzü* (Ankara: Türk Tarih Kurumu, 1983). Neither Orel or Yuca are scholars; Orel was a well-known diplomat. They have not published any other works. It is doubtful that a work examining what are a number of highly difficult technical questions in a considerably detailed and professional manner would have actually been written by two authors who had never before (nor after) put pen to page in such a fashion. For this reason, we felt the need to research the matter more deeply, and this is what we discovered: as we suspected, their book was not actually written by them, but was instead prepared by a team of researchers under the direction of the Turkish Foreign Ministry. The ministry official Kamuran Gürün (author of the widely-distributed work *The Armenian File* defending the Turkish "official version" of history) played a crucial role in its publication. Initially, it was thought to publish the work without authorship as a sort of government issued "white paper," but the names of Orel and Yuca, both of whom served on the aforementioned team, were eventually given authorship.

The work itself has been deemed by Turkish Foreign Ministry officials to be one of the most important works on the Armenian question, and when one considers its decades-long impact on the field of Armenian Genocide studies, the officials' estimation of the book's value cannot be denied.

The Story and Authenticity of Naim Efendi and His Memoirs

HOW THE TEXT HAS COME DOWN TO US

Until now, it was believed that the Naim Efendi Memoirs and documents published by Andonian were complete, but as will be understood from the text in our possession, the text published by Andonian was *not* the complete text supplied by Naim Efendi, but only a part of it.[1]

The person who first found the original document now in our possession was the priest, Krikor Guerguerian, who came across the original memoir and several different documents during a visit to the Boghos Nubar Library in Paris in 1950 and promptly photographed them.[2] According to his description, the memoirs actually consisted of three separate drafts, consisting of 16, 12, and seven pages, respectively, and bound together by a pin.[3] Apart from the Naim Efendi memoirs, Guerguerian claims that "three heretofore unpublished original pieces of official documentation concerning the death of Krikor Zohrab" are to be found in the library as well.[4] Today, except for two documents related to Zohrab's death, neither Naim Efendi's memoirs, nor the original telegrams accompanying them are still there, and their current location is unknown.[5]

In regard to the sections that he *did* publish, Andonian did not remain faithful to the order in which the memoirs were written; the passages that he deemed important were placed within his own text in a manner that he felt best served his narrative. At times, instead of faithfully relating Naim's words, he preferred to summarize them. In a few rare cases, some sentences that do not appear in his memoirs are given as having been his

© The Author(s) 2018
T. Akçam, *Killing Orders*, Palgrave Studies in the History of Genocide,
https://doi.org/10.1007/978-3-319-69787-1_3

words, but these are mostly small insertions meant to clarify the account, such as when the identity is supplied for signatures at the end of documents.

In fact, we can state that what Andonian published in his book was not exactly Naim's memoirs, but large excepts of these memoirs that he saw as important. Nevertheless, at the beginning of his book he says that he is providing informed comments and annotations: "It is not possible to publish Naim Bey's memoirs without some analysis. In certain sections, the necessary explanations must be provided, because the events and persons mentioned or alluded to in those sections are generally unknown in Europe." [6]

Since, in Andonian's Armenian-language version, the sections that he took from Naim's memoirs are written with different characters, it is very easy to compare the sections that he published with the text in our possession. When comparing these two texts, the first thing that we noticed was not the fact that a significant part of the memoirs had not been published by Andonian, but that a great many passages found in the Andonian edition were not to be found in the original text. We have collected these passages in Appendix A.

Andonian's failure to publish a significant portion of Naim's memoirs is understandable. We might conclude that he did not feel it necessary to do so. The question remains, however, as to the fate of those parts of the memoirs used by Andonian, but not discovered by Krikor Guerguerian.

Before discussing the subject in detail, it will be advantageous to discuss another matter having to do with the memoirs. As explained above, there are photographic images of 18 of the original 52 documents included in the memoirs. Of these 18 documents, seven are cipher telegrams that contain only numbers, not words. In the Armenian version of his work, Andonian published reproductions of 14 of these 18 documents. In the text in our possession, there are handwritten copies of 32 of the documents, of which we possess only seven images.

When we compare the handwritten copies of the documents in the memoir with the document images, it quickly becomes apparent that they are identical, word for word.[7] This reveals to us another important truth: Naim did not hand write these documents from memory; rather, he made copies of the originals. If this work had been done from memory, it is certain that some words or sentences would have been different.

The fact that the document images and the descriptions of them found in the published memoirs are one and the same topples one of Orel and

Yuca's principal arguments for the inauthenticity of the documents. They compared the English and French translations of the document copies in the memoirs with the printed Ottoman text images, and saw serious differences, both between the English and French translations and between two translations and the Ottoman texts. It was these discrepancies that they used to support their argument of inauthenticity. "The document forgeries reveal a number of differences in the French and English editions of Andonian's book, so much so that it is not possible to characterize these differences as wrong translations or as the factual errors [of the publishers]."[8] In the wake of the points listed above, we can now consider this issue as resolved. The descriptions in both the handwritten copies found in the memoirs and the document images are one and the same.

WHERE ARE THE MEMOIR AND DOCUMENT ORIGINALS NOW?

So, what happened to the memoirs and documents published by Aram Andonian that we no longer possess? The answer to this question can be found in two different letters published here in the appendices. One of the letters, dated 6 October 1925, is from Dr. Avedis Nakkashian to Aram Andonian (see Appendix B),[9] while the other was written on 28 July 1937 by Andonian to Mrs. Mary Terzian in Geneva (see Appendix C).

The relevant information in these two letters can be summarized thusly: Andonian brought the collection of memoirs and documents to London in 1920 for sake of the English edition. Afterward, he selected from these "some of the original documents that he had not finished photographing." The others he left "in London, because they needed to prepare photographs for the edition." In August 1920, Avedis Nakkashian, who was working as a doctor in Istanbul at the time, appealed to Andonian through the Armenian Patriarch, Zaven, for assistance in the Istanbul Court-Martial war crimes trial against Abdülahad Nuri [Tengirşenk].[10] Abdülahad Nuri had served as Director of Deportation in the Settlement Branch of the Directorate of Tribal and Immigrant Settlement in Aleppo during the war years.[11]

Naim worked as secretary at this directorate at the time and was intimately familiar with Abdülahad Nuri. In his memoirs, Naim provides a good deal of information and documents on Abdülahad Nuri.

Dr. Avedis Nakkashian had heard many stories about Abdülahad Nuri from fellow Armenians who had survived the deportations and then lived around Aleppo. He knew that the survivors had sought him out everywhere in order to apprehend him. Dr. Nakkashian had picked up his trail in Istanbul completely by accident and succeeded in having him arrested. It was in this period, in August 1920, that he came into possession of Andonian's book, where he first read about "Talat and Abdul Ahad Nuri's correspondence with one another." He then decided to request from Andonian, through the intermediary of the Armenian Patriarch Zaven, the documents that he had published regarding Abdülahad Nuri.

Andonian recounted the rest of the story in a letter he wrote to a certain Mrs. Terzian in 1937:

> ... I received a letter... pertaining to this matter and immediately wrote to the Armenian Bureau in London for them to send all the original versions they had to the Patriarchate, which they did. At the same time, I sent a long essay that Naim Bey had written in pencil concerning Abdulahad Nuri Bey, an incriminating document for his sinister superior, as well as a few of the original versions I had at home in which Abdulahad Nuri Bey was mentioned.

From the Istanbul press at the time, we learn that a trial was opened against Abdülahad Nuri and that these documents were indeed used in the trial. In its 19 September 1919 edition, the Armenian daily, *Joghovurti Tzayn* ("The Voice of the People"), contained a news report saying that "A trial has recently been held in the First Court-Martial against the notorious butcher Abdül Ahad Nuri." According to the article, "Dr. Nakkashian has taken part in the [prosecution's] case and [submitted] striking documents against the well-known murderer." Apart from the doctor, some of the documents sent by Andonian were read into the record.[12]

Abdülahad Nuri's trial would be adjourned before it had concluded, and the defendant was "allowed" to escape custody and make his way to Anatolia. In his letter, Dr. Nakkashian gives a lengthy account as to why Abdülahad Nuri's trial was so suddenly ended, according to which, on one of the days in which the court was in session, an unknown priest arrived from Ankara on a visit. "I am Father Dajjad," he said. "I have come here at the expense of the National Government in Ankara in order to free Abdul Ahad Nuri." He then gave the warning: "That beast is the brother of Yusuf Kemal, the head of the Ministry of Foreign Affairs in Ankara. You are about to hang a dog here, and if you do, 2,000–3,000 Armenians will be annihilated there. I beg you, let this man go free."[13]

In his letter, Dr. Nakkashian also writes that: "While we were working to find a solution and organize our efforts, Ferid Pasha's cabinet was dismissed, and a government sympathetic to the nationalists took its place," adding that the composition of the panel of Court-Martial judges also changed, with the former Chief Judge, Kürt Mustafa Pasha, who had had Abdülahad Nuri arrested in the first place, now being arrested himself. The account given in the letter is confirmed in the daily press. Ferid's government resigned on 17 October 1920,[14] and Kürt Mustafa Pasha would be arrested less than a month later, on November 15.[15] According Dr. Nakkashian, he was briefly held for having been the one to initiate the case in the first place.

In a letter to Mary Terzian, dated 28 July 1937, Andonian replied to her inquiry as to what had happened to the memoirs and documents that he had sent to Istanbul. "Regarding the documents sent to the Patriarchate either from London or by me directly—and which were added to the file for the case brought against Abdulahad Nuri—they, of course, stayed there. I never learned what happened to them." We still do not know what happened to these documents, but as they were supposed to have been included in the aforementioned case file, there is compelling reason to assume that, if they were not destroyed like all of the other case files for these trials, then they must be stored away somewhere, either in the Prime Minister's Ottoman Archives in Istanbul or Military Archive in Ankara, known as ATASE (Archives of the Turkish General Staff, Military History and Strategic Studies).[16]

Some parts of the remaining (i.e., unsent) documents disappeared or were lost over the course of the Soghomon Tehlirian Trial in Berlin. Tehlirian was arrested and tried for the March 1921 murder of Talat Pasha, who had sought refuge in Berlin after the war. Tehlirian's defense attorneys sought help from Andonian, who consented, traveling to Berlin with some of the documents in his possession. According to Andonian, "the originals of two letters and several telegraphic cables [written by Bahaettin Şakir] were included in Tehlirian's case dossier."[17]

A number of clarifications should be made here. The documents brought by Andonian to Berlin for the trial were not actually included as evidence in the case file, as they were not directly connected to the trial. What is more, the court did not summon Andonian to testify, despite his presence in Berlin. In the judges' opinion, there was no need to debate Talat Pasha's responsibility for the deportations and what followed, because from the standpoint of the trial, it was sufficient that Tehlirian *saw*

Talat Pasha as individually responsible for the annihilation of the Armenians.[18]

The failure of the documents to be utilized in Tehlirian's trial was used by Orel and Yuca as evidence of having been fabricated.[19] This argument is incorrect. The Berlin court had no wish to either discuss the documents nor the role of Talat Pasha (and, by extension, the Turkish Government) in the killing of Armenians. If such a discussion had indeed been held, the court would have confirmed by its own hand that the documents were real and the role of Germany in the genocide would have come to the fore. In the wake of both the Versailles Treaty and its onerous terms and the social and economic instability then besetting the country, this was a potentially volatile subject, of which the German Government wished to steer clear.

It was specifically for this reason that Walter Rössler, who had served as Germany's consul in Aleppo during the Genocide, was not given permission to testify during the trial.[20] In a letter to the German Foreign Ministry, Rössler informed his superiors that, should he be allowed to do so, he would be obliged to state both that the Andonian documents were real and that Talat Pasha (and the Ottoman Government) were directly responsible for the murders (and other war crimes).

It will be of some benefit to quote Rössler at length.

> If the German Foreign Office should give its permission that I be examined as a witness in the proceedings against the murderer of Talaat Pasha, I would have to be released from official secrecy and would be obliged to answer all of the presiding judge's questions under the oath I would swear as a witness. I would not be able to avoid expressing my conviction that Talaat Pasha is, in fact, one of those Turkish statesmen who wanted the Armenians to be annihilated and carried this out according to plan. All of the softening effects that might arise, for example from my depiction of the exceptional danger that the Armenian question was, in fact, for Turkey as it was to be used by Russia as a means of dividing up Turkey, would recede to the background compared with the main impression that my testimony would make. I suppose that the court will present me with documents that were published by the Armenian, Aram Andonian, and which contain accounts of Talaat Pasha's orders in the matter concerning the deportation and annihilation. I would have to give testimony to the effect that these documents are, in all probability, genuine. I would also have to testify that a remark made to me by the Commissioner of Deportations, who was sent from Constantinople to Aleppo, was actually made, "You do not understand what we want: we want an Armenia without Armenians".[21]

After his return to Paris, Andonian would make several attempts to have the documents he left in Berlin returned to him, but without result. Unfortunately, these documents, which normally should still be found among the case file in question, are today nowhere to be found. As best as can be understood from Andonian's account[s], a part of Naim's memoirs and documents should have still been in the Boghos Nubar Pasha Library in Paris. As was mentioned above, when Father Guerguerian visited the library in 1950 he found handwritten drafts bound together and a number of documents as well, which he promptly photographed. Neither Yves Ternon, nor Vahakn Dadrian, who visited the library in the 1970s and 1980s, respectively, found the originals of any of these documents. Where they ended up is not clear. The only traces of the originals of both the memoirs and the documents are the photographs of the originals taken by Guerguerian, which we are publishing here.

CHALLENGES TO THE AUTHENTICITY OF THE TEXT

In their 1983 book, Orel and Yuca questioned the very existence of an Ottoman official by the name of Naim Efendi, and claimed that both the memoirs attributed to him and the accompanying documents had been fabricated by their editor/publisher, Aram Andonian. Although Vahakn Dadrian attempted to prove their authenticity in a 1986 article,[22] ever since the appearance of Orel and Yuca's work, the Naim-Andonian texts have been generally met with skepticism, not only in academic circles, but also among the general public. They were increasingly referred to not as the *Naim Efendi* documents, but the *Andonian* documents, implying the latter's actual authorship. Apart from the general aversion to their use in scholarly works, their inauthenticity has featured as one of the principal arguments by those defending the official Turkish view in political debates, and mention of their "fabrication by Armenian circles" is constantly made. It is thus possible to claim today that the interested public is in broad agreement that both the Naim Efendi memoirs and the accompanying documents are forgeries.

What is interesting here is that there has not been a single new work on the subject since Orel and Yuca's work, more than 30 years ago. Those writers defending the state's official version, who have subsequently written on the topic, such as Kamuran Gürün,[23] Türkkaya Ataöv,[24] Guenther Lewy,[25] and Maxime Gauin,[26] have done no more than to repeat Orel and Yuca's findings. Even those scholars of the period who have not directly addressed the topic have largely accepted the falsity of Andonian's documents as a given and have said as much. Erik Zürcher,[27] Bernard Lewis,[28] Andrew Mango,[29] Norman Stone,[30] and Michael Gunter,[31] are but a few of the dozens of examples that could be given in this regard.

As mentioned above, critical historians have taken heed not to touch the subject of Naim Efendi in their works, or to use either the memoirs or the attached documents, instead giving the whole subject a wide berth, and, even if they find other similar documents, prefer to employ these instead, or to limit themselves to statements that the subject needs further discussion and investigation.[32] And to be fair, my personal stance was along these same lines when I began this study. I was fully open to the possibility that the documents under review were indeed forgeries.[33] In a subsequent work, I stated simply that I "would not enter into a discussion of the topic," but when I discovered documents with similar content, I vowed to use the documents published by Andonian as well.[34] Thus, in my later work, I went further, stating that the whole debate needed to be reopened.[35]

THE THREE FUNDAMENTAL RESERVATIONS ABOUT THE NAIM EFENDI MEMOIRS

Orel and Yuca based their claims that the memoirs and documents were fabricated by Andonian on three main arguments: (1) It was unlikely that there was an individual by the name of Naim Efendi; (2) It is unclear whether or not Naim Efendi's memoirs were an original text; (3) The published documents contain many errors, such as signatures and dates; they are forgeries produced by the Armenian journalist Aram Andonian. In order to back up their first claim, the authors present research they have done in the Ottoman archives. They claim to have researched "Ottoman almanacs… Collections of Imperial Laws and Decrees, and the first private Ottoman newspaper, as well as law codes," but never to have encountered the name "Naim Efendi."[36] For this reason, "It is not possible to arrive at a decisive judgment as to whether Naim Bey was a person who actually existed." Orel and Yuca offer three possibilities: "A—Naim Bey is an imaginary person; B—Naim Bey is a fictitious name; C—Naim Bey is a real person," but "the only thing that can be firmly established is that if such a person as Naim Bey actually existed, he was in all events an insignificant bureaucrat…[and] would not have been in a position where he could have access to these documents that were top secret and very important."[37]

Since they doubt the existence of such a person, Orel and Yuca do not accept Naim Efendi's authorship of the memoirs attributed to him. Indeed, throughout their work, when referencing the memoirs published by Andonian, they always signal their disbelief by putting the words "memory" and "recollection" in quotation marks.[38] For them, the entire memoirs and accompanying documents are the work of Andonian,[39] arguing that "Andonian acted carelessly when he edited the forged documents," and asserting that "Andonian hastily scribbled down the alleged documents."[40] The authors state that the purpose of their work is to show how Andonian produced the documents and argue that, through their work they have "destroyed the very foundations of a system that had been established by Andonian for producing forged documents."[41] According to Orel and Yuca, "Armenian circles" have perpetrated "a crime…by putting together these forged documents."[42]

Perhaps the harshest judgment of the documents was expressed by Kamuran Gürün:

> If [a] sentence of documents claimed to be authentic is false, the entire book then becomes [nothing more than] a documentation of an international forgery.… I wonder: were these forged documents that were prepared by an "immoral" Naim Bey and examined by an Armenian organization seen as such when they were purchased? We will never know. Nevertheless, it is worth considering that this person called "Naim Bey" may have only lived in someone's imagination and that these forgeries were actually concocted by Andonian[43]

Was There an Ottoman Official by the Name of Naim Efendi?

The first and most important question that must be answered in regard to the authenticity of the memoirs and documents is whether or not there ever actually was an Ottoman official by the name of Naim Efendi. We can confidently answer in the affirmative. There was indeed an Ottoman official by the name of Naim Efendi, and it is possible to establish this from a number of different sources. At the head of these are the documents published by the Turkish General Staff's Military Archive (ATASE).[44] The second source—also important—is the three separate Ottoman documents in which the name "Naim Efendi" occurs. One of these is published by Andonian; the other two are documents concerning the Armenian parliamentary deputy, Krikor Zohrab, the originals of which are still to be found in the Boghos Nubar Library in Paris.[45] On the basis of these documents we can confidently assert that a person by the name of Naim Efendi served in the Deportation Office in both the camp of Meskene and in Aleppo.

The Ottoman documents published by ATASE deal with investigations of military and civil bureaucrats who took bribes from Armenians in the refugee camp of Meskene and its environs in the summer of 1916. The reason for the investigation was reports that the deportation office officials, in exchange for bribes, had been turning a blind eye toward Armenians who, having been slated for deportation from Aleppo to Deyr-i Zor, were producing travel documents and fleeing elsewhere.[46]

Heading the list of Ottoman officials against whom investigations were conducted was Lieutenant Colonel Galip (henceforth Colonel). Colonel Galip had been appointed as the commander of the Office of Logistical Support (of the Army), and his job was to deport the Armenians who had concentrated in great number along the banks of the Euphrates River (including Meskene camp) and were thus seen as a threat to military transports there, and to resettle them further east in Deyr-i Zor. Related to this, he was also entrusted with the task of separating out the craftsmen among Armenians so as to have them work for Ottoman military.[47] Instead of doing this, however, Colonel Galip and those around him had taken bribes from hundreds of Armenians in exchange for special travel documents and then turned a blind eye while they fled toward Aleppo instead of Deyr-i Zor.

Aleppo Governor Mustafa Abdülhalik was incensed at goings-on around Meskene and brought his complaints to the attention of Istanbul through a series of telegraphic cables.[48]

A portion of the Armenians who are to be deported from here [i.e., Aleppo] to Deyr-i Zor have fled and returned [here] by the passive acquiescence of the deportation officials and guards, and their exploitation of their lack of documents and have thereby transformed the deportation question into vicious circle.

In the governor's view, "the officials and guards have grasped the opportunity and abused their authority" and that, in order "to prevent abuses," he had therefore called a temporary "pause to the deportations to Deyr-i Zor until such time as they could be carried out in an orderly and proper manner." The governor also complained about the establishment of an orphanage in Meskene for Armenian children.[49]

Similar complaints were made by Salih Zeki, the District Governor of Deyr-i Zor, about things transpiring on the route from Aleppo to Deyr-i Zor. In a cable dated 19 July 1916, he informed his superiors in the capital that, of the seven persons ordered by the Aleppo Police Directorate to be sent to Deyr-i Zor with gendarmerie accompaniment for being "harmful individuals," only one had actually been brought there. The remaining six individuals had been allowed to escape somewhere along the way. In similar fashion, of a convoy of 72 Armenians who had been deported from Aleppo to Deyr-i Zor, only three had actually arrived at their intended destination. Almost the entire convoy had been allowed to go free by the gendarmerie escort before reaching the district of Deyr-i Zor. Zeki requested that the behavior of the gendarmes be reported to the authorities in Aleppo and to the other responsible parties.[50]

Talat, after receiving these complaints from the governor of Aleppo and district governor of Deyr-i Zor, sent a cable to the former on July 19, requesting a list "of names of those officials whose abuses were witnessed during the Armenian deportations, in order that the necessary measures may be taken against them," and ordered that an immediate end be put "to the employment of those whom the provincial [government has the] authority to remove."[51] In his reply, Governor Mustafa Abdülhalik mentioned that the "convoys deported to [Deyr-i] Zor under guard are even dispersing on the way [there]" and demanded that a broad investigation be undertaken regarding those who fled, and that the responsible parties be sent to the Court-Martial.

The governor requested that Hakkı Bey, who had been appointed to oversee the (now suspended) deportations to Deyr-i Zor once they were to be recommenced, be sent at the soonest possible opportunity.[52] In a cable dated 4 August 1916, Talat informed the Aleppo governor that "Hakkı Bey had already set out 15 days before."[53] The decision to open an investigation per the governor's request was taken on August 8. Hakkı Bey, who began his duties in Aleppo with the title "Assistant Director of the Deportation Office," would travel to the camp of Meskene and prepare a report on the situation there.[54] In time, Hakkı Bey would also restart the deportations/resettlement to Deyr-i Zor.[55]

The report from the investigation into corruption and impropriety was completed on 5–6 October 1916, and the testimonies of persons involved began to be recorded the following month.[56] Over the course of the interviews and interrogations, one of the persons whose testimony was sought was a certain Naim Efendi, who gave his account on 14–15 November 1916. In this draft deposition, his personal information was recorded as

"Naim Efendi, the son of Hüseyin Nuri, 26 years of age, from Silifke, former Dispatch Official for Meskene, currently the official in charge of Municipal Grain Storage Depots."[57]

In his testimony, Naim Efendi said that Colonel Galip had met with deportation officials in the camp of Meskene "one day after he came from Jarabulus (Cerablus) to Meskene as the commander in charge of the Office of Logistic Support" and showed them "one of two telegrams written [and sent] by the Ministry of War....In these cables [the Minister of War] speaks of the need to exploit [the skills] of those Armenians with certain professions who were settled in the Euphrates region, and to protect the orphans." Because of these orders, Colonel Galip requested that he be given the names of "all of the [Armenians] with certain professions, as well as [those of] wagon drivers then in the deportation center," and added that "registries [be created] for any children who are without parents or guardians."[58]

According to several Ottoman documents in our possession, Colonel Galip spoke truthfully to Naim Efendi. Talat Pasha sent a cable to the District Governor of Deyr-i Zor on 7 August 1916, in which he mentioned the policy of exploiting the services of Armenian craftsmen. Nevertheless, the interior minister also stated that the local camp commandant [i.e., Colonel Galip] could not simply make arbitrary decisions as to who the craftsmen to be selected were.[59] In another cable, dated 29 July 1916, Talat stated that the presence of large numbers of Armenians in the area of the Euphrates basin were a threat to military transport and requested that they be deported. The necessary wagons and drivers were to be secured from the Armenians, who would perform this task.[60] In other words, the issues raised by Talat Pasha in these cables were the subjects of the investigation.

In his testimony, Naim stated that almost all of the Armenians had registered themselves as having a profession, but that he had not been personally involved whatsoever in these events. He even claimed that he had told Colonel Galip, "[T]his is not correct. The return of those persons subjected to the general deportation is subject to the orders of the Interior Ministry. We do not do this." Even so, he did not fail to defend Colonel Galip, adding that "I never heard a thing about this changing [of deportation destinations] in exchange for money."

Naim Efendi denied that he had turned a blind eye to the providing of Armenians with documents so that they could flee to Aleppo: "There were never instances of fleeing during my time [of service]. The deportations were delayed for a limited period, and the deportation offices [in Meskene] were temporarily closed. During that period, a few Armenians fled and came to Aleppo. How did they get there? Through [the paying of] money, or through some other means? I have no information about this."[61] Naim Efendi's denial of any involvement—even knowledge of the reported goings-on—is an understandable position for him to have taken, since he himself had been one of the bureaucrats who had allowed Armenians to flee to Aleppo in exchange for bribes, and the "fees" charged for this service had been great indeed.

In the memoirs of a number of Armenians who managed to survive their time in Meskene camp, Colonel Galip and those in his retinue are said to have taken much money in bribes, both during the process of selecting Armenian craftsmen and in separating the wagon drivers. For example, Krikor Ankut, who was in Meskene during that period, wrote:

> Galip Bey was appointed…as Commander for Logistical Support on the lines leading from Meskene to Deyr-i Zor. He began his [new] task by deciding to select craftsmen and workers from among th[ose in th]e Armenian deportation convoys, for this allowed him the possibility of acquiring a significant amount of bribes. Since all of the [Armenians'] heads were mindful of the horrors and brutality of Deyr-i Zor, everyone promised Galip Bey—even competed [for the privilege]—that they could provide him with a bribe, so that they could remain [together] as a family in Hamam or one of the military camps: for every family [that wished to stay] they gave about five Ottoman lira.[62]

All of this shows that the information that Andonian and Naim provided about the events in Meskene during the summer of 1916 was true. The time that Naim began to discuss with Andonian the question of a group of wealthy Armenians being allowed to flee to Aleppo is in conformity with the dates above.

THE OTTOMAN DOCUMENTS BEARING THE NAME "NAIM EFENDI"

As already mentioned, we are in possession of three Ottoman documents bearing the name Naim Efendi. Two of these concerns the killing of the prominent Armenian thinker and parliamentary deputy, Krikor Zohrab.[63] The originals of these documents are still found in the Boghos Nubar Library in Paris. They are not mentioned, either in Naim's memoirs, or in the book published by Andonian, however.[64] Chronologically speaking, the first was written on 11 November 1915, and is a letter from Aleppo Governor Mustafa Abdülhalik to Assistant Director of the Deportation Office, Abdülahad Nuri. In a note added to the letter by Nuri, he writes, "Naim Efendi, my son, go to Eyüp Bey; it must be registered there somewhere. Investigate it thoroughly. Additionally, write down [your findings] on paper."[65]

The second document in question is a cable dated 17 November 1915, sent by Interior Minister Talat Pasha to the Governor of Aleppo. In it, Talat says that reports have been received that Kirkor Zohrab, whose continued presence in Istanbul was seen as undesirable, and who had therefore been sent to the region under command of the Sixth Army, "had perished as the result of an accident," and stated that an investigation into the matter had been made "by the district governor of Urfa and the Euphrates Logistical Support Line Commander." Since the relevant documents of inquiry had been sent to the "Aleppo Logistical Support Line Commander," the governor of Aleppo was asked to appoint an official to investigate the matter.[66] Governor Mustafa Abdülhalik, who received the telegram, passed on information and wrote a note of reference to Abdülahad Nuri on November 19 with the attached note: "I spoke [to him] verbally yesterday. I think that these papers are with Corps Commander Şevki Pasha. Look for them there." The same day Abdülahad Nuri turned to Naim Efendi and asked him to investigate the situation. He added the note on November 22 that inquiry "documents weren't with Şevki Pasha," and inserted another note at the end of the document on November 24 saying, "Store this away, Naim Efendi."[67]

The third document is a message sent by Talat Pasha on 1 December 1915, of which a hand-written copy is found in Naim's memoirs. There is a photographic image of it, and it is used in all three editions of Andonian's book.[68] In the cable, Talat Pasha states that certain information has been procured by the American consulates in various areas regarding the manner in which Armenians have been deported. He deduced that this procurement was being organized secretly from the memorandum he received from the American Embassy in Istanbul, which was acting on direct orders of its government, and requested that special attention be paid that there be no occurrences that might draw attention during the deportation of Armenians in areas close to cities, towns, and other population centers. For Talat, the purpose was to produce the belief among the foreigners wandering around in those parts that the purpose of the deportations was nothing other than the relocation. To achieve this, the temporary implementation of compassionate treatment was necessary for political reasons, and the usual measures—meaning killings—should be implemented in the appropriate regions.

Additionally, Talat requested that those who are supplying information to the American consuls be found, arrested, and tried. On 3, 4, and 5 December, Governor Mustafa Abdülhalik and Abdülahad Nuri wrote notes at the end of these documents, in particular regarding what needed to be done in order to investigate those persons supplying information to the U.S. consuls. These notes concluded with the inscriptions, "Write to Naim Efendi ... he has been written to."[69]

All of these documents provide incontrovertible evidence that there indeed existed an Ottoman official by the name of Naim Efendi.

THE PLACES THAT NAIM EFENDI WAS STATIONED AND HIS RELATIONSHIP WITH ANDONIAN

Unfortunately, we have very little information about Naim Efendi's personal and professional life. The only real source for this is his own writings and the previously mentioned document published by the Office of the Turkish General Staff. In his memoirs published by Andonian (i.e., the ones of which we do not possess originals), Naim states that before he was appointed to the Office of Deportation, he was the Regie Secretary in Ras-ul-Ayn.[70] He also claims that he was assigned to Aleppo a few days after Abdülahad Nuri arrived and that he was assigned to his service: "I arrived in Aleppo. Fate arranged it so that I was appointed to office as chief secretary to Abdülahad Nuri Bey, who arrived only three or four days ago as assistant to the general director of deportations."[71]

We do not possess precise information regarding Abdülahad Nuri's appointment date in this position. Şükrü Bey,[72] who had previously been appointed to the task as Director of Tribal and Immigrant Affairs(the Deportation Office) in Aleppo, wrote in a cable dated 8 October 1915 that he wanted someone appointed to work in the Directorate of Deportation. He said that "it was necessary for an individual to be sent who could either assist the governor [of Aleppo] or be given the title and position to be able to dispatch [deportees] and oversee [the deportations] in his capacity as Assistant to the Governor."[73] In a cable of reply dated 13 October 1915, Interior Minister Talat asked Şükrü Bey his opinion "about the appointment of Abdülahad Nuri Bey to the Directorate-General,"[74] which shows that he must have been appointed by this date. Thus, even if we do not know the exact date, on the basis of existing documents, we can state with some confidence that he must have begun his new task in early November.

Nuri departed Istanbul for Aleppo on 1 November 1915 with the province's new governor, Mustafa Abdülhalik. Two days earlier, on October 30, the interior minister (Talat) sent a cable to Şükrü Bey, informing him that "The Governor of Aleppo and Abdülahad Nuri Bey will depart on Monday."[75] Another telegram, this one sent from Aleppo on November 7, reported that the new governor had reached Aleppo that evening.[76] In light of this information, we may conclude that Naim began his duties some three or four days later.

In his memoirs, Naim states that he was later to be dispatched to the camp at Meskene to deal with the further deportations from there. Although he does not provide a date, he mentions that, after being "sent to Meskene as an official [for the] deportation of deportees," he "remained there for two months."[77] From what we can glean from the interrogations of summer 1916 published by the Turkish Military Archives, ATASE, Colonel Galip summoned him to speak at the beginning of May, meaning that Naim was in Meskene at the time.[78] The reason for his being dispatched to Meskene was that the deportations from the camp and its surrounding area were being done in a disorderly fashion. In a section of the memoirs of which the originals are not in our possession, he states that "before departing, Eyüp Bey called me to his side":

"Naim Efendi," he said, "we saw no good from any of the deportation officials sent to Meskene. You found yourself in the matter; you are aware of the orders which came. See that you do not allow these people (the Armenians) to remain alive: if necessary, kill with your own hands. And killing them is a delight."[79]

In November 1915, during the period in which testimony was being taken in the Colonel Galip investigation, Naim was no longer an official in charge of deportations, but of the municipal grain silos in Aleppo. We have no information whatsoever on what prompted this new appointment, nor when his work there was concluded. In regard to his removal from the earlier position, he claims that he was promoted, since the desired deportations had not been carried out after all. Again, in the part of his memoir published by Andonian, he states that "I remained two months there. I only carried out a deportation of exiles once. The number of people I sent did not exceed thirty." Andonian largely supports this claim, and makes similar ones himself, "Since he was not a wicked man, Naim Bey was not the man for this task. He arranged a few deportations to Deyr-i Zor for show, but before long they lost faith in him and he was recalled....[b]ecause he failed to empty out the camp."[80]

The aforementioned cable from Aleppo Governor Mustafa Abdülhalik (11 July 1916) and investigations that were carried out show that the things Naim had to say about the disorderly manner in which the deportations from Meskene were carried out were true. The German Consul in Aleppo, Rössler, also provided similar information in the report he wrote about Andonian's book for the Tehlirian trial in Berlin:

Many particular events with which I am familiar are portrayed with absolute accuracy; others with which I was not yet familiar provide an explanation for phenomena that I observed but could not explain at the time. This is the case, for example, with the fact that, for a time, large numbers of Armenians returned to Aleppo from Meskene. The explanation is now provided convincingly by the author on page 13 of the book, in that Naim Bey, like Hussein [Hüseyin] Bey, the Mudir [Müdür -director] of Meskene, did not carry out the terrible orders they were given.[81]

Another account that supports Naim's is that of Hakkı Bey, the Assistant Director of Deportations in Aleppo. Hakkı Bey, who had been sent from Aleppo to Meskene on 8 August 1916, in order to address the complaints that had arisen in regard to the deportation and corruption problems and to prepare a report thereon, gave his testimony within the framework of the investigation of Colonel Galip and his friends. In it, he said:

The task was given to me to undertake an investigation of the numerous reports submitted by the Main Office of Deportations in Meskene to the governor [of Aleppo] in regard to the fact that deportations from Meskene were not proceeding [according to plan]. The investigation into the matter was begun immediately by going to Meskene and beginning with the Main Office of Deportations. It was learned that deportations [from there] were not being carried out in a regular, orderly fashion, [as there were] reports that bribes were being received [both in] the market place and from the wagon drivers...that, under the guise of being tradesmen a great many Armenian deportees were not being deported [further].[82]

From Hakkı Bey's account, we may conclude that Naim's removal from his position was connected with the bribes that had been received, and with the fact that the deportations in and from Meskene had come to a complete halt. Andonian, likewise, wrote in the notes he took about the camps around Aleppo (although it did not make it into the published book), that Naim was questioned because he had allowed a number of Armenian families to flee Meskene and had taken bribes. But when he was questioned, Naim protected Andonian and other Armenians and did not give his questioners a single name, despite being asked to do so.

> Naim Sefa Bey was summoned from Meskene to Aleppo and confronted with these families [who had fled the camp]. He was asked whether or not he knew them, or whether or not he had encountered them during the time he was in Meskene. Naim Bey swore (in those conversations he frequently used the term "vallahi"—"by my God [I swear]) fervently insisting that this was the first time he had seen them. Despite playing dumb in this manner, Naim Bey was forced to leave his position shortly thereafter."[83]

Whether a subsequent investigation was made that resulted in Naim's being removed from his position, or this investigation was in any way connected with the one of Colonel Galip and his friends, we will likely never know for certain. From the General Staff documents it can be understood that by the time of the Galip investigations, Naim was no longer serving in his former position. He was in Aleppo during this period, however, and was summoned as a witness in the matter. For this reason, it is entirely possible that he was removed from his position in connection with another investigation. A cable sent by Talat Pasha to the District Governor of Urfa, Fethi Bey, on 5 July 1916 reveals that investigations and the removal of officials from their positions continued throughout the summer. In his message, Talat mentions an investigation "that is being carried out about abuse [of office] and bribery in regard to the resettlement and provisioning of the deportees," and informs the district governor that certain officials "have been removed from their positions... in the sub-district of Rakka after [these] investigations have shown this to be necessary."[84]

From the relevant correspondence on this matter, it can be understood that the investigations into the corruption and improprieties in Rakka had already begun in March of that year.[85] As we showed above, Interior Minister Talat sent a telegram to Aleppo on 19 July 1916, requesting that an end be put to the employment of those officials who were seen to be abusing their positions for gain.[86] From all of the correspondence, what becomes clear is that throughout the spring and summer of 1916, a great number of Armenians succeeded in escaping from the places to which they had been deported by the payment of bribes, and that investigations into the matter had been launched. It may have been that Naim was summoned to Aleppo and terminated as a result of this process.

In his notes from Meskene, Andonian provides detailed information on his encounter with Naim and its aftermath. We do not know the month that Andonian arrived in Meskene. The author does not mention a date. In Rita Kuyumjian's biography of Andonian, she states that it was "probably [in] February 1916."[87] Andonian states: "[A]fter my arrival in Meskene, two other [persons]" arrived, having been assigned there "as functionaries." One of these was Naim Efendi. According to Andonian, Naim was a person "who earned quite a reputation for himself among the deportees... He drank and was an inveterate gambler, and due to his constant need for money, he loved [to take] bribes. He was the person in a position ... to inform the deportees that it was not impossible for families who were willing to making financial sacrifices to flee to Aleppo. And it was due to him that a great many wealthy families, most of them from Adana and Konya, succeeded in leaving Meskene and going to Aleppo."[88]

Andonian remained in the camp for five months. He left Meskene for Aleppo at the end of June 1916.[89] Krikor Ankut, who wrote his recollections of his time in Meskene, says that after he received a letter from Andonian on June 9, he went to Meskene and saw him there.[90] While he was at Meskene, Andonian stayed in the tent of the Boyajians, a family from Konya, and even used their surname while he was there.[91] It is likely that he negotiated with Naim during May regarding 16 wealthy Armenian families traveling to Aleppo.[92]

In his personal notes about Meskene, Andonian speaks of his acquaintance with Naim and what happened afterward

[Naim] came to lunch in the tent of one of the families from Adana, and when the time came for coffee, he informed them in blunt and unsparing language that all of the Armenians who traveled south [to Deyr-i Zor] would be killed, and that the best solution was to wait here a little while longer and to find a way to flee, at the first opportunity, to Aleppo, and that, in his opinion, this plan of action appeared entirely possible.[93]

Neither the families nor Andonian trusted Naim, but they had no other option.[94] In the end, Naim prepared an escape plan and asked Andonian to go to Aleppo to see an Arab wagon driver by the name of Nakhli

(Nahli). Andonian provides a detailed account, both of the route they followed and the things they needed to look out for on the way. After a four or five day walk, Andonian arrived in Aleppo and located the wagon driver. In the end, the flight was successful:

> Later on, some members of these families were caught in Aleppo as persons having [illegally] fled Meskene. I was also arrested, but I was quickly allowed to go free, due to the document that my friends had secured for me. The others were put in front of Naim Bey, who had returned to Aleppo. He made it easier for them to be set free by swearing in God's name that he had never seen them in Meskene. The wagon driver, Nakhli, who had been reported on and arrested himself, also vehemently denied [any knowledge or involvement], as the Arabs know how to do very well, but they held him in prison for months, even though he had not given anyone away.[95]

The relationship between Andonian and Naim would continue beyond this, as well. Naim did not blackmail the Armenian families whom he had helped to escape; he simply asked for more money when he was short, through the agency of Andonian, and according to the latter, "the amounts that Naim Bey requested were very small."[96] As a result, a relationship of trust developed between Andonian and Naim, which resulted, in November 1918, in Andonian purchasing Naim's aforementioned memoirs and related documents.

The last point that should be mentioned here is that the agreement of the information provided by Andonian with that found in the investigation documents published by the Turkish General Staff is not limited simply to the questions of corruption and the escape of Armenian deportees to Aleppo. For instance, during their interrogation, Colonel Galip and his friends give ample testimony on the killing of an Armenian family by the name of Sofyan and the sale of their property in the market place. In their notes on the period, both Andonian and Krikor Ankut provide detailed accounts of this very event.[97] It is significant that the information in all the accounts is in agreement.

THE QUESTION OF NAIM EFENDI'S PERSONALITY AND CHARACTER

Aram Andonian paints a highly favorable picture of Naim, both in the book he published and in the lengthy letter he wrote on 10 June 1921 to the attorney of Soghomon Tehlirian during the latter's trial for the murder of Talat Pasha (see Appendix E). In the book, he describes him as "the voice of conscience." In both cases he knowingly lies, denying that Naim Efendi received bribes from the deportees, either during their flight from Meskene or while they were in Aleppo. In his book, we read the following lines:

> When we were again arrested in Aleppo with [our] false names, the government nevertheless came up empty handed in trying to prove that we had fled Meskene. Naim Bey's testimony may have been singularly important in this regard, but he did not deliver us up, nor did he demand a thing in exchange for his silence. The truth is, he could have received anything he wanted from those wealthy families, because [they knew that] if they were sent off into the wastes a second time, it would mean a death sentence from which there could be no escape.[98]

Likewise, in his letter to Tehlirian's attorneys, Andonian describes Naim Efendi as "an extraordinarily good and harmless man." But, as we have seen, in his notes from 1918, Andonian describes him as a man given over to strong drink and gambling, and who continued to ask for money from the escapees in Aleppo after their flight.

Years later, in his letter to Mary Terzian (26 July 1937), Andonian admits that the Naim Efendi that he describes in his book and in the letter to Tehlirian's attorneys was intentionally misleading. He tells Terzian:

> I am writing all of this in strict confidence with my only intention being to satisfy your curiosity. I sketched an entirely different portrait of Naim Bey in my book, and the reestablishment of pure truth, in what concerns him personally, cannot be for nothing. Naim Bey was a completely amoral being.

Similarly, Andonian confessed to Terzian that:

> In a memorandum that I gave to Tehlirian's lawyers in Berlin, a copy of which you will find enclosed, you will see described a few of the circumstances through which we were able to procure the documents reproduced in my book. This Memorandum is not complete. There were matters that I could not divulge in my book or to Tehlirian's lawyers in order not to discredit the man that was Naim Bey, who was not entirely clean.[99]

Why did Andonian hide his true thoughts about Naim? We can glean from the letter above that the author's principle concern was not whether Naim was a dissolute official, given over to liquor and gambling, or the information provided by such a person would be considered reliable. According to Andonian, "he [Naim] didn't constitute an exception among the administrative staff of the city of Aleppo, which contained some real scoundrels, persons who, in comparison, made Naim Bey look like a saint."[100]

Andonian is not wrong about this. The aforementioned report sent by Major Azmi to Istanbul on 20 June 1916 regarding Aleppo's Baron Hotel (where Andonian was also hiding) relays the following information about Ottoman bureaucrats in Aleppo:

> You should be sure that, apart from the governor, all of the relevant parties in Aleppo are accepting prodigious amounts of money. Just acknowledge this to be true. Every single individual is stealing as if it were [the] perfectly natural [thing to do], from those in whom we have placed the greatest trust down to those whom we have not yet managed to meet. There is no need to even name names.[101]

It was not only corruption and bribery; drinking and gambling were also rife among the bureaucrats. Talat Pasha, who had heard many rumors about the Baron Hotel, sent a cable to the Governor of Aleppo on 22 July 1916, in which he wrote:

> Reports have been received that an Armenian foreign national by the name of Baron and who runs a hotel of the same name in Aleppo is using his hotel less for hospitality to travelers than as a gambling den, and, just as the afore-mentioned has served to provide for the pleasures of officials in high positions who come there from both near and far, has given [them] large sums [in the form] of loans equal to their gambling debts; by virtue of this method, and by using various other means to exercise influence over some of the officials in the provincial administration, he succeeds in achieving his aims.

Talat then requests a list of the names of these officials who came under the influence of the hotel owner by means of drinking and gambling.[102]

In response to the interior minister's request, Aleppo Governor Mustafa Abdülhalik confirms that "the reports regarding Baron are correct," and adds that

> Baron has gained fame for winning the support of those in high position and the control of those in low positions. For the sake of this support and con-

trol he resorts to any and all means; he gambles in the hotel at every opportunity and he tries to ensure that those in high position participate in the
gambling....Every official who cannot resist women and gambling is ultimately forced to become Baron's friend.[103]

If the problem for Andonian was not that Naim was someone who took
bribes, was a drunk or a gambler, then why did he choose to lie about it?
In order to explain this, we need to look more closely at the things that he
said about the personality of Naim.

> Naim Bey was a completely amoral being. He had vices because of which he
> was inclined to sell many things, but not everything. The difference is con-
> siderable. I have not forgotten that he never lied over the course of the long
> relationship I had with him. In a word, his character was made up of entirely
> contradictory elements, both good and bad. You can get a sense from what
> I have written that we were able to benefit from the first, without being
> bothered by the second. I think about him constantly and always with a kind
> of sympathy that time has not been able to lessen. It is because I often stuck
> my neck out in my relationship with him—a dangerous exercise, but true to
> my adventurous spirit—and he never betrayed me.[104]

It was for these reasons that Andonian trusted Naim: "In the final analysis, he was a good man. Despite the calamity within which he found
himself, more than anything else, he communicated trust. He could always
be relied upon."[105]

From his writings, we can understand then that the fundamental question for Andonian was not Naim's drinking or acceptance of bribes. Rather,
it was, in his words, Naim's having "become an informer in our hands who
betrayed his own country." His being an "inveterate drinker and gambler...
were his faults" and these led to his committing "treason."[106] Andonian
thought that any information provided by a person who thought that he
had betrayed his own country could not be seen as reliable, and it was for
this reason that he hid his true opinion about Naim for so long.

In fact, it was both his addiction to gambling and drinking and
Andonian's own dishonesty regarding Naim that formed the basis of Orel
and Yuca's argument that the documents he provided could not therefore
be seen as reliable. Most other researchers and writers have since followed
suit, using Naim's character flaws as the most significant proof of the lack
of the documents' veracity. Orel and Yuca explained the reasons for
Andonian's behavior thus:

The first answer that might come to mind is that the personality of Naim Efendi raises doubts about his "memoirs" and the "documents" that he sold and give force to their persuasiveness. Andonian certainly must have known that he could not expect regard to be given to the memoirs of a person who was an alcoholic, a gambler, and without scruples.[107]

Needless to say, the question of the reliability of information relayed in the memoirs of a corrupt drunk or of the documents he provided is debatable, and ultimately subject to speculation. According to the authors' logic, one could also claim one could not have found a single official in Aleppo at the time who could give reliable information. It is painfully clear that the memoirs and documents supplied by persons with such characteristics could just as easily be authentic as they could be false. Likewise, it is equally possible that, instead of an all or nothing proposition, *some* of the material mentioned is authentic and *some* of it is false. Luckily, we have other means, beyond the simple question of the personality of Naim Efendi, that can show us if the material in question is authentic.

NOTES

1. One reason that this belief has taken root is that Krikor Guerguerian's aforementioned 1965 article in Armenian did not get the scholarly attention that it deserved. In this article, Guerguerian wrote very clearly that "Aram Andonian did not provide the entire memoirs of Naim Sefa Efendi in any of the editions that he published: not in the Armenian original, nor in the French or English translations. A portion of these recollections are stored away within three notebooks in the Nubarian Library. There are also a number of yet untranslated and unpublished details to be found there." Guerguerian then expressed "the hope that [these sections] will be published." Krieger, "Aram Andoniani Hradaragadz...", 236. Fifty years after he wrote this, his hope is finally being realized.
2. In a private correspondence from Guerguerian to Vahakn Dadrian, dated 24 August 1984, we read these lines: "At least [as late as] in 1950, there were three notebooks of the documents copied by Naim [Efendi] in the Nubarian Library: I took photographs of all of these in their original form." (The letter is currently in my private collection.)
3. Krieger, "Aram Andoniani Hradaragadz...", 236.
4. Ibid.
5. According to Raymond Kévorkian, who served as director of the Boghos Nubar Library in Paris between 1986 and 2013, both Naim's memoirs and some of the original images of the documents disappeared during the

period between Guerguerian's visit in 1950 and the 1975 visit by Yves Ternon. Neither Ternon, nor Vahakn Dadrian, who visited the library in the early 1980s, were able to see the originals of this material. The question of their fate remains a complete mystery to Raymond Kévorkian.

6. Aram Andonian, *Medz Vojirĕ*, 15.
7. The copies of the documents are not completely error-free. For example, there is a difference between the dates of the original document (numbered 803) and the copy made by Naim. The date on the original is 25 December 1915; in the memoirs, it is given as 25 January 1917.
8. Orel and Yuca, *Talat Paşa'ya Atfedilen*, 130. In the course of their comparisons, the authors make such observations as "It is rather close to the Turkish text" (p. 31); "...despite the nuances, they appear to be in conformity" (p. 33); "they seem to be similar" (p. 51); and "they are generally in conformity" (p. 65); "some of the nuances and discrepancies are striking" (p. 42) and that "supplements and additions" (p. 42) were made. They thereby express their doubts about the memoirs and arrive at the conclusion that the differences cannot simply be described as "errors in translation or transcription" (p. 130).
9. Dr. Avedis Nakkashian (1868(?)–1943) was a member of Istanbul's Armenian intelligentsia and was arrested on 24 April 1915. He was released on July 23 of that year and served in the Ottoman Army with the rank of captain for the duration of the war. For his successes, he received the highest medal of service. After the Armistice, he returned to Istanbul but left again in 1922, traveling first to Egypt, and eventually going to the United States in 1924. He compiled and published in Armenian all of his memoirs from the period that he was held in Ayaş (*Ayashi Pandu*, Boston: Hairenik, 1925), and the following year published all of his memoirs (*Zuart Patmutiwnner*, New York: n.p., 1926). These would appear in English translation some 14 years later as *A Man Who Found a Country* (New York: Thomas Y. Crowell Company, 1940). The latter work can be accessed online: http://avedis.telf.com/.
10. Abdülahad Nuri [Tengirşenk] Bey (?–1927), was the elder brother of Yusuf Kemal [Tengirşenk], who between the years 1920 and 1933 would serve, alternately, as Minister of Economics, Foreign Affairs, and Justice. In the years 1915–1916 Abdülahad Nuri served as Director of the Deportation Office (*Sevkiyat Müdürü*) in Aleppo. During the Armistice period he traveled to Istanbul, where he was arrested by the occupation forces. While still in custody, he would be allowed to flee from the hospital where he was being held, after which, in 1921, he would make his way to Anatolia to join the Nationalist Forces. In 1922, after the Nationalist Forces had entered Istanbul, he would return to his old pre-war job in the city's Shipping and Sea Transport Administration. For more information

on Nuri and his life, see Cevdet Yakupoğlu, "Bir Sürgün Kahramanı
Abdülahad Nuri Bey: Hayatı, Eserleri ve Selçuklu-Beylikler Tarihi Üzerine
Çalışmaları," *Ankara Üniversitesi Osmanlı Tarihi Araştırma ve Uygulama
Merkezi Dergisi*, 21 (2007): 169–189.

11. Abdülahad Nuri was appointed as Assistant Director in the branch, most
likely in October 1915, and replaced the then-director Şükrü Bey when
he left the position. In the Ottoman documents from the earlier months
of the year, he is referred to as "Assistant Director," and only later as
"Director." There is strong evidence that this change of position occurred
in the last part of November. In that month, the responsibility for dispatches in Aleppo passed from the Deportation Office to the office of the
provincial governor of Aleppo (BOA.DH.ŞFR., 58/56 and 66). In a
November 13 cable sent by Dispatch Director Şükrü Bey to Interior
Minister Talat Pasha, the director reports that he has turned over his
duties to the Governor of Aleppo (BOA.DH.ŞFR., 497/43). In a reply
sent five days later (18 November 1915), Talat requests of Şükrü Bey that
he depart by the first possible means available in order to assume his new
position in Istanbul, "Since the matter of dispatches has [already] been
handed over to the Governor of Aleppo" (BOA.DH.ŞFR., 58/60).
Nevertheless, from another cable, dated 21 November 1915, we learn
that Şükrü Bey had still not left Aleppo (BOA.DH.ŞFR., 498/62). When
Şükrü does finally return to Istanbul, Abdülahad Nuri succeeds him.

12. *Joghovurti Tzayn*, 19 September 1919. One important aspect of the trial
is the witness testimony of Kilis County Executive (*Kaymakamı*) Ihsan
Bey. In his account, the former official made the following statement:
"In the official orders the families of soldiers, Protestants, Catholics,
and the infirm were exempt [from deportation] … and permission [was
given] for these persons … to remain together as a family." In response,
the Governor of Aleppo wrote a letter to Istanbul requesting that Ihsan
Bey be removed from his position. Ihsan Bey then traveled to Aleppo and
met there with Abdülahad Nuri. During their meeting, Nuri told him: "I
received the order personally from Talat Bey. The aim of the deportation
is to fundamentally extirpate [the Armenians]. The welfare of the homeland necessitates this." Ihsan Bey's testimony is important because a similar, written testimony by him was used in the indictment in the post-war
trials of the Unionist leaders (*Takvimi Vekayi*, no. 3540, 5 May 1919). In
a great number of Armenian memoirs of this period, Ihsan Bey is mentioned as having saved the lives of many Armenians. Apraham Kasahyan,
for instance, recounts that Ihsan saved 33 members of his family from
death. Apraham Kasapyan, *Kaç Kişisiniz Boğos Efendi, Bir Ermeninin
Hatıra Defteri* (Istanbul: Aras Yayıncılık, 2015), 24–31.

THE STORY AND AUTHENTICITY OF NAIM EFENDI AND HIS MEMOIRS

13. Orel and Yuca have used the argument that, in the months when the event occurred, Yusuf Kemal Tengirshenk was not serving in the Ottoman Foreign Ministry as proof that Andonian's information is fabricated (Orel and Yuca, *Ermenilerce Talat Paşa'ya Atfedilen*, 20–21). They are incorrect for two reasons: First, Andonian had no direct connection with the events in question. Rather, he simply transmitted the things written by Dr. Nakkashian. Orel and Yuca erroneously blame Andonian because they were unaware of this letter. Second, they do not provide correct information about Yusuf Kemal Tengirshenk. The latter may not have *technically* been foreign minister during the months in question, but he was a member of the Turkish government committee that undertook to carry out the *duties* of the foreign ministry, and he was constantly traveling abroad, performing the function of a foreign minister. Tengirshenk would in time serve as a member of the 15-person Executive Committee selected on 25 April 1920, and as a member of the first eight-person temporary cabinet selected the same day (the first official Turkish Government of Nationalists in Ankara), and, while on the Executive Committee, would assume the task of Minister of Economics. He was also on the official delegation that traveled to Moscow in June 1920, and would continue his meetings with the Bolsheviks on behalf of the Ankara-Nationalist government afterward, until 19 May 1921, when he was appointed Foreign Minister. During the Abdülahad Nuri incident, he was constantly holding meetings abroad like a foreign minister. Thus, despite the fact that he was *not* foreign minister, Tengirshenk was one of those signing the 16 March 1921 Moscow Treaty on behalf of the Turkish Government (More detailed information on Tengirshenk can be found in Ömer Akdağ, "Millî Mücadele Şahsiyetlerinden Yusuf Kemal Bey (TENGİRŞENK)," Atatürk Araştırma Merkezi Dergisi, Cilt XIV, no. 40, March 1998; http://www.atam.gov.tr/dergi/sayi-40/milli-mucadele-sahsiyetlerinden-yusuf-kemal-bey-tengirsenk (Accessed 14 February 2016)).

14. Tarık Zafer Tunaya, *Türkiye'de Siyasal Partiler Cilt 2, Mütareke Dönemi, 1918–1922* (Istanbul: İletişim, 2015), 61.

15. For news of Kurt Mustafa Pasha's arrest, see *Vakit gazetesi*, no. 1056, 16 November 1920. Kürt ["Kurdish"] Mustafa Pasha, who was also known as Nemrut Mustafa Pasha, was the presiding judge in Istanbul's First Military Tribunal/Court-Martial (*Divan-i Harb-i Örfi*) that heard some of the cases against the Union and Progress officials between the years 1919 and 1921. While serving in this capacity, Mustafa Pasha was arrested in October 1920 on the charge of having intentionally forged documents in the trial of Nusret, the Bayburt County Executive (*Kaymakam*) and Governor (*Mutasarrıf*) of the Provincial District of Urfa, so as to be able

to sentence him to death (Nusret had been convicted, sentenced to death, and executed in August 1920). As a result of this charge, Mustafa Pasha was convicted and sent to prison, but he would later be pardoned by the Sultan. Fearing that he might be rearrested when Istanbul was captured by the Turkish Nationalist Forces in 1922, he fled to Cairo. For the court case against Mustafa Pasha, see Dadrian and Akçam, *Judgment at Istanbul*, 305–306.

16. For an illuminating article explaining how the military's archival materials were transported, even sold or burnt, see: Gültekin Yıldız, "Osmanlı Evrakını Önce Yaktılar sonra Depolara Kapattılar," *Derin Tarih* (June 2014): 112–119.

17. See Appendix C: Andonian's letter to Mary Terzian.

18. Concerning how the matter was taken up at the trial, see Tessa Hofmann (ed.), *Der Völkermord an den Armeniern vor Gericht, Der Prozess Talaat Pascha* (Göttingen: Gesellschaft für bedrohte Völker, 1980), 68–69, 86.

19. Orel and Yuca, *Ermenilerce Talat Paşa'ya*, 17–19.

20. The person who appealed to the Berlin court to allow Rössler to testify was none other than the Protestant missionary and orientalist Johannes Lepsius. Lepsius had earlier sent Rössler a copy of Andonian's book and asked his opinion on the authenticity of the documents contained therein. Rössler replied to Lepsius, giving his opinion in a lengthy letter, but also after receiving a promise that it not be published (see Appendix D).

21. http://www.armenocide.net/armenocide/armgende.nsf/$$AllDocs-en/1921-05-30-DE-001?OpenDocument (Accessed 15 February 2016).

22. Vahakn N. Dadrian, "The Naim-Andonian Documents on the World War I..."

23. Kamuran Gürün, *The Armenian File, The Myth of Innocence Exposed* (Nicosia, Cyprus: K. Rustem & Brother, 1985), 237–239.

24. Türkkaya Ataöv, *Talat Paşa'ya atfedilen Andonian "Belgeleri" Sahtedir* (Ankara: Siyasal Bilgiler Fakültesi Yayını, 1984).

25. Guenther Lewy, *The Armenian Massacres in Ottoman Turkey, A Disputed Genocide* (Salt Lake City: University of Utah Press, 2005), 63–73.

26. Maxime Gauin, "Aram Andonian's 'Memoirs of Naim Bey' and the Contemporary Attempts to Defend their 'Authenticity'," *Review of Armenian Studies*, 23 (2011): 233–293.

27. "The Turkish side... points out that the official records of the Ottoman government do not, as far as is known, contain any documents that demonstrate government involvement in the killings. The Armenian side has tried to demonstrate this involvement, but some of the documents it has produced (the so-called Andonian papers) have been shown to be forgeries." Erik-Jan Zürcher, *Turkey: A Modern History* (London: I. B. Tauris, 2004), 115–116.

28. "There are some celebrated historical fabrications.... There are the so-called Protocols of the Elders of Zion, the Talat Pasha telegrams, and others of the same kind." Bernard Lewis, *From Babel to Dragomans: Interpreting the Middle East* (New York: Oxford University Press, 2004), 388–389.

29. "...quotes the telegrams dubiously attributed to the Ottoman wartime Minister of the Interior, Talat Pasha..." Andrew Mango, "Turks and Kurds," *Middle Eastern Studies* 30 (1994): 985.

30. "There is forged evidence. In 1920 some documents were handed to the British by a journalist called Andonian. She [*sic*] claimed that he had been given them by an Ottoman official called Naim. The documents have been published as a book (in English and French) and if you take them at face value they are devastating: here is Talaat Pasha as minister of the Interior telling the governors to exterminate the Armenians, not to forget to exterminate the children in orphanages, but to keep it all secret. But the documents are very obviously a forgery—elementary mistakes as regards dates and signatures." Norman Stone, "'There Is No Armenian Genocide'," *JTW News* (Saturday, 21 October 2006), URL: http://historynewsnetwork.org/article/31085 (Accessed 23 January 2016).

31. "Lewy takes on what many who back the Armenian contentions consider to be some of the most damning evidences of a premeditated genocide and shows how they are 'materials of highly questionable authenticity. These suspect documents include ... the Naim Bey 'telegrams allegedly sent out by minister of the interior Talaat Pasha, ordering the extermination of the Armenians' and published by a minor military censor at that time, Aram Andonian." Michael Gunter, *Review Article, International Journal of Middle East Studies*, 38, no. 4 (2006): 598–599; "...the notorious forgeries produced after World War I by Aram Andonian." Michael Gunter, *Review Article, International Journal of Middle East Studies*, 21, no. 3 (August 1989): 422.

32. Hilmar Kaiser was the first scholar to express the opinion that the Andonian documents need to be debated anew. H. Kaiser, "The Baghdad Railway and the Armenian Genocide 1915–1916: A Case Study of German Resistance and Complicity," in Richard Hovannisian (ed.), *Remembrance and Denial* (Detroit: Wayne State University Press, 1998), 108, no. 78.

33. "In fact, feeling immense pressure to find and publish [incriminating] documents, there have even been individuals who published documents which some have claimed to be fake." Taner Akçam, *Türk Ulusal Kimliği ve Ermeni Sorunu* (Istanbul: İletişim Yayınları, 1992), 118–119.

34. Taner Akçam, *İnsan Hakları ve Ermeni Sorunu* [Human Rights and the Armenian Question] (Ankara: İmge Yayınevi, 1999), 33.
35. Taner Akçam, *The Young Turks' Crime against Humanity: The Armenian Genocide and Ethnic Cleansing in the Ottoman Empire* (Princeton and Oxford: Princeton University Press, 2012): xix.
36. Orel and Yuca, *Ermenilerce Talat Paşa'ya Atfedilen...*, 23–24. Here are the Ottoman Original names of the sources that they claimed have searched: *Salname; İrade-i Seniye Defterleri; Ruzname-i Ceride-i Havadisler* and *Düstur*.
37. Ibid.
38. For examples, see ibid., 1, 8, 11, 24, 25.
39. Ibid., 26, 76.
40. Ibid., 75, 60.
41. Ibid., 48, 81.
42. Ibid., 130. As the authors put it: "There is a term in criminology known as "the perfect crime." This term is correct. Every crime has to leave behind some traces, some clues. In perpetrating the crime of putting together these fabricated documents—and it is a crime to try and besmirch [the honor of] an entire nation—they left behind a great many clues, and they have been caught through this evidence of guilt."
43. Kamuran Gürün, *Ermeni Dosyası*, 333 "*...otantik diye iddia edilen vesikaların cümlesi de sahte olunca, kitabın tamamı milletlerarası bir sahtekarlık vesikası haline dönüşmüş bulunmaktadır... Acaba bu sahte vesikalar 'ahlaksız' bir Naim Bey tarafından hazırlanıp da Ermeni örgütünce tetkik edilip, sahici sanılarak satın mı alındı?). Bunu hiç öğrenemeyeceğiz. Ne var ki Naim Bey diye bir insanın sadece hayalde yaşatılmış olması, bu sahte vesikaların Andonian tarafından tanzim edilmiş olması da düşünülebilecek bir husustur.*" It should be noted that this passage does not appear in the book's English translation.
44. Genelkurmay Başkanlığı, *Arşiv Belgeleriyle Ermeni Faaliyetleri (1914–1918), Cilt VII (1914–1915)* (Ankara: Genelkurmay Basımevi, 2007).
45. To this list we must of course add Naim Efendi's own memoirs, and even though Naim's name is not directly mentioned, the information relayed by Krikor Ankut and Simon Onbachian from Bandırma in the Meskene camp where Aram Andonian himself worked should be added as an important historical source for the period. The testimonies of these individuals can be found in Raymond Kévorkian, *L'extermination des déportés Arméniens ottomans dans les camps de concentration de Syrie-Mésopotamie, La deuxième phase du genocide (1915–1916)*, Tome II, 1988; there is an electronic version of this source, URL: http://www.imprescriptible.fr/rhac/tome2/. We used the page numbers from the Turkish translation of the book: Raymond Kévorkian, *Soykırımın İkinci Safhası, Sürgüne*

Gönderilen Osmanlı Ermenilerinin Suriye-Mezopotamya Toplama Kamplarında İmha Edilmeleri (Istanbul: Belge Yayınları, 2011), 233–235, 243–245, 274–278.

46. The dimension of bribery and the plunder of Armenian properties during the destruction process is indeed striking and needs special treatment. One of the main reasons for this high percentage in bribery and plunder is the lack of ideological mass support for Government policies toward extermination. The leaders of the Union and Progress Party (CUP) were aware of this deficiency on the ideological level and tried to manipulate the cupidity of bureaucrats and the broad masses to gain their participation in the genocidal process. Whenever the bribery and plunder became a risk for the implementation of the overall genocidal scheme, they launched investigations and even established Courts Martial and punished the individuals. The overall policy was to bridle the cupidity within the limits of genocidal policies. The investigation in and around the Meskene-Aleppo area, which is the topic here, is a perfect example of this dilemma.

47. The claim that the Armenians constituted a threat to military transport was merely a pretext. The real reason for resettling the Armenians to Deyr-i Zor was their annihilation. See Akçam, *Young Turks' Crime Against Humanity*, 264–285; Kévorkian, *The Armenian Genocide*, 625–699. Kévorkian calls the developments in Syria in fall 1915 and 1916 the "second stage" of the Genocide.

48. Mustafa Abdülhalik [Renda] was the brother-in-law of Talat Pasha. He was appointed to replace Mazhar as governor of Bitlis in April 1915, and subsequently governor of Aleppo (1915–1916), whence he force-marched surviving Armenians to Mesopotamia. After the war, he was arrested by the British and sent to Malta, but was eventually released without being tried. He would later serve in Republican governments as Minister of Defense, Finance, and Education, as President of the Turkish National Parliament (TBMM), and, upon the death of Atatürk, President of the Republic for one day.

49. Genelkurmay Başkanlığı, *Arşiv Belgeleriyle Ermeni Faaliyetleri (1914–1918), Cilt VIII* (Ankara: Genelkurmay Basımevi, 2007), 115.

50. BOA.DH.ŞFR., 525/106, Cipher cable, dated 19 July 1916, from Deyr-i Zor District Governor Zeki to the Ottoman Interior Ministry.

51. BOA.DH.ŞFR., 66/24, Cipher cable, dated 19 July 1916, from Interior Minister Talat to the Province of Aleppo.

52. BOA.DH.ŞFR., 526/60, Cipher cable, dated 26 July 1916, from [Aleppo] Governor Mustafa Abdülhalik to the Interior Ministry; the same cable can be found in: Genelkurmay Başkanlığı, *Arşiv Belgeleriyle Ermeni Faaliyetleri (1914–1918) Cilt VII*, 145.

53. BOA.DH.ŞFR., 66/136, Cipher cable, dated 4 August 1916, from Interior Minister Talat to the Province of Aleppo.
54. Ibid., 70. The task of conducting the investigation was given to Hakkı Bey and Colonel (*Albay*) Nuri, Inspector for the Euphrates region. For one of the pair's reports on the matter, see BOA.DH.EUM.KLU., 16/28-1, Report by Assistant Director-General of Dispatches/ Deportations Hakkı and Euphrates Region Inspector Colonel (*Miralay*) Nuri, dated 20 September 1916.
55. BOA.DH.ŞFR., 73/8, Cipher Cable, dated 14 February 1917, from Interior Minister Talat to the Province of Aleppo.
56. The testimony of some of the suspects had been taken earlier, but these persons were nevertheless obliged to give it a second time in November.
57. Genelkurmay Başkanlığı, *Arşiv Belgeleriyle, Cilt VII*, 95.
58. Ibid. We understand from the testimonies of both Colonel Galip and Çerkez Hüseyin Efendi, the official in charge of deportations for Meskene and who was recorded as a witness, that the period discussed by Naim Efendi was May 1916. For example, in his testimony, Çerkez Hüseyin Efendi stated that reserve officer candidate Ahmet (*Yedek Subay adayı*), who was attached to Colonel Galip, came to him "at the beginning of May 1916." See ibid., 75, 89.
59. BOA.DH.ŞFR., 66/159, Cipher cable, dated 7 August 1916, from the Interior Ministry's Directorate-General of Security to the District Governor of [Deyr-i] Zor. The full text of the telegram reads: "The Office of the General Staff has reported in response that the Sixth Army Command was informed of the need to ensure both that the craftsmen and tradesmen that are to be taken from among the Armenians not be separated out by the camp commander by their own volition and that the civilian and military branches work in unison [in this matter]."
60. BOA.DH.ŞFR., 66/94, Cipher Cable, dated 29 July 1916, from the Interior Ministry's Directorate-General of Security to the District Governor of [Deyr-i] Zor. "It has been reported that the necessary measures have been taken for the placement and settlement of the Armenians in appropriate locales, since the presence of large groups of them in the Euphrates basin and on military [supply & transport] routes is dangerous for military transports. It has been reported by the High Command to the Sixth Army Command that labor battalions have been ordered to be formed from the remaining individuals, and that the need for wagons is to be met from the Armenians and that only Muslims are to be appointed to drive these wagons."
61. Genelkurmay Başkanlığı, *Arşiv Belgeleriyle, Cilt VII*, 95–96.
62. Bandırmalı Simon Onbaşıyan [Onbashian] relates similar information in his account. Raymond Kévorkian, *Soykırımın İkinci Safhası*, 274–278.

63. For further information on the killing of Kirkor Zohrab, see Preface of this work and Haigazn K. Kazarian, "The Murder of 6 Armenian Members of the Ottoman Parliament," *Armenian Review* 22 (Winter 1970): 26–33; Nesim Ovadya İzrail, *1915 Bir Ölüm Yolculuğu—Krikor Zohrab.*

64. As we know, all other documents given by Naim and mentioned in Andonian's book have vanished. Why did those published documents vanish, but those not published survive? Could it be a coincidence? There is no clear answer at this time.

65. Bibliothèque Nubar, Fonds Andonian, Matériaux pour l'histoire du génocide: "Déportations et massacres: Zohrab, Vartkès et divers."

66. Ibid.

67. Ibid.

68. Aram Andonian, *Medz Vojirě*, 136; in the French edition, 6; in the English edition, 52. The full text is provided below in the section titled "The American Consulates and the Photographs Taken on the Roads." Also see Appendix A.2.

69. Ibid., and Appendix A.1.

70. Ibid., 20 and Attachment 1-B. Re'is ül-Ayin, or Sari Kani, in Syria, is located across the Turkish border from Ceylanpınar, and northwest of Hassake, in whose administrative jurisdiction it currently lies. The Turkish term for Regie is Reji, and it was formerly the name given to the tobacco monopoly in the Ottoman Empire.

71. Ibid., 21 and Attachment 1-B.

72. Şükrü [Kaya] (1883–1959) was a Unionist functionary who headed the Ottoman Interior Ministry's Directorate of Tribal and Immigrant Resettlement (*Iskan-i Aşair ve Muhaciran Muduriyeti*) early in the war and during the deportations. He was sent to Aleppo in the summer of 1915 (August-September) to directly coordinate the deportation and resettlement efforts. Abdülahad Nuri [Tengirshenk] was appointed his assistant. He would be one of the former officials arrested by the British occupation forces and interned on Malta, but he was eventually released and joined the nationalist movement in Anatolia. He would serve variously as Minister of Agriculture, Foreign Affairs, and the Interior in the early Republican period (1924–1928).

73. BOA.DH.ŞFR., 429/90, Cipher cable, dated 8 October 1915, from Director of Migrants/Refugees (*Muhacirin*) in Aleppo Şükrü Bey to Interior Minister Talat.

74. BOA.DH.ŞFR., 56/385, Cipher cable, dated 13 October 1915, from Interior Minister Talat to Director of Immigrant and Resettlement in Aleppo, Şükrü Bey.

75. BOA.DH.ŞFR., 57/191, Cipher cable, dated 30 October 1915, from Interior Minister Talat to Şükrü Bey.
76. BOA.DH.ŞFR. 496/53, Cipher cable, dated 7 November 1915, from Director-General of Security, Emniyeti İsmail Canpolat to the Ministry of the Interior.
77. Aram Andonian, *Medz Vojirĕ*, 102.
78. Genelkurmay Başkanlığı, *Arşiv Belgeleriyle, Cilt VII*, 95.
79. Aram Andonian, *Medz Vojirĕ*, 102; Attachment 1-B.
80. Ibid., 7, 105.
81. See Appendix D.
82. Genelkurmay Başkanlığı, *Arşiv Belgeleriyle*, 99.
83. Raymond Kévorkian, *Soykırımın İkinci Safhası*, 235. As we have already seen, Andonian states openly, both in the published work and in his unpublished notes, that Naim was removed from his position. Neverthless, V. N. Dadrian claims that this is an error, and was not actually the case.V.N. Dadrian, "The Naim-Andonian Documents on the World War I...", 346.
84. BOA.DH.EUM.6.Şb. 8/24-01, Cipher cable, dated 5 July 1916, from Interior Minister Talat to the District Governor of Urfa.
85. BOA.DH.EUM.6.Şb. 8/24. The entire correspondence can be found in this file.
86. BOA.DH.ŞFR., 66/24, Cipher cable, dated 16 July 1916, from Interior Minister Talat to the Provincial Governor of Aleppo.
87. Rita Soulahian Kuyumjian, The Survivor: Biography of Aram Andonian (London: Gomidas Institute, 2010), 19.
88. Kévorkian, *Soykırımın İkinci Safhası*, 234.
89. Kuyumjian, *The Survivor*, footnotes 26, 86.
90. Kévorkian, *Soykırımın İkinci Safhası*, 269.
91. Ibid., 241.
92. While Andonian was negotiating with Naim Efendi, Salih Zeki, who had been appointed as District Governor of Deyr-i Zor, was circulating in the environs of Aleppo and Meskene. Salih Zeki was appointed on 26 April 1916, and his appointment was approved three days later (BOA.BEO., 4410-330741-01-01, Written communication, dated 29 April 1916, from the Grand Vezier's Chancery Office). Thus, it appears entirely reasonable that the events recounted here occurred in the second half of May or the beginning of June. Similarly, in a report on the Baron Hotel in Aleppo, sent by Major Azmi to Istanbul on 20 June 1916, he stated that he went to the aforementioned hotel with Salih Zeki at the beginning of June (BOA.DH.EUM. 2. Şube, 26/9, Report from Aleppo, dated 20 June 1916, by Major Azmi). The Armenian survivor, M. Aghazaryan, who kept a journal during those months that he was in

Deyr-i Zor, gives 18 June 1916 in his journal as the date that Salih Zeki came to Deyr-i Zor (M. Aghazaryan, *Aksoragani Husher* [Memories of the Deportations] (Adana: Hay Tzayn Matbaası, 1919), 13.

93. Kévorkian, *Soykırımın İkinci Safhası*, 269.

94. In fact, the families were initially in favor of bribing the District Governor of Deyr-i Zor, Salih Zeki, in order to go to Deyr-i Zor. Zeki agreed and accepted the bribe, but suggested to the families that they should not go there in his company, but come to Deyr-i Zor after his arrival there. However, Andonian's acquaintance with Salih Zeki changed all these plans. Having known Andonian from his youth, Zeki shared with Andonian the facts of the massacres, and warned him, "Be careful that you don't come [down here] to Deyr-i Zor." Andonian explained [the situation] to the families and convinced them to opt for Aleppo instead by bribing Naim. For Andonian's encounter with Salih Zeki, see Ibid., 239–245.

95. Aram Andonian's letter to Mary Terzian (Appendix C).

96. Ibid.

97. Genelkurmay Başkanlığı, *Arşiv Belgeleriyle, Cilt VII*, 69–140; Kévorkian, *Soykırımın İkinci Safhası*, 257–260, 267–268.

98. Aram Andonian, *Medz Vojirĕ*, 8.

99. Andonian's letter to Mary Terzian (see Appendix C).

100. Ibid.

101. BOA.DH.EUM 2. Şube, 26/9, Report by Major Azmi from Aleppo, dated 20 June 1916.

102. BOA.DH.ŞFR., 66/56, Cipher cable, dated 22 July 1916, from Interior Minister Talat to the Provincial Governor of Aleppo.

103. BOA.DH.EUM., 2.Şb. 26/9-7, Cipher cable, dated 26 July 1916, from Aleppo Provincial Governor Mustafa Abdülhalik to the Interior Ministry.

104. Andonian's letter to Mary Terzian (see Appendix C).

105. Ibid.

106. Ibid.

107. Orel and Yuca, *Talat Paşa'ya Atfedilen*, 8, 9.

Even If the Memoirs Are Authentic, Could the Documents Still Be Forgeries?

We may summarize the discussion up to this point thus: the argument that the telegrams attributed to Talat Pasha are forgeries is based first and foremost on the premise that there was no such official by the name of Naim Efendi, and, since such a person never existed, he cannot have written his memoirs (nor have handed documents to Andonian), and the memoirs are therefore entirely the product of Andonian's hand. But this premise is wrong. There was indeed a late Ottoman official by the name of Naim, and the memoirs that exist came from his own pen. Andonian did not fabricate them or change them. However, he did choose to publish only a part of the documents that he had received.

On the other hand, even if what we have said is true, there is still one important question that remains unanswered: Is it not possible that Naim himself fabricated his memoirs and the accompanying documents? Knowing as he did that the Armenians were tirelessly searching for documentary evidence of the massacres, might not Naim, who was chronically insolvent, have "made them to order," simply to earn money?

Orel and Yuca summarized their thesis on the falseness of the documents provided by Naim in 12 basic points.[1] Of these, eight key points directly concern the question of authenticity, as follows: (1) the signatures on the documents are forged; (2–3) there are serious errors in the dates on the documents; (4) the dates and numbers on the documents have no connection to reality; (5) the cipher telegrams, which are composed of a

© The Author(s) 2018
T. Akçam, *Killing Orders*, Palgrave Studies in the History of Genocide,
https://doi.org/10.1007/978-3-319-69787-1_4

group of figures that have nothing to do with real cryptographic methods; (6) the "bismillah" marks on the documents are false; (7) some explanations and descriptions are to be found on the documents that are not used in Ottoman; (8) the type of paper used for these documents is not the kind used by Ottoman bureaucrats.

Each one of these claims is no doubt important and needs to be addressed separately, but the claims made in numbers four and five must be acknowledged as carrying particular weight.

THE REGISTRY NOTEBOOK OF THE INTERIOR MINISTRY'S CIPHER OFFICE

In regard to point number four above, namely, that the dates and document numbers found on Naim's documents do not jibe with existing documents in the Ottoman archive, Orel and Yuca offer several pages from the Interior Ministry's Registry Notebooks of Incoming and Outgoing Messages, in which the cipher telegrams sent by the Interior Ministry to Aleppo are recorded.[2] The dates and numbers of the documents that are recorded in these pages of Registry Notebooks are different from those on the documents produced by Naim. In other words, the latter are not recorded in the Registry Notebooks. The authors assert on these grounds that the documents provided by Naim are fake.

A noteworthy point here is this: the notebooks in the archives that the authors mention are not available to researchers. We are thus confronted with the strange situation that, not only are the registry notebooks being hidden from researchers, but also that the numbers and dates of the some of the documents found in these "hidden" registry notebooks are used as evidence. Clearly, if researchers are not allowed access to the registry notebooks in question, then the claims of Orel and Yuca are not verifiable and become far less convincing. Those who would base their arguments on the Ottoman Interior Ministry's registry of incoming and outgoing cipher cables must first advocate for and ensure that these registries are actually accessible to all researchers.

Another noteworthy point on this matter is the fact that the telegrams going to Aleppo were sent not only from the Ministry of the Interior. Many sources have confirmed that Interior Minister Talat, who had earlier been a postal official, had a private telegraph line set up in his house and used it like he was at a post office. He communicated with the provinces and was informed as to what was going on there through this means. For instance, in his memoirs, then-Foreign Minister Halil Menteşe wrote that:

> one morning I went to the house in Yerebatan where [Talat] lived.... Something about him looked unnatural. The coal black eyes in his head were bloodshot as could be.
>
> "Good Lord, Talat, what happened? You look to be in a pretty bad state," I said. "Don't ask," he replied. "I received a few telegrams from [Erzurum Governor] Tahsin about the Armenians, and it set my nerves on edge. I wasn't able to sleep all night."[3]

American Ambassador Henry Morgenthau provided a similar account. One day when he went to the interior minister's house to ask him for his help, Talat told him:

> "I am going to help you," and "turned around to his table and began working his telegraph instrument." Morgenthau recalls; "I shall never forget the picture; this huge Turk, sitting there in his gray pajamas and his red fez, working industriously his own telegraph key, his young wife gazing at him through a little window and the late afternoon sun streaming into the room. ... A piece of news which Talaat received at that moment over the wire almost ruined my case. After a prolonged thumping of his instrument, in the course of which Talaat's face lost its geniality and became almost savage..."[4]

Morgenthau claims that for the more than two hours that he was there, his conversation with Talat was continually interrupted by the telegrams that arrived.[5]

Nor must we rely on the testimonies of outside observers. The testimony of Talat's own wife, Hayriye Hanım, also confirms what Menteshe and Morgenthau saw. In a 1982 interview, she stated that there was indeed a "telegraph machine" in their house that was used by Talat. When asked, she replied, "Of course he used it. He gave all the [provincial] governors orders [by means of it]."[6] What sort of numbering system did Talat use for the telegrams he sent from his house? We will most likely never be able to answer this question, but it raises the possibility that the numbering on Naim's documents are legitimate.

CIPHER TELEGRAMS AND CODING TECHNIQUES

Regarding the authenticity of Naim's telegrams, the most important of Orel and Yuca's claims is that the coding technique on those cables that consist of only numbers is incorrect. Altogether Naim provided Aram Andonian with seven cipher telegrams, five with double-digit and two with triple-digit codes. These are, in chronological order: (1) 29 September 1915 [triple-digit]; (2) 9 December 1915 [double-digit];[7] (3) 26 December 1915 [double-digit]; (4) 20 March 1916 [triple-digit]; (5) 20 March 1916 [double-digit]; (6) 23 January 1917 [double-digit]; (7)? March 1917 [double-digit].[8]

Orel and Yuca claim that all of these ciphers, both the double- and triple-digit codes, were produced by Andonian, not Naim. The documents that "Andonian offered as cipher cables, consisting as they did of groups of numbers, and with the hope that they might thus be seen as credible, actually have no connection with the actual cryptologic techniques used during that period."[9] The authors put forth two important arguments to support this claim. The first is that every coding system was used only for a short period. According to them, this period never exceeded six months, because it was inconceivable that they would "use the coding system within war[time] without any changes."[10] They do not provide any explanation at all, however, on when these periods began or ended.[11] The greatest evidence for Naim (or Andonian) not knowing the encryption techniques of the period is that the time differential between the dates of the cipher documents written with the same digit groupings is almost six months. The authors give the dates of Naim's two triple-digit documents (29 September 1915 and 20 March 1916) as their proof. According to the authors, this is impossible, and so the documents are forgeries.

Orel and Yuca's second argument is that, at any given period, cipher messages were encrypted with only a single group of digits. In other words, two different digit-groups would not be employed within the same time period. For example, the authors claim that from 26 August to 11 December 1915, the encryption was done with five-digit number groupings and no others. According to the authors, the four-digit number groupings were in use only from March 1916 onward. The authors do not give an exact day. According to their reasoning, any telegraphic message sent within a given period and possessing a different number of digits that was used during this period must, by definition, be a forgery.

For example, since five-digit groupings was the coding system of the period between August 26 and December 11, the two different telegrams, which fall within this time period (29 September 1915 with triple-digit and 9 December two-digit) provided by Naim are obvious forgeries. In short, Orel and Yuca based their argument that the encrypted telegrams given by Naim to Andonian are forgeries on the claim that only a single specific group of digits would be used as an encryption technique within any given (less than six-month) period.

These claims are entirely incorrect and are without any material basis. But before we examine the authors' thesis in depth, it will assist us in understanding the subject at hand to offer some of our own observations on the cipher cables currently found in the Ottoman Archives.[12]

SOME GENERAL OBSERVATIONS ON THE ENCRYPTING SYSTEM

We have examined a great number of the tens of thousands of encrypted telegrams sent between the Ottoman entry into the First World War in October 1914 until March 1918. One thing that was striking is that the Interior Ministry had its own method of encryption, one not shared by the other government ministries and departments. The ministry did not like to share its encryption method with the government's other ministries. For instance, in a cable sent by the ministry to the provincial governor of Aleppo on 3 December 1914, Governor Celal Bey, who had given Fourth Army Commander Cemal Pasha (in Syria) the encryption notebooks for Deyr-i Zor, is warned that the interior ministry did not permit the deciphering key used in its encryption methods to be shared with anyone else.[13] A similar order was sent in 1918, wherein the ministry again demanded that its methods not be shared, stating that "it is not possible for the [decryption] keys belonging to the [Interior] Ministry be given to the [army] commanders."[14] Of course, in certain situations, other ministries and institutions were permitted to communicate by means of the interior ministry's codes. On 10 March 1918, for instance, a telegram sent to the Ottoman consul in Süleymaniye [Sulaymaniyah], Mahmut Bey, reads: "Since the [decryption] key at the ministry has been cancelled, it is necessary for you to continue communicating with the code key of the Interior Ministry."[15]

The interior ministry itself used various encryption methods for its local civilian officials to communicate with other institutions, especially with the army and defense ministry. A message sent to all of the provinces on 6 December 1914, for example, reported that it was seen as acceptable for "secret communications between the Defense Ministry and civilian officials to be conducted by means of the encryption methods [usually] reserved for communication with the corps commanders."[16] In instances in which one of the existing encryption methods was not used, special encryption keys were created only for this type of communication. For example, a circular from 11 May 1915 states that "a new encryption key has been prepared and implemented by the Interior Ministry exclusively for the communications between provinces/provincial districts and the War Ministry," and requests that "the cipher communications to be written to the Ministry of War and the Office of General Provisioning be undertaken with this key." The specific reminder was also given that, in this type of communication, "the [encryption] key of the [Interior] Ministry not be used."[17]

In some cases, one of the encryption methods used by the interior ministry was designated specifically for the purpose of communication between the army commanders in various regions and the local officials. An example of this phenomenon was the interior ministry report in March 1916 that "the encryption code of the sixth type is being given [to Vehip Pasha, the Commander of the Third Army] in order to communicate with various provinces and provincial districts."[18] We encounter a similar situation in 1918. On October 9 of that year, a circular sent to all of the provinces requested that "the encryption key of the sixth type should be partially used in communication with the Ministry of Provisioning and Supply."[19]

Again, we can glean from the existing documents that special encryption methods were developed for the functionaries whose duties had them dispatched to the provinces or abroad in an official capacity. Two examples are the special encryption methods that were used for Süleyman Askeri, who traveled to Baghdad as a functionary of the Special Organization (*Teşkilat-ı Mahsusa*),[20] and for Halil Menteşe,[21] who traveled to Germany on official business during the war. We can glean similar information from some memoirs. One of the well-known Ottoman bureaucrats, A. Faik Hurshit Günday, informs us that when he was employed in Baghdad, he knew that Enver Pasha (one of the triumvirate) sent a special encryption key-book to one of the leading Arab politicians for special communications.[22]

Even within the interior ministry, different encryption methods were used. The cipher used by provinces and provincial districts in communication with their associated districts was different, for instance, from the one they used for communications with Istanbul. On 9 March 1915, the interior ministry sent a cable to Izmit and Menteşe, containing the following explanation on the subject:

> [T]he encryption keys that were sent previously and are currently in use are reserved for [your] communication with the surrounding provincial districts and sub-districts. The [encryption] key that is now being sent is for communication between the Sublime Porte and the provinces and associated provincial districts. You will therefore use the other [key] when communicating with provincial districts. There needs to be a clarification of this issue.[23]

Basically, the interior ministry used two separate types of encryption techniques. The first was a technique consisting of various digit groupings; the other encryption technique consisted of combinations of letters and was called *huruf-ı mukatta* (letter substitution). From the documents we now possess, we can understand that the second method was used primarily in communications with Istanbul and with the provinces that had many associated provincial districts. Since the letter substitution method was very easy to decipher, an order was sent out to all of the provinces and provincial districts on 25 April 1915, requesting that the method no longer be used. "As it has been learned that certain regions have been communicating with their surrounding counties and townships by means of the encryption key made up of letters, [this method] is no longer to be used for the protecting of secrecy [in communications], since this type of encryption can be very easily cracked."[24] In another circular from 2 August 1915, the order was given that the codes belonging to this encryption method be burned. "Please burn under your surveillance the encryption key notebooks, which contain the *Huruf-u Mukatta* [letter substitution] that is used for the communication of the provincial districts with Bab-ı Ali [government] and the provinces. Inform us about the status."[25]

Regarding the encryption techniques using the digit groups, throughout the period in question, the methods used employed digit-groups ranging from two to five figures. Although in our own combing of the archives we came across numerous mentions of six, seven, eight, and even nine types of encryption systems being used, we never actually encountered a single telegram written with these number groups. One prime example is a memo by the Interior Ministry's Office of the Special Secreteriat on 10 April 1915, requesting that "on account of the Provincial District of Niğde and the County of Eskishehir being turned into an independent provincial district, one or two copies of the sixth, seventh, and eighth type of encryption key for exclusive use in communicating with the general provinces and independent districts should be sent to the aforementioned provincial district governors."[26]

Another cable, sent to the interior ministry from Erzurum on 6 September, mentions "we inform you that the seventh type of encryption key notebook has arrived."[27] For the ninth type of encryption key, we may give the example of the cipher cable sent from Deyr-i Zor to the interior ministry on 28 July 1918, informing the ministry that "it has been learned, as the result of an investigation, that the [message] was written in the name of 'Office for the Resettlement of Immigrants' and with the ninth type of cipher group."[28]

As stated above, we have only encountered encrypted documents with from two- to five-digit groups but none of six-, seven-, eight- or nine-digit groups. One possible reason for this is that the number groups six, seven, eight and nine are not related to different digit groups but to a different numbering system within each digit group, and most probably only within 4 and 5 digit-groups. Indeed, every digit-group has several different numbering systems; this means several different encryption combinations. As we will discuss below, there are at least nine different encryption combinations for the four digit-group, for example.[29] Another example is the Director-General of Immigrant Affairs; this office used the two-digit group, and there are at least 15 different encryption techniques. Based on this information, one can argue that the number-groups six, seven, eight, or nine might not concern the question of digit groups to encrypt a telegram, but how to decipher the documents within a given digit-group.[30]

A related observation we made is that, regardless of the digit-group with which it was encrypted, each telegram indicates at the beginning by which numbering system it should be deciphered. For example, in a cable encrypted with the five-digit group, sent to Istanbul on 25 December 1915, the Governor of Aleppo provided the following instructions:

"Number five. I am acting today in order to turn over the southwestern and southern parts of the province...[the code that I will send] is to be deciphered with the sixth type of encryption."[31] This shows clearly that the governor encrypted his five-digit group telegram according to code number five and informed Istanbul that he would continue to send five-digit telegrams, but that they should be read according to code number six! This is the reason we often find the phrases, "number two, three, four, five, six, seven or nine" at the beginning of the documents, and the documents themselves appear to have been encrypted with the four- and five-digit code. Another example can be given for documents with two-digit groups; at the beginning of some of the documents with two digits we read the phrase, "[encrypted] with the Immigrant [Resettlement Office] cipher number 15."[32]

Our final observation regarding the cipher techniques is that different offices and departments within the interior ministry used different digit groups for encryption. Most of the cables that Naim gave to Andonian, for instance, were written with the two-digit group. This is not surprising, since the two-digit encryption method was used by the Directorate for Tribal and Immigrant Settlement (also frequently referred to as the directorate for deportations) and the Commissions on Abandoned Properties, as we have already seen above. This fact alone is another strong piece of evidence pointing toward the authenticity of the Naim documents.

In many situations, the encryption done with this digit-group is mentioned along with the name of the relevant office. Two telegraphic messages sent to Istanbul on 2 September and 21 November 1915 by Şükrü Bey, the Director of Office of Immigrant Resettlement (at the time, in Aleppo), bear the description "to be deciphered with the Immigrant [Resettlement] Office Encryption."[33] A cable from Trebizond also has the note inserted: "[encrypted] with the Immigrant [Resettlement Office] cipher number 15".[34] These two cables are also encrypted with the two-digit group.

There might be some changes over the years regarding which office used which digit-groups. For example, it seems that after September 1916, the two-digit group encryptions are understood to have been also used in communications between the interior ministry and the army.[35]

Sometimes, certain departments were warned not to use other departments' cipher methods. For example, in a circular sent to the commissions on abandoned property in some regions, the recipients are requested not to use the "ministry's [encryption] key" for their written communications and instead that "communication be conducted with the existing cipher of the Immigrant [Resettlement] Office."[36] Ciphers exclusive to the commissions were sent separately and specially delivered to the provinces. A cable sent to the "President of the Commission on Abandoned Property" in Niğde on 22 September 1915, which states that the "encryption key [notebook] is in the mail," is a good example of this.[37]

In the places and situations where the relevant encryption keys did not reach, the local officials were given permission to use the encryption key used by the provincial government: "Since the encryption key has not yet been sent to the Presidents of the Commissions on Abandoned Properties, it is mandatory that the relevant ciphers be written with the ministry's cipher." The provincial governments were informed of this situation through a special order that was sent out, and they were requested to supply the aforementioned commissions with their ciphers: "The provinces have been communicated with by telegram that they should give a form of the aforementioned cipher [keys] to the presidents of the Commissions on Abandoned Properties."[38]

There were also some special encryption systems that deviate from the cases that we mentioned above. An encrypted cable sent from Berlin by Finance Minister Cavit Bey on 27 May 1915 is a perfect example of this. The telegram was encrypted with the five-digit number group. There is no specific mention at the beginning of telegram according to which number group it should be deciphered. The official in Istanbul deciphered the telegram as if it were encrypted with the four-digit group. That is, he took the first four numbers of the first five-digit group and deciphered it; he then took the fifth number and combined it with the first three numbers of the second five-digit group, thereby creating a four-digit group, and deciphered it. The second five-digit group now had two numbers remaining. The official took these two numbers and combined them with the third five-digit group, and so on[39] (see Image 1).

More information on the subject could only be obtained by publishing the so-called "Encryption Key Notebooks" (*Şifre Miftahı Defteri*) containing encryption keys for all of the different digit groups. These notebooks, which pertain to the war years, have unfortunately remained off-limits to researchers.

Image 1 DH.ŞFR., 472/111-1, coded cable from Finance Minister Cavit from Berlin

THE QUESTION OF SPECIFIC PERIODS FOR ENCRYPTION METHODS

Against this general background, we can now examine more closely Orel and Yuca's central claim regarding the encryption number groups. They argue that "In the years 1331–1332 [1915–1916] ciphers composed of two-, four-, and five-digit number groups were used, but the three-digit group was not used."[40] However, as we will see again and again, their claim in regard to the three-digit encryption method is incorrect. The three-digit number group was used for encryption—albeit rarely—throughout 1915.

But let us leave this subject aside for now and focus on another point. As we have shown above, Orel and Yuca's claim that the telegrams given to Andonian by Naim were false rests on the argument that encryption techniques were only used for periods of less than six months. During our own forays into the Ottoman archives, we never encountered a single document stating that a given number group would remain in use for less than or up to six months. Moreover, we also never came across any information as to which number groups would be valid for any given period. From the Encryption Key Registry Notebook of 1914 that we possess, we learn that encryption was reorganized on a yearly basis.

On the first page of this notebook, we see the headings: "the encryption key reserved for communication with all the provinces" and "encryption key specific to Sublime Porte." We read also the instructions, "it is necessary that the provincial governors and other esteemed officials pay special attention to guarding the Encryption Key Registry Notebooks so that the keys do not pass into untrustworthy hands." The digit numbers with which the key registry was encrypted are also specifically explained.[41]

One can easily conclude from the encryption keys being sent to the various provincial governments on different dates that certain changes were made to it over the course of the year, but it is difficult to discern a clear pattern in the type of changes or in the manner that they were made. From some of the cables it can be concluded that they were reorganized or changed on a yearly basis, as we have seen in the examples above—or at least that they were so renamed. For instance, a cable sent to the Province of Van on 4 May 1915 reads: "Because it was not reported [whether or not] the new encryption key that was sent on 28 February [1]330 had arrived, it is was not understood [whether the present] key is for last year or for this year."[42] However—and for reasons we will list at greater length—it is difficult to arrive at a final judgment on the subject simply from the account and dates found within the documents, even if we can make some firm conclusions, such as the fact that the encryption keys were changed in March, the beginning of the Ottoman year.

What we may conclude from the encrypted cables sent between November 1914 and March 1918 is that those encryption methods using two-, four-, and five-digit number groups were continually used throughout this period, and their use was *not* restricted to given periods of time. However, at certain periods there were changes in the frequency of their use, particularly for the four- and five-digit groups. At the beginning of this period (November 1914) the five-digit group was used most frequently.

The second-most common were encryptions with the four-digit number group. Only infrequently do we encounter encryptions with the two- and three-digit groups. In the middle of January 1915, the number of four-digit encryptions grew steadily, so that by February it became the number group used most frequently.

In June, the increased frequency of the five-digit number group can once again be discerned, and by the middle of July, this group once again became the principal method of encryption. This state of affairs continued until February 1916. By March and April, the four-digit encryption method began to show increase again, so that it once again became the most widely used method by May 1916. From this point until the end of March 1918 (where our own archival research stopped), the four-digit group would remain the predominant method for encryption. In short, the four- and five-digit encryption methods were used steadily throughout this period, with only the proportional frequency of their employment changing. But these changes were not sudden, taking place gradually over a period of weeks or months, and in any case, there were no limits or restrictions on their use in regard to time periods.

The principal reasons that the four- and five-digit methods were used simultaneously—albeit with changes in frequency of use—were the delays and lack of uniformity in sending and receiving the new encryption key registries. Countless examples can be provided of this phenomenon.

For example, we learn from a circular sent to all the provincial governments on 16 December 1914 that a new encryption key registry for communication between the provinces had been sent out long before December. The message included the request of the provincial and district governors that they "be extraordinarily cautious in protecting the new encryption keys,"[43] but also inquired if all the encryption registries in question had arrived in their respective regions. Throughout the months of December and January, the inquiries continued about who would receive the encryption key notebooks and when. For instance, a cable sent to the provincial governor of Baghdad, Süleyman Nazif, on 29 December 1915, requested that "the new encryption key, which is in the possession of Reshit Bey, should be taken, and he should be communicated with in this way; the old key is absolutely not to be used."[44] Several different cables, sent on 4 January 1915 to the Provinces of Bolu, Ankara and Diyarbekir, state that the encryption key registries that were sent had not yet reached their destinations or had not been picked up, and requested that they be ordered picked up at the soonest possible moment.[45]

A similar situation appeared in March 1915 in regard to a new encryption key registry that was sent for the purpose of securing communications between the provincial governments and their respective districts. A cable on 31 March to the provinces of Konya, Adana, and Antalya assured the recipients that the encryption key registries were on the way to them.[46] The "new encryption key for province-provincial district communications" for Sivas, Mamuretülaziz (Elazığ), Bitlis, Van, and Kayseri was reported sent on 7 April 1915, and these administrators were requested to report back when the registries arrived.[47] The registries for the Province of Aleppo and associated districts was only sent on 17 April, however.[48] The registries destined for Kütahya, a district not so distant from Istanbul, were only actually received on 28 April 1915.[49] Another cable dated 1 May 1915 asked of a great many provinces and districts whether or not the encryption key registries had arrived yet;[50] the Provinces of Van and Bitlis were asked the same thing in a message dated 26 May 1915.[51] By 2 June 1915, the registries to Diyarbekir, Siverek, [Deyr-i] Zor, Baghdad, and Basra had yet to arrive.[52] New encryption keys began to be sent out on July 8.[53]

Perhaps the most interesting example of this situation is a document we discovered regarding when the registries of the sixth, seventh, and eighth type of encryption keys were sent to the provinces. According to a list prepared by the interior ministry, they were sent between the relatively broad time span of 11 March and 21 August 1915. The first place that the registry was sent was the city of Bursa. It was sent there on 11 March 1915, followed by the one to Balıkesir two days later. To give but a few of the other provincial and district capitals to which the registry was sent: Edirne (20 March), Aydın (12 April), Urfa (15 April), Deyr-i Zor [6th & 7th type] (12 May) [8th type] (31 May), Trebizond (3 June), Kastamonu (8 July), Hijaz and Yemen (21 August).[54]

Another important discovery made during our research in the archive is that, despite the changes of the type of encryption key for each digit group, these different numbering combinations were also used in a very mixed way. For example, we discovered at least six different coding systems regarding ciphers with two-digit groups (Please note that the Director-General of Immigrant Affairs had 15 different numbering groups). Most of the documents we discovered in the Ottoman Archive were with the fifteenth encryption technique (or number combination 15). We found around 100 documents of this type. This numbering group was used throughout the period, without any time limitation. For example, a telegram from Eskisehir, dated 3 September 1915 (DH.ŞFR., 486/138), and a telegram from Samsun, dated 6 July 1916 (DH.ŞFR., 524/105), are both written with the same numbering group. The time interval between these two documents is more than 10 months. During the same time, the other numbering groups belonging to the two-digit code were also used.

Another example can be given with the four-digit encryption system. As we mentioned, there were at least nine different numbering combinations for the four-digit group. Different numbering groups were used simultaneously throughout this period. For example, a telegram sent from Ankara on 6 July 1915 (DH.ŞFR., 478/110) was encrypted with the four-digit group with numbering system of five. Another telegram with the same digit group and numbering system was sent on 7 September 1916 (DH.ŞFR., 531/46). As we see, the time interval is more than 13 months. And we have several four-digit group telegrams encrypted with different numbering systems during exact the same time period.

Because of all this disorder and irregularity in the distribution of the new codes, it is possible to find countless documents in the archives that report on the need "to communicate with the old encryption key until the new one, which is being put in order, is sent."[55] In some situations, one reads that, due to the delays, the provincial governments will be able to correspond with one another with the encryption number group of their choice. An order sent to Bursa on 30 November 1914 (from its language we can surmise that it was also sent to other regional governments) states that "notice has not been given for the old encryption keys to be returned. The Provincial and District Governors may communicate with their own subordinate administrative districts/sub-districts with the ciphers that they choose."[56] From what we have been able to observe in these documents, it is difficult to speak of a systematic process. In fact, utter disorder would appear to be the order of the day.

The Evidence Offered as Proof of the Inauthenticity of Naim Efendi's Telegrams

After having closely examined the information contained in the individual cipher telegrams from the Ottoman archives, we may now take a closer look at the claims forwarded by Orel and Yuca regarding the number groups in the Naim cables, namely, that they do not agree with Ottoman Interior Ministry practice and are therefore forgeries.

The two three-digit encrypted telegrams whose photographic images were published by Andonian are dated 29 September 1915 and 20 March 1916. The authors claim that the period of time between these two documents is too long to be valid:

> [By] this situation we understand that the same encryption code was in use for up to six months; but it is not possible during wartime for an encryption key to be preserved for such a long period without being changed at all.[57]

Their assertion, which is based on the period of time between the two telegrams in question, is a serious error. There exist in the Ottoman archives telegrams encrypted with the three-digit method that are dated at an interval far greater than these two messages. To give but a few examples, there is a cable sent by Dersim District Governor (*Mutasarrıf*) Sabit on 8 April 1914 (DH.ŞFR., 423/27), and another sent by Provincial Governor of Van Cevdet on 5 November 1914 (DH.ŞFR., 451/134), a time difference of seven months. By Orel and Yuca's logic, at least one of these cables must be a forgery.

The objection might be made, of course, that the first communication is from the period before the Ottoman entry into the First World War and that the six months' time interval would start with the beginning of war, but other such examples can be given as well; if we take the 5 November 1914 telegram of Cevdet, Governor of Van, (DH.ŞFR., 451/134) as the first date, we have a 17 April 1915 cable with three-digit encryption from former Necef District Governor Sami (DH.ŞFR., 467/114) and another three-digit encryption by Fuat, the Civil Service Inspector for the Province of Hüdavendigar (Bursa), sent on 7 December 1915 (DH.ŞFR., 500/53). The difference between Governer Cevdet's and Inspector Fuat's telegrams is 13 months; and that between Sami's April 1915 telegram and Fuat's December 1915 telegram is eight months, once again flying in the face of the authors' claim.

The authors' claim of the "impossibility" of the same number group being used for encryption for six months would naturally cover not only three-digit methods but also two-, four- and five-digit methods. For example, if we were to find two-digit encrypted cables during the same time period as the three-digit ones offered by Naim, by Orel and Yuca's logic this, too, would compel us to believe that a forgery had taken place. And yet, as we showed above, not only the same digit groups, but also the different numbering groups for each digit group had been used throughout this period without any time limitation.

Let us give an additional example. There is a six-month interval between the 28 September 1915 cable sent from Aleppo by Immigrant Resettlement Director Şükrü (DH.ŞFR., 491/24) and one sent by the Commission for the Liquidation of Abandoned Property on 26 March 1916. Another "forgery"? In fact, it is unnecessary to belabor the point further. As we said previously, the Ottoman archives contain literally tens of thousands of two-, three-, (and especially) four- and five-digit encrypted telegrams that were sent throughout the entire war, without specific time limitations.

Orel and Yuca have also strived to prove from another angle that the three-digit encrypted cable of 29 September 1915 given by Naim is a forgery:

> [T]here is no connection between the real encryption system used on 16 September 1331 [29 September 1915], the date on which the forged cable was sent, and the system that was used by Andonian, since the five-digit number group was in use at that time, not the three-digit [one].[58]

In order to prove their claim, the authors publish two encrypted cables sent by Talat on 26 August and 11 December 1915. They then state, with reference to the Naim telegram of 29 September 1915, "the inauthenticity of the Andonian cables is clear, since they fall within the dates of the two-digit cables [being used]."[59]

Leaving aside the awkwardness of the two dates themselves, the authors' claim of a rule that there be a single time period for a given encryption method, on the basis of two cables they discovered in the General Staff archives, is simply fanciful. There is no such rule, and the claim of such is a concoction by the authors with no basis in empirical reality. Moreover, the Ottoman archives are replete with hundreds of cables sent during the period of their example that feature two-, three-, four-, and five-digit encryption methods. If we were to accept Orel and Yuca's argument, we would have to conclude that the majority of these cables are forgeries. To give but one example, a cable sent by the aforementioned Civil Service Inspector Fuat from Bursa on 7 December 1915 ("I have arrived in Bursa. After tomorrow I will go to Gemlik."), which is encrypted with the three-digit method, would be a fabrication[60] (see Image 2).

The same is true for two-digit encryptions. The Office of the Director of Immigrant Resettlement in Aleppo, Şükrü Bey, sent a cable on 12 October 1915 concerning the removal of Armenians who had been arriving in Aleppo throughout the deportations,[61] and another on 21 November

DH.ŞFR.00500.00053.001

Image 2 DH.ŞFR., 500/53, coded cable from Civil Service Inspector Fuat

concerning the refusing of permission for the deportees from concentrating at the train station and other population centers and stating the efforts to remove them had begun[62] (see Image 3). If we are to follow Orel and Yuca's argument, these and dozens more just like them must be seen as forgeries.[63]

Hundreds of examples can be given of telegrams encrypted using the four-digit numbers method between the period of 26 August and 11 December 1915. To give but a few examples of telegrams for each month between August and December to prove my point: the documents dated 29 August 1915 from Diyarbekir (DH.ŞFR., 486/25); 30 August 1915 from Urfa (DH.ŞFR., 486/4); 3 September 1915 from Yemen (DH.

DH.ŞFR.00490.00096.001

Image 3 DH.ŞFR., 490/96, coded cable from Director of Immigrant Resettlement Şükrü, 12 October 1915

ŞFR., 487/51); 30 September 1915 Adana (DH.ŞFR., 491/97); 19 October 1915 from Sivas (DH.ŞFR., 494/25); 30 October 1915 from Konya (DH.ŞFR., 495/33); 2 November 1915, from Sivas (DH.ŞFR., 495/85) 16 and 23 November 1915 from Kayseri (DH.ŞFR., 497/82; 498/63); 2 December 1915 from Mosul (DH.ŞFR., 499/77).

Orel and Yuca claim that only the five-digit number group was used for encryption during this period, which would make hundreds of documents with four-digit numbers forgeries. The short answer is this: Orel and Yuca's claim in regard to Naim's 29 September 1915 document, namely, that "there is no connection between the actual encryption system that was used and the one used by Andonian, since during that period the five-digit groupings were in use" is simply wrong. And their claim that "the forged nature of the Andonian telegrams is clear,"[64] which is based on this argument, is thus without foundation.[65]

For the Naim telegram of 20 March 1916, encrypted with the three-digit method, the authors make a similar claim: "the encryption system then in use was the four-digit number group system," and add that:

> [t]his is proven by authentic documents that are found in the General Staff Archives, Cabinet 139, Binder 1762, File 187. As for Andonian, since he had no possibility of knowing the actual encryption system in use on that date, he wrote the forged cable—or had it written for him—using the three-digit number group.[66]

This is a strange position to take. It is highly problematic to cite a source, which is unavailable to anybody else and thus its legitimacy impossible to ascertain, and to utilize this source as proof that all other documents are invalid. Orel and Yuca are asking for a *prima facie* acceptance of their claims without making this source available; this is unacceptable. Apart from this, their claim that "the four-digit encryption system was in effect" in March 1916 is fanciful. We counted each and every document from March in the Ottoman archives. There are 216 cipher telegrams from the period of 1–31 March 1916, and the great majority of them are encrypted not with the four-digit, but the five-digit number group. There are also four examples of the two-digit encryption method to be found among these.[67] More to our point, however, is the fact that there are at least 10 cables that were sent on 20 March, the date of the Naim document in question. Of these, four are of the five-digit group and the other six are of the four-digit group.[68] How does this jibe with the authors' claim of period-specific encryption methods? Are the two- and five-digit cables all forgeries? (see Images 4 and 5).

I would also like to add here that, since all number groups from two to five digits were used widely for cipher telegrams sent internally, cables encrypted with different groups were often sent and arrived on the same day! This alone is enough to show just how groundless are the arguments of Orel and Yuca. Here are but a few of the dozens of examples from each of the years in question:

- 26 December 1914: three-digit (450/86), four-digit (450/69) and five-digit (450/71) cipher cables;
- 18 & 20 March 1915: (Province of Van) three-digit (DH.ŞFR., 464/16); (Provinces of Izmit and Muğla) four-digit (DH.ŞFR., 464/25 ve /27); and (Province of Sivas) five-digit (DH.ŞFR., 464/40) cipher cables;

DH.ŞFR.00513.00073.001

Image 4   DH.ŞFR., 513/73, coded cable from Niğde, 18 March 1916

- 6 May 1916: (Province of Marash) five-digit (518/79); (Provincial District of Canik) two-digit (DH.ŞFR., 518/90); and (Province of Kastamonu) four-digit (518/94) cipher cables!

All of these examples point unambiguously to one truth: Every single one of Orel and Yuca's arguments regarding the Ottoman Empire's wartime encryption techniques and practices is false and thus cannot be used to prove or disprove the authenticity of the Naim cables. As the archival documents have shown, the documents said to have been provided by Naim are in accordance with Ottoman wartime encryption practices.

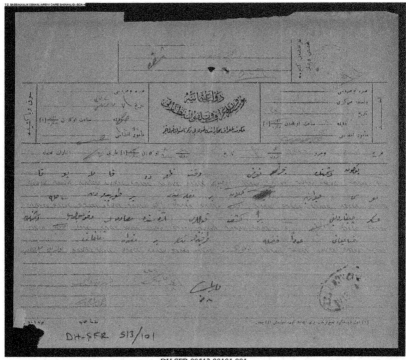

DH.ŞFR.00513.00101.001

Image 5 DH.ŞFR., 513/101, coded cable from Trebizond, 20 March 1915

THE QUESTION OF THE USE OF LINED PAPER

Another of Orel and Yuca's arguments for the inauthenticity of Naim's documents has to do with the paper on which they are written. They claim that the fact that one of them is written on lined paper is proof of it being a forgery:

> One of these "documents" was written on a piece of paper bearing the document number 76 but does not bear any official mark. Such a piece of paper, which more greatly resembles the type used in calligraphic lessons at French schools, cannot be expected to be found in use as official stationery in Ottoman [administrative] offices.[69]

The photograph of this telegram, which was sent by the Director of the Deportation Office Abdülahad Nuri to the Interior Ministry on 20 March

1916 and is encrypted with the two-digit number group, was published by Andonian in the Armenian and French editions of his book. Naim deciphers this document in his memoir thus: "It is understood from the information received that up to the present, 35,000 in the area of Bab and Meskene, 10,000 in Aleppo's deportation site (Karlık), 20,000 in the area around Dipsi, Abuharrar and Hamam, [and] 35,000 in Ras-ul-Ayn, in all 95,000 Armenians, have died of various causes."[70]

The authors' judgment that lined paper "cannot be expected to be found in use as official stationary in Ottoman [administrative] offices" and their use of this fact as evidence of forgery is simply incomprehensible. Lined paper *was* in fact used within the Ottoman bureaucracy during the period in question, and the Ottoman archives are simply full of documents requesting lined paper for use in various departments of the Ottoman Interior Ministry. To give but a few examples: "...the demand that 100 units of lined paper of the type be sent from the General Security Directorate's Office of Supply;"[71] "...the Accounting Department's demand for lined paper;"[72] "The payment of the price for the lined paper purchased for the Private Secretariat."[73]

But the most important bit of information contained in these and other, similar documents is the request on the part of the interior ministry that encrypted cables, in particular, be written on lined paper. The reason for this is clear. Only in this way could officials be certain not to confuse the rows of digits to be encrypted/deciphered and to prevent errors in the same. Unnecessary correspondence to correct errors could thus be avoided. A general circular to this effect was sent to all regional administrative offices already in October 1913—long before the outbreak of the war.

The first ones to bring this subject to the attention of the government was the office of the grand vizier, which wrote to the interior ministry on 29 October 1913. Titling the communication "Concerning the Organizing of Ciphers on Lined Paper and Their Delivery to the [Regional Administrative] Centers," the vezirate reported that it had observed that "the two big groups of telegraphic messages, each one of which consists of hundreds of telegrams that were earlier written by the District Official (*Kaymakam*) for Gevar and sent to the Province of Van and the Provincial District of Hakkari, and which was then delivered to the local telegraph office, were written in a very dense [and thus, hard-to-read] way, and in a manner that allows for errors at the time of its composition." After expressing concern that "such conditions as these will be repeated in other regions and districts," the vezirate requests that a communication be sent out to all of the provincial and other smaller administrative centers stating that encrypted telegrams be written on lined paper.

In the same communication, the Office of Grand Vezirate claims that the Foreign Ministry also uses lined paper in its encrypted correspondence.[74] The Grand Vezirate would subsequently send a message with similar content to the President of the State Council.[75] In response to the grand vizier's message, the Interior Ministry issued on 21 November 1913, by means of a circular to "all of the provinces and non-attached [i.e., independent provincial] districts," the order that lined paper be used in all encrypted telegrams to the provinces in an attempt to ameliorate the problem:

> Since the lines of encrypted telegrams in some places are very tight and are composed in a manner that allows for a great number of errors [to occur] during their writing, all administrative units are hereby notified of the necessity that ciphers be written on [well-]spaced lined paper so as to avoid these types of errors that have appeared thus far and to prevent unnecessary additional correspondence [in the future].[76]

As will be understood below, Orel and Yuca's claim is entirely wrong that the lined paper found in one of Naim's documents proves it to be a forgery. Encrypted correspondence was not smooth or straight, so using lined paper provided a useful foundation for such. Thus, the fact that one of the documents provided by Naim was on lined paper does nothing to prove that it is a forgery—on the contrary, it far more shows it to be authentic.

A FINAL OBSERVATION

As we have seen this far, the encrypted cables given by Naim to Andonian are similar to ciphers found in the Ottoman archives; indeed, there is *nothing* in them that would invalidate their authenticity, and they may very well be the original documents. Naim himself worked in the Office of Deportations, and this office made official use of the two-digit number group for encrypting their messages. Thus, it is entirely reasonable for him to have provided Andonian with cables using this encryption method, the method used in the majority of the copied cables in question. The principal difficulty with this subject is that, even today, we do not know the encryption key that was used in that period, since the encryption keys and the registries in which the rules for solving the codes are laid down are still closed to researchers.

In the Ottoman archives, only the encryption key registry for 1914 is to be found. This notebook reveals the three-digit encryption method only for 1914, as we have seen.[77] This system was used until March 1915 (the beginning of the Ottoman year), and subsequently removed "theoretically" from use. An order sent to all provinces and regions except for Hijaz, Yemen, and Medina on 7 March 1915 requests that "since the third type of [encryption] key, which was previously used for communication between the Sublime Porte and the provinces, was cancelled and burned, the copies [of the key] that still exist there be burned in your presence and the situation then reported [back to Istanbul]." In the various cables sent by the provincial and district governors to Istanbul in response, they reported the "burning of the third type" of key per the government's request.[78]

Yet, despite this request (and alleged compliance thereto), the three-digit number group continued to be used in cipher communications, for instance, in messages by Cevdet, the Provincial Governor of Van (17, 18, and 22 March 1915) (DH.ŞFR., 465/60, 91, 126); by the Registrar Besim, acting in the name of the acting governor of Mosul (3 April 1915) (DH.ŞFR., 466/146) (6 April 1915) (DH.ŞFR., 467/23); and by Sami, the former Governor of the Provincial District of Neced (5 April 1915) (DH.ŞFR., 467/10). As a result, the order requesting to have the third type of encryption key registries burned was repeated in another cable sent on 2 August 1915.[79] However, just as before, this order was not fully complied with, as can be seen in the aforementioned 7 December 1915 cable from the Civil Service Inspector Fuat (DH.ŞFR., 500/53). We should also add the information that none of the three-digit ciphered documents that we discovered in the archive were encrypted with the 1914 encryption key. This means clearly that in 1915 a new encryption key was produced for the three-digit group!

In conclusion, no final, decisive judgment can be given in regard to the two- and three-digit cipher cables that Naim gave to Andonian without first seeing the relevant encryption key registries. In order to shed further light on this topic, the registries for the years 1915–1918 must first be published and made available to researchers. Certain documents that we came across in the archives have led us to believe that these registries do indeed exist and that they have been used by those working in the archives.

Those scholars who work in the archive know that the cables that were sent from the various administrative centers in the provinces arrived in encrypted form, and that the officials of the period deciphered them on the same page that they received. The ability of researchers to read these documents is enabled by the deciphering that is written above the numbers themselves. However, there are some cables upon which no deciphering has been done. One perfect example of this is DH.ŞFR., 523/90; it is a three-page cable dated 21 June 1916, encrypted with the four-digit method. It does not appear to have been deciphered, and, as such, is currently of no use to researchers. Yet, in the catalogue of archival holdings, the document's contents are described as "reporting that the enemy has begun to bombard Jeddah, and that skirmishes have continued between [Ottoman] soldiers and the rebels." There is only one possible explanation for this: the encryption key registry for this digit group of 1916 still exists and has been consulted by archive employees, thereby allowing them to decipher such documents and to write summaries thereof, thus begging the question—why are these registries still denied to researchers?

Why indeed? The decision to deny researchers access to such vital material as the encryption key registries for the period after 1914, despite the passage of a full century at this point, is a crucial question. We have every reason to be suspicious. This situation may be seen—indeed, *must* be seen—as evidence of the accuracy or authenticity of the incriminating Naim documents. We would assert that if the encryption system in these registries were to show the cables and other documents to be forgeries, researchers or authors who had been granted the privilege of using the restricted documents in General Staff Archives would have published their findings long ago. Thus, the fact that these registries have not been made generally available to researchers must be seen as compelling evidence for the authenticity of the Naim documents.

THE QUESTION OF THE DATES ON THE DOCUMENTS AND THE SIGNATURES OF THE GOVERNOR

Basing our arguments on Ottoman archival documents, we have shown that there did indeed exist an Ottoman official by the name of Naim Efendi, that he wrote a memoir, and that events of which he writes were real events, which he, himself, had experienced. Likewise—and again, on the basis of evidence found in the Ottoman archives—we have revealed that the encryption techniques found in the telegraphic cables that Naim sold to Andonian are the same as those used by the Ottoman Government. Above all, we have showed that the use of lined paper for these cables sent from Aleppo and the employment of the two-digit encryption technique in their writing—both of which had been previous held up as proof of the documents' inauthenticity—did not actually bring into question their authenticity, but instead confirms it.

Only one point of dispute remains: the claims that the date on one of the seven deciphered documents that were reproduced in Naim's memoir was erroneous and that the signature of Aleppo Provincial Governor Mustafa Abdülhalik on these documents was forged. Orel and Yuca's claims on this matter are similar to their other claims of inauthenticity, and in both cases, they are incorrect.

In order to allow the reader to more easily follow the discussion of this matter, let us reiterate the important points: Naim gave Andonian approximately 24 documents in total. Of these, seven were encrypted telegrams using two- and three-digit encryption techniques. In his book, Andonian reproduced photographs of five of these seven cables. There were 12 deciphered documents bearing the signature of the aforementioned Governor Mustafa Abdülhalik, of which 10 are mentioned in the memoir. Of these 10 documents, Andonian provides photographs of seven in the book. The remaining two documents concern the Ottoman parliamentary deputy Krikor Zohrab and are found in the Boghos Nubar Pasha Library. We have already discredited the claims that these encrypted telegrams were forgeries based on the lined paper and encryption techniques used. The only remaining question that needs to be elucidated is the claim of the documents' inauthenticity based on the date of one document and signatures on the 12 deciphered cables.

Do the Dates on the Documents Prove Their Forgery?

Orel and Yuca argue that the date on telegraphic cable number 502, allegedly sent from Istanbul to Aleppo on 16 September, is proof that the document is a forgery, because next to the governor's signature, the phrase "5 *minhü*" is written, meaning the fifth [eighteenth] of the month of September.[80] In fact, Mustafa Abdülhalik was appointed to the position only on 3 October 1915, and only actually arrived in Aleppo to assume his duties on 7 November.[81] Orel and Yuca thus claim that a document signed by a governor before he actually assumed his position must be a forgery.

Orel and Yuca raised the claim of inauthenticity due to the dating error on one document alone, but there are in fact five such documents that are similarly problematic. In other words, all five bear the signature of Mustafa Abdülhalik, but bear dates from before he became governor. Four of these are mentioned in Naim's memoir: (1) 16 September 1915, (2) 12 October 1915, (3) 16 October 1915, and (4) 25 October 1915.[82] (5) There is also a document not mentioned in the memoir, regarding the killing of Armenian parliamentary deputy Krikor Zohrab, dated 17 October 1915; the original is held in the Boghos Nubar Library.

If we follow Orel and Yuca's logic, we must regard these five documents bearing the pre-appointment signature of Mustafa Abdülhalik as inauthentic. But such a claim would be incorrect, and there are several reasons for this. In his memoir, Naim states he "was by chance appointed as Chief Secretary to Abdülahad Nuri Bey, who had only taken up his duties as Acting Director General of Immigrants in Aleppo three or four days previously."[83] Governor Mustafa Abdülhalik and Deportation Office Director Abdülahad [Nuri] had come to Aleppo together, which is to say that Naim began his position around mid-November 1915. If Naim, as one who knew when the governor and director of deportations had arrived in Aleppo, had wished to forge documents, he obviously would have dated them *after* the date that the new governor had arrived. We believe that the large number of documents (namely, five) does not prove them a forgery, but, on the contrary, points to their authentic nature. Orel and Yuca's greatest error is not in believing that the document was given by Naim, but that it was fabricated by Andonian.

Second, a dating error on a document cannot alone be taken as incontrovertible evidence of the document's forgery. On the contrary, an incorrect date can be seen as evidence of a document's authenticity. If we were to categorically declare any document bearing an inaccurate date to be false, we would have to conclude that the Ottoman State Archives are replete with false and forged documents.

As support for this claim, I would offer the following three documents. The first is a telegram sent by a certain Şükrü (in the name of the Interior Minister) to the Province of Van on 1 April 1915, requesting information on the situation of the Kurds in the region. In the document, the author asks about "relations between the Kurds and the population of the Turkish villages and towns that were reported [on] in the cipher dated 10 February

1916." Clearly, a message written on 1 April 1915 could not actually be referring to a communication written 10 months hence. Rather, the author of the April telegram must have actually written it on 1 April 1916, or the date of the communication referred to should be 10 February 1915. The years cited are simply a clerical error on the part of the person who sent it.[84]

The second example is a communication from the Ottoman Foreign Ministry to the Interior Ministry, dated 1 December 1915. Within the text of the message, an event is mentioned as having occurred on 13 December 1915. Another date is also mentioned in the text, "31 November" (*31 Teşrinisani*), which simply doesn't exist. Again, it goes without saying that either the date of the report or the dates within the text (one, at the very least) are inaccurate.[85]

The third and final example is a cable sent from Aleppo, bearing the date[s] 24/25 February 1332 [1916]. However, such dates do not exist on the Ottoman calendar. As is well known, the Ottoman Government employed the "Rumi" calendar,[86] and there was a 13-day difference from the Gregorian one. During the war, the government took the decision that, after 15 February 1332 [1916], the remaining days of the month would simply be erased from the calendar and the following day, 16 February, would be replaced by 1 March, at which point the new dating would begin. As a result, the document's dates of "24/25 February 1332" simply did not exist.

To repeat, if we were to use dating errors as grounds for rejecting a document's authenticity, all of the aforementioned documents would have to be classified as forgeries. But such an action would be wrong. As we have shown, the Ottoman archives contain dozens of documents containing dating errors like these and they can be found with ease.

The third important argument that can be used to show that incorrect dating alone is insufficient grounds for rejecting the documents' authenticity is the contents of said documents. Not a single one of these documents, whose language and reasoning are in all other aspects completely in line with that of the Ottoman bureaucracy, contain an order concerning the murder or annihilation of the Armenian population. In other words, there is no information in these documents that would lead one to believe that there would be a motive for them to be forged. For example, in one of them, dated 16 September 1915, it states that "It is suggested that the treatment, previously communicated as to be carried out in regard to the male population of certain known individuals, be expanded to also apply

to their women and children and that it be employed by reliable officials."
Another of these documents, dated 16 September 1915, reads as follows:
"Reports have been received that a number of the [local] population and
officials have married some of the Armenian women. It is strongly urged
that [these marriages] be forcefully prevented and that such women be
deported separately."

One of the most striking examples of this phenomenon is to be found
in the document dated 25 October 1915. In this document, the Interior
Minister requests of the provincial authorities in Aleppo that "*within a
week the papers that were [originally] requested in secret correspondence
number 1923 and dated 25 September [1]331 be assembled together and sent
off.*" It is clear that there could be no sense in forging a document simply
dealing with the request for papers previously requested. As we showed
above, the photographic image of this document, dated 25 October 1915,
was neither used by Andonian nor included in the book he published.

The same situation exists in regard to the document dated 17 October
1915, found in the Boghos Nubar Pasha Library. The document contains
a request for the papers from the investigation into the killing of the
Armenian parliamentary deputy for Istanbul, Krikor Zohrab, and states
that "*Istanbul Deputy Krikor Zohrab Efendi died as the result of an accident
[that befell him] while traveling.*" To claim that such a document is a forgery is laughable, because it could be used to disprove that Zohbrab was
murdered, if taken out of context. And yet, Orel and Yuca claim that "the
fundamental goal of the book [published by Andonian] is to circulate
'official evidence that would incriminate the Turks'."[87] If this were indeed
the case, their claim that the aforementioned document is a forgery—a
document which states that Zohrab Efendi was not murdered but died as
the result of an accident—comes across as more than a little strange. We
must add here that, as in the case of a document written by Enver Pasha,
Andonian did not hesitate to publish in his book documents other than
those provided by Naim. It would seem that Andonian felt that the content of this telegram, given to him by Naim, did not necessitate its inclu-
sion in the book.[88]

What remains to be explained, however, is how and why the signature
of Mustafa Abdülhalik appears on these telegrams when he had yet to
assume the duties of his new position. The answer is surprisingly simple.
He most likely read the documents in question *after* the date he began his
duties and sent them on to the Department of Deportations where Naim
was employed. This would also explain how Naim was able to come into

possession of these documents. In fact, the situation here was frequently encountered within the Ottoman state bureaucracy.

Before Mustafa Abdülhalik was appointed to the position, the provincial governor of Aleppo was Bekir Sami, whose appointment ended on 3 October 1915.[89] The documents under discussion here (apart from the one dated 16 September 1915) are all from the period after Bekir Sami left his position.[90] Between the period of Bekir Sami's departure and the start of the new governor's term, the Qadi (Islamic religious court judge) Halit served as acting governor. From the archival documents in our possession, we can understand that the Qadi Halit responded only to the communications that came from Istanbul in the form of a question or to problems demanding an immediate solution. Papers that came in the form of suggestions for future actions or policy directions were left for the incoming governor.[91]

If we look more closely at the telegrams provided by Naim from the months of September and October, we can see that they dealt with advice and significant proposals on certain matters. After his appointment, the new governor read these cables and sent them to the relevant offices and parties. In short, the content of these telegrams was not so revelatory as to motivate their forgery; and the repetition of a request for papers and a report on Zohrab's "accidental" death are not the stuff of "damning evidence" that one could reasonably expect to have been falsified.

THE SIGNATURES OF GOVERNOR MUSTAFA ABDÜLHALIK

Another argument put forward by Orel and Yuca for the inauthenticity of the Naim documents is that the signature of Governor Mustafa Abdülhalik on these documents is forged. The authors support their claim by providing a sample of the governor's signature from a document in the Ottoman archives (among the papers of the Interior Ministry's Second Department), and in truth, there are some minor differences between the signature on this document and the ones provided by Naim. Nevertheless, we found other signatures of the Governor in two different places. The first group of such signatures is found among the documents of the Cipher Office of the Interior Ministry (in the Ottoman Archive), and the second group of signatures are in the 7th and 8th volumes of the collection of archival documents published by the Turkish military's Institute for Military History and Strategic Studies (Askeri Tarih ve Stratejik Etüt Başkanlığı, or ATASE), *"Armenian Activities in the Archive Document 1914–1918."*

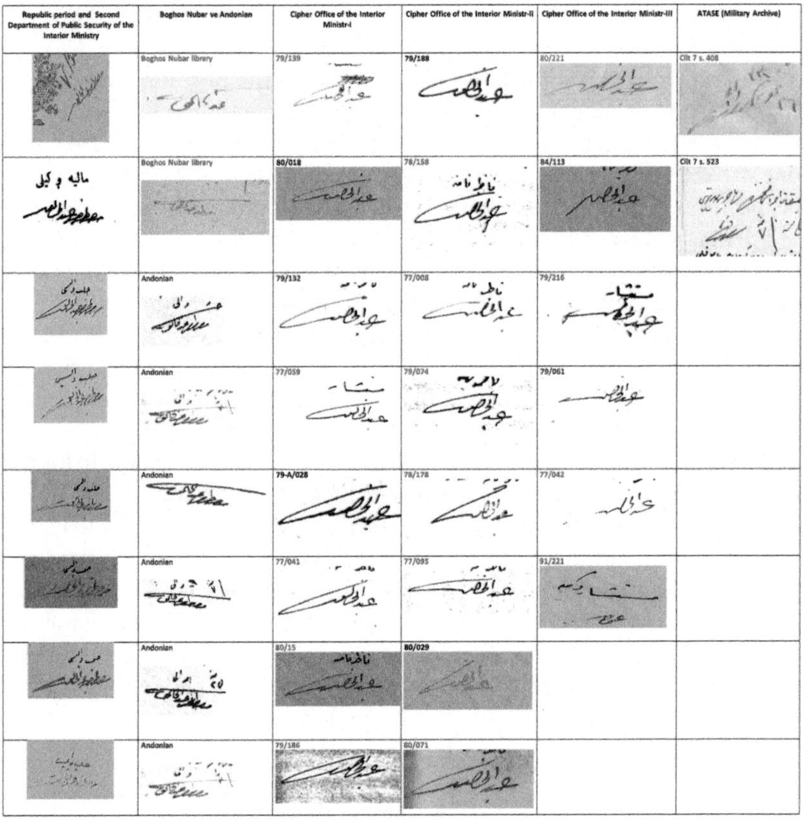

Image 6   Table of signatures of Governor Mustafa Abdulhalik

When compared with these signatures, we found the differences between the signatures in the Naim documents and those of the Second Department appear insignificant. In fact, in a comparison of the two sets of signatures, what catches the eye is not their differences but their similarities. The greatest differences appear in fact between the documents from the Second Department and from Naim on one hand, and those found in the Cipher Office on the other. The signature in the ATASE publication is totally different than all above (see Image 6).

As will quickly be understood from the table of signatures produced here, Mustafa Abdülhalik used at least four or five different styles of signature, all of which were quite distinct from one another. The reason for this is that he sometime wrote his signature using both parts of his name and at other times, only one. The signatures of the Interior Ministry's Second Department papers offered by Orel and Yuca and the ones on the Naim Efendi documents all feature both parts of his name. A close look at these signatures, written in the Arabic script, shows that the two parts of his name can be identified separately. The first part of his signature, with its series of loops, corresponds in its shape to the word Mustafa. As for the second part of the signature, it corresponds to the abbreviated version of "Abdülhalik," so we have the whole name in the signature. For their part, the signatures on the papers from the Interior Ministry's Cipher Office only bear the name "Abdülhalik," and the documents from the ATASE publication, only the name "Mustafa."

In both the Second Department and the Naim signatures, the "Mustafa" portion is similar; but the second part, namely the abbreviated version of "Abdülhalik," is slightly different. The most striking difference on the Naim documents is that there is a long line drawn sharply curving straight backward from the left, "sheltering" the name under it. In comparison, this line is very sharp and short in the signatures on the Second Department documents and does not span the entire signature, instead ending somewhere above the word Abdülhalik. It is on the basis of these differences that Orel and Yuca make their claim that the Naim documents were forgeries by Andonian.

As with all their other claims, Orel and Yuca are incorrect here as well, and the argument that they put forward is flawed for many reasons. Before recounting these, however, it should first be added that, not only do the signatures on the Second Department documents offered by Orel and Yuca differ from those of the Naim documents, but they also contain partial differences from one another. In some of the Second Department documents, the line that runs above the signature is hard and straight; in others, it forms an arc. Similarly, in some of the signatures that he used mostly during the republic period (the first two signatures on the first column) there is no line at all or on the same level or going downward. We are thus persuaded that one cannot use these differences in the signatures alone to decide the authenticity of the documents containing them.

The most important piece of evidence for our claim that the Naim documents are not forgeries is that we found *different* signatures of the governor on them. For instance, the signature on the document dated 11 November 1915, concerning the fate of Krikor Zohrab, is completely different from those on the other documents (See Signature Table: first signature in the Naim Efendi column). All of the other documents provided by Naim contain both parts of Mustafa Abdülhalik's name, whereas the signature on the aforementioned document reads only "Abdülhalik." Let us stop and consider: is not the one thing a person wishing to pass off forged documents on the basis of their signature *would not* do is to sign these documents with *different* signatures?

The second main reason that the aforementioned signatures should not be considered forgeries is the existence of similar signatures matching that of the 11 November 1915 document on documents we have discovered in the Ottoman archives. These documents were found among the papers of the Interior Ministry's Cipher Office, which are signed merely "Abdülhalik." Among these papers we were able to identify approximately 100 such signatures belonging to Mustafa Abdülhalik. The reason for such a plethora of signatures is that Abdülhalik worked as undersecretary to the Interior Ministry between April 1917 and September 1918. The encrypted telegrams that were to be sent to the various provincial officials were all signed by him before being encrypted. At least one of them, dated 24 September 1918, was actually written out by him as well.

The third argument for the authenticity of the signatures in the documents provided by Naim is that there are serious differences even among and within the various signatures on the Interior Ministry Cipher Office documents, as can clearly be seen in the table provided. The first six different signatures in the column (*Cipher Office of the Interior Ministry-III*— second column from right) by Mustafa Abdülhalik are not only very different from the signatures of the Second Department, Naim, and the ATASE documents, but also greatly differ from the signatures on the other Cihper Office documents.[92] Leaving aside the other sets of document signatures (Second Department, ATASE, Naim), on the basis of these six signatures alone, we could easily claim that all other signatures on the Cipher Office documents were forgeries.

The fourth important piece of evidence for their authenticity is the great similarity between the "Abdülhalik" portion of the signatures on both the Cipher Office documents and those provided by Naim. On the great majority of the Cipher Office documents, the signatures have a line over the entire name as in the Naim documents.

The fifth piece of evidence for the signatures' authenticity is the strikingly different signatures of Mustafa Abdülhalik that we discovered in the seventh volume of the previously mentioned ATASE publication, *Armenian Activities in the Archive Document 1914–1918*. In the two signatures we discovered in Volume 7, Mustafa Abdülhalik signs only his first name. This is totally different from all the other signatures (see the last column on our list).[93]

If we accept as our points of departure Orel and Yuca's logic in claiming that the signatures on the Naim Efendi documents are forgeries based on the signature found on one of the Second Department papers, we would have to conclude that all of the signatures on the documents from both ATASE and the Interior Ministry's Cipher Office are forgeries. Even if we were to focus only on the signatures on the six Cipher Office documents, we could easily argue that they were *all* forgeries. Likewise, we could, on the basis of the ATASE signature, argue that all of Mustafa Abdülhalik's *other* signatures were forgeries. In short, whichever of these different signature styles one chooses as "authentic," the others can therefore be asserted to be false.

We cannot answer the question of why Mustafa Abdülhalik employed such markedly different signatures, but we would assert that the different styles are the product of conscious choice on his part. That is, Mustafa Abdülhalik knowingly wrote his signature differently. This is in fact the sixth point we would assert for the authenticity of the signatures on the Naim documents, the main evidence being the signature on Ottoman archival document DH.ŞFR., 79/139 (see the first line of the signature table, *Interior Ministry Cipher Office—I*). As can be understood from the signature on this document, Mustafa Abdülhalik begins with his first name (Mustafa), but then draws a line through it and decided it would suffice to simply sign with the second part (Abdülhalik). As we have seen above, all of the signatures from the Cipher Office documents have this characteristic. If we put together the last name signatures here with the crossed out first names, what appears are full signatures quite similar to those on the Naim Efendi documents. This is yet another proof that Mustafa Abdülhalik knowingly used different signatures at different times.

We possess still another very strong piece of evidence that the signatures on the Naim signatures (and therefore, the documents upon which they are written) are not forgeries. This is the handwritten notes of Mustafa Abdülhalik upon these documents. When viewing the Naim documents with the naked eye, two different handwritings are readily apparent (see Image 7). The first is the one used for the actual text of the document and is that of the Aleppo official who deciphered the encrypted telegrams coming from Istanbul. The second handwriting appears under the main text and is simply short notes or instructions by the governor, primarily for the intended addressee, such as "To the Assistant Director General of Refugee Affairs." On others, he writes a brief note about what needs to be done. To give but a few examples: "Have you met with the Gendarmerie commander?;" "Meet with the Police Director;" "Speak with the Police Director but do not mention the cipher [telegram?]. Are there actually

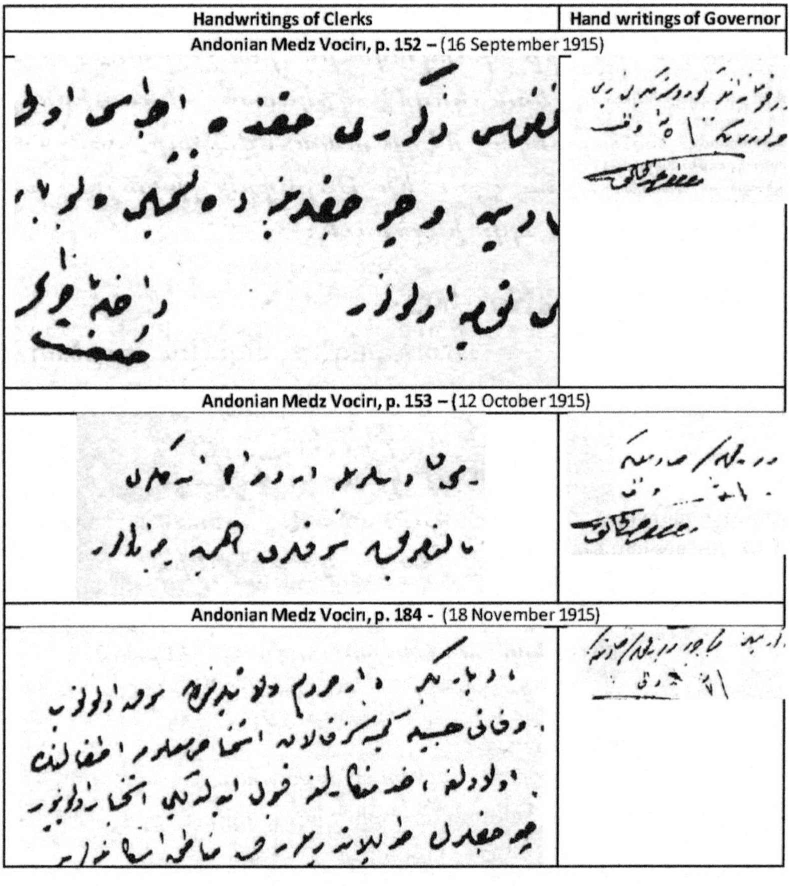

Handwritings of Clerks	Hand writings of Governor
Andonian Medz Vocırı, p. 152 – (16 September 1915)	

Andonian Medz Vocırı, p. 153 – (12 October 1915)	

Andonian Medz Vocırı, p. 184 - (18 November 1915)	

Image 7   Governor Abdulhalik's and Ottoman Clerk's handwriting comparison

organized people [such]as[those] mentioned here?; "It's very important, is it not? To the Assistant Director General of Refugee Affairs."[94]

When viewed with the naked eye, these referral notes on all of the documents appear to resemble one another closely. And these notes are of a very different writing manner than that of the text of the document. There is information in our hands that would show that these handwritten notes are from the hand of Aleppo Governor Mustafa Abdülhalik. We can see some other examples of the governor's handwriting, both in the documents from the Interior Ministry's Cipher Office and in those from the

ATASE publication. Even without close inspection, one can easily see the similarities between this writing and the handwritten notations found on the Naim documents (see Image 8). The document found among the Cipher Office papers was a cable sent by Mustafa Abdülhalik to Batum. In

Boghos Nubar Library: document dated 17 October 1915	DH.ŞFR. 91/221: document dated 24 September 1918
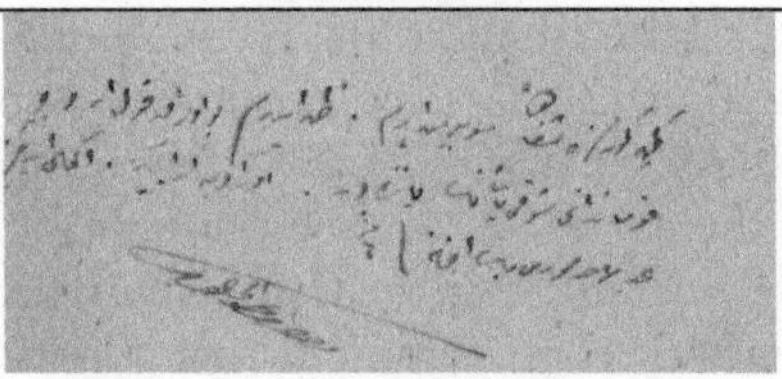	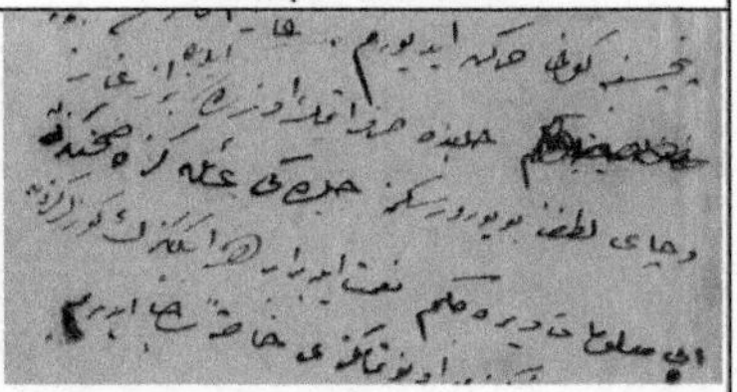
Andonian, Medz Vojire, p. 136 : document dated 1 December 1915	Military Archive Volume 7 p. 408, document dated 8 August 1916
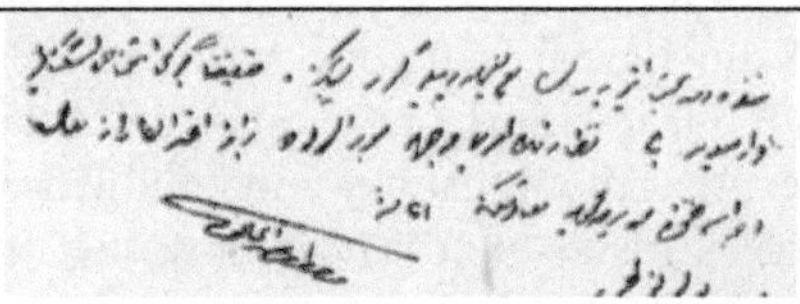	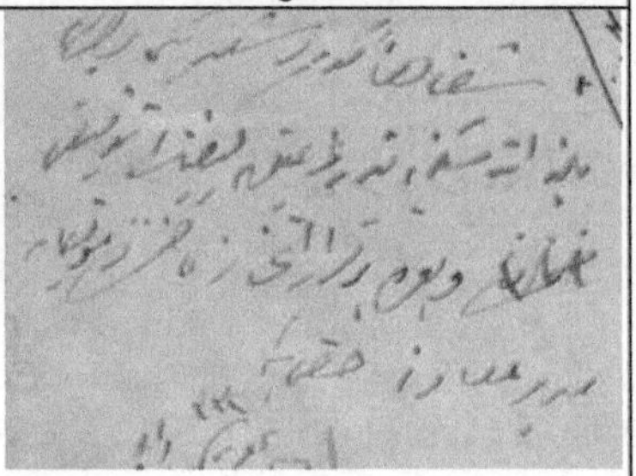
Andonian, Medz Vojire, p. 152 document dated 16 September 1915	Military Archive Volume 7 p. 523, document dated 18 January 1917
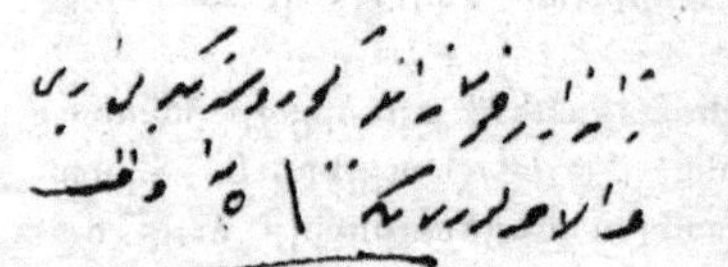	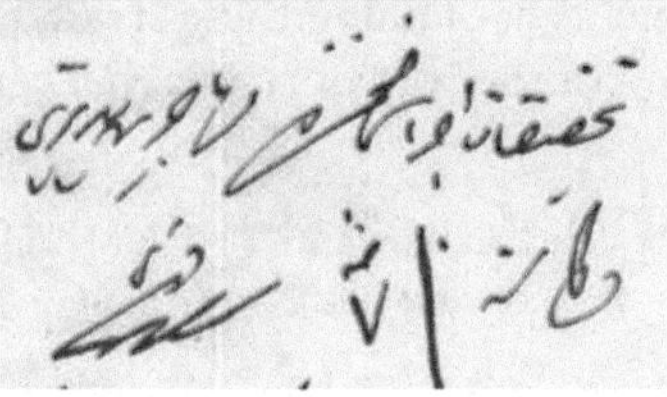

Image 8 Handwritings of Governor Abdulhalik in comparison as published in Andonian and the Ottoman Archive

the cable, Abdülhalik states that he was again appointed governor of Aleppo and that it is necessary for him to set out immediately.[95] We discovered at least five different hand-written letters and two referral notes belonging to the governor in ATASE publication volumes seven and eight.[96] The content of some of these is identical to some of the ciphered telegrams we discovered in the Ottoman Archives, leaving no doubt that this handwriting belongs to the governor. For example, the handwritten note by Mustafa Abdülhalik on the telegram dated 26 July 1916, found in volume seven of the ATASE publication, is the same document as the cipher cable DH.ŞFR. 526/60 found in the Cipher Office documents. His full name appears at the bottom of the cable. We can see the similarities between the referals in ATASE and the documents in the Ottoman Archive. For an example of one of these referals, it reads: "Upon further considerations, it is hereby decided that the Assistant Deputy Director of Deportation, Hakkı Bey, be sent to Maskanah for a further investigation of the situation."[97] This note refers to the investigations being conducted in Meskene that we examined earlier under the heading, "Was There an Ottoman Official by the name of Naim Efendi." In conclusion, all these writings of Mustafa Abdülhalik are identical with the notes and referrals in the Naim Efendi documents. To assert that the signatures and handwriting on Naim Efendi documents are forgeries is as good as claiming that the documents found in the Ottoman archives are also inauthentic.

Lastly, it should be added that the handwriting in the main text of the documents provided by Naim also contain differences from one another that are discernable to the naked eye. It shows, among other things, that deciphering of the documents was performed by different officials. To imagine that Naim possessed the ability to write in four or five different handwriting styles, and that he employed this skill to produce forged documents containing these styles, is the stuff of a conspiratorial mind. These are not the sort of claims that can or should be taken seriously.

A FINAL ADDENDUM TO THE MATTER OF CONDEMNING THE DOCUMENTS

The central reason for Orel and Yuca's assertion that the documents provided by Naim are forgeries is the argument that they contain orders directly concerning the annihilation of the Armenians. Let us recall here that Orel and Yuca's principal argument is as follows: "The assertion that the Armenians were 'murdered' by the Ottoman Government during the

First World War..." is simply a smear campaign that has been perpetrated "against Turkey for years." The Armenians—and Andonian chief among them—have produced documents "whose aim is to tar all Turks with the same [shameful] brush."

For their part, the authors Orel and Yuca explain that the goal of their work is to "closely examine, both from the aspect of form and content, every single document found in Andonian's book and claimed to be 'official,' and to show them all to be forgeries."[98]

Because the subject was debated in this context, the perception would later be created among the public that first, all of the documents were produced/fabricated by the Armenians; second, the documents that contained orders to kill the Armenians—especially the ones signed by Mustafa Abdülhalik and whose photographic images were printed in Andonian's work—were forgeries. We have shown that these documents were not produced by Andonian, but were sold to him by Naim. But these documents have another, crucial importance. Not a single one of the communications signed by Mustafa Abdülhalik contain direct orders to kill or massacre anyone.[99] In regard to the question of their authenticity, this is of the utmost significance; the false image created among the public needs to be corrected.

When one closely reads the content of all the telegrams in Naim's memoirs, the following picture emerges: there are eight documents containing the direct order to annihilate the Armenians. Two of these are encrypted with the three-digit method and have photographic images. There are no photos of the other six documents, which only exist in Naim's memoirs as reproductions of handwritten copies. Four of these six documents are found in the version of the memoirs in our possession; the other two are found in the section of the memoirs published by Andonian that we do not possess. Among these eight documents containing direct orders to kill, none of them is a deciphered document bearing the signature of Mustafa Abdülhalik. In other words, none of those signed by the provincial governor of Aleppo deals directly with the killing orders.

Five of the seven documents whose photographic plates appear in the book deal with the measures that needed to be taken vis-à-vis the deported women and children. One of these discusses the decision to make Deyr-i Zor a site for Armenian resettlement, while the other is about the activities of American consuls in the region. Of the three documents bearing Abdülhalik's signature that were not used by Andonian, one is a request for documents previously requested, another contains the demand that persons be prevented from taking photographs along the deportation routes, and the third instructs that any telegrams of complaint by the Armenian deportees be submitted in the places to which they are heading.

As we explained above, the two documents bearing Mustafa Abdülhalik's signature and found in the Boghos Nubar Pasha Libary deal with the death of Armenian deputy Krikor Zohrab. One of these mentions that he perished in an accident along the route, the other contains a list of questions about Zohrab: when did he arrive in Aleppo? what hotel did he stay at?, etc. In other words, there would be no good rationale for fabricating these documents, of which similar communications can be found with ease in the Ottoman archives. In light of these new facts, we are now obliged to more closely reexamine Naim Efendi's memoir.

NOTES

1. Şinasi and Yuca, *Talat Paşa'ya Atfedilen*, 129–130.
2. For examples of the registries of outgoing cipher cables (*Şifre Telgraf Giden Defter*), see ibid., 49, 58, 61, 62, 67–71, 75, 76.
3. Halil Menteşe, *Osmanlı Mebusan Meclisi Reisi Halil Menteşe'nin Anıları* (Istanbul: Hürriyet Vakfi Yayınları, 1986), 216.
4. Henry Morgenthau, *Ambassador Morgenthau's Story* (Garden City, New York: Doubleday, Page & Co., 1918), 143–144.
5. Ibid., 145.
6. Murat Bardakçı, *Talat Paşa'nın Evrakı Metrukesi* (Istanbul: Everest, 2008), 211.
7. Andonian did not use the photographic image of this cipher telegram. The document was published by Krikor Guerguerian (Krieger, "Aram Andoniani Hradaragadz Turk Başdonagan Vaverakreri"). The translation of the document is found on the same paper below the groups of numbers, and reads: "there are almost 400 children in the orphanage and these will be sent to the areas of resettlement separately from the convoys." The deciphered version of the cable is to be found in the version of Naim's memoirs published by Andonian (and that we no longer possess). See, Aram Andonian, *Medz Vojirě*, 183, 185.
8. This telegram is related to the killing of Armenian deputy Zohrab and was not used by Andonian. The Ottoman date on the document is 17 February 1332, which is a mistake. There was a 13 days' difference between the Ottoman Rumi calendar and the Gregorian calendar. To avoid this 13-day difference, the Ottoman Government decided to eliminate the dates between 16 February 1332 and 1 March 1333 (which is the first day of a

new year according to the Ottoman calendar). Beginning with 1 March 1333, Ottoman and Gregorian calendars have the same dates, which is a source of confusion even today.

9. Ozel and Yuca, *Talat Paşa'ya Atfedilen*, 129.
10. İbid.
11. Ibid., 76, 129.
12. To the best of our knowledge, no study has ever been done of the encryption methods used by Ottoman governments for their own internal correspondence. What we can offer here is only some limited observations. The subject is of sufficient import to merit a specific study in its own right.
13. BOA.DH.ŞFR., 47/302 Cipher cable, dated 3 December 1914, from the Interior Ministry to the Province of Aleppo.
14. BOA.DH.ŞFR., 92/71, Cipher cable, dated 7 October 1918, from the Interior Ministry to the Province of Mamuretülaziz.
15. BOA.DH.ŞFR., DH.ŞFR. 85/62, Cipher cable, dated 10 March 1918, from the Foreign Ministry to Consul Mahmut Bey.
16. BOA.DH.ŞFR., 47/355, Cipher cable, dated 6 December 1914, from the Interior Ministry to the Provinces of Edirne, Erzurum, Adana, Ankara, Aydın, Bitlis, Basra, Baghdad, Beirut, Hicaz, Aleppo, Hüdavendigar (Bursa), Diyarbekir, Syria, Sivas, Trebizond, Kastamonu, Konya, Mamuretülaziz (Elazığ), Mosul, Van, and Yemen and to the Provincial Districts of Urfa, Izmit, Bolu, Canik, Çatalca, [Deyr-i] Zor, Asîr, Karesi, Kudüs-i Sherif (Jerusalem), Kale-i Sultaniye (Gallipoli), Menteşe, Teke (Antalya), Kayseri, Karahisar-ı Sahib (Afyon Karahisar); and the Sanctuary of Medina.
17. BOA.DH.ŞFR., 52/228, Cipher cable, dated 11 May 1915, from the Interior Ministry to the Provinces of Edirne, Erzurum, Adana, Ankara, Aydın, Bitlis, Basra, Baghdad, Beirut, Hicaz, Halep, Hüdavendigar (Bursa), Diyarbekir, Syria, Sivas, Trebizond, Kastamonu, Konya, Mamuretülaziz (Elazığ), Mosul, Van, and Yemen; and to the Provincial Districts of Urfa, Izmit, Bolu, Canik, Çatalca, [Deyr-i]Zor, Asîr, Karesi, Kudüs-i Sherif (Jerusalem), Kale-i Sultaniye (Dardanelles), Menteşe, Teke (Antalya), Kayseri, Karahisar-ı Sahib (Afyon Karahisar), Eskishehir, İçel, Kütahya, Marash, and Niğde; and the Sanctuary of Medina.
18. BOA.DH.ŞFR., 61/280, Written message from the Cipher Office of the Interior Ministry, dated 1 March 1916.
19. BOA.DH.ŞFR., 92/82, Cipher cable, dated 9 October 1918, from the Interior Ministry to the Provinces of Edirne, Erzurum, Adana, Ankara, Aydın, Bitlis, Aleppo, Hüdavendigar (Bursa), Diyarbekir, Sivas, Trebizond, Kastamonu, Konya, Mamuretülaziz (Elazığ), Mosul, and Van; and to the Provincial District of Urfa, Izmit, Bolu, Canik, Çatalca, Zor, Karesi, Kale-i Sultaniye, Menteşe, Teke (Antalya), Kayseri, Kütahya, Karahisar-ı Sahib (Afyon Karahisar), İçel, Marash, Niğde, and Eskishehir.

20. BOA.DH.ŞFR., 48/199, Cipher cable, dated 29 December 1914, from the Interior Ministry to Süleyman Askeri Bey. In the telegram, Süleyman Askeri is requested not to use the special code that he has with him: [Please] use the new encryption code that is in Cavid Pasha's possession to communicate [with the Ministry]; by no means is the special encryption key to be used, as this key can be encrypted by everyone.

21. BOA.DH.ŞFR., 50/262, Cipher cable, dated 21 March 1915, from the Special Secretariat of the Interior Ministry to the Interior Ministry. In the cable, it is reported that "a certain type of encryption key has been created" for the communication between the "[interior] minister and Halil Beyefendi, who was in Europe on official business."

22. A. Faik Hurşit Günday, *Hayat ve Hatıralarım*, volume 1 (Istanbul: Çelikcilt Matbaası, 1960), 97–98.

23. BOA.DH.KMS., 24-2-05-03, Cipher cable, dated 9 March 1915, from the Interior Ministry to the Provincial Districts of Izmit and Menteşe. The same document can be found in the archives as BOA.DH.ŞFR., 50/219.

24. BOA.DH.ŞFR. 52/107, Cipher cable, dated 25 April 1915, from the Interior Ministry to the Provinces of Istanbul, Edirne, Erzurum, Adana, Ankara, Aydın, Bitlis, Basra, Baghdad, Beirut, Hicaz, Aleppo, Hüdavendigar (Bursa), Diyarbekir, Syria, Sivas, Trebizond, Kastamonu, Konya, Mamuretülaziz (Elazığ), Mosul, Van, and Yemen; and to the Provincial Districts of Urfa, Izmit, Bolu, Canik, Çatalca, [Deyr-i]Zor, Asîr, Karesi, Kudüs-i Sherif (Jerusalem), Kale-i Sultaniye (Dardanelles), Menteşe, Teke (Antalya), Kayseri, Kütahya, Karahisar-ı Sahib (Afyon Karahisar), İçel, Marash, and Niğde; and to the Sanctuary of Medina.

25. BOA.DH.KMS., 24-2-44.

26. BOA.DH.ŞFR., 50/262-2 Written message, dated 10 April 1915, by the Directorate of the Interior Ministry's Special Secretariat.

27. BOA.DH.ŞFR., 531/35, Cipher cable, dated 6 September 1916, from Erzurum Provincial Governor Midhat to the Interior Ministry.

28. BOA.DH.ŞFR., 591/3 Cipher cable, dated 29 July 1918, from the Acting Deputy District Governor of [Deyr-i] Zor, Ömer Zeki to the Interior Ministry.

29. Here some examples of four-digit telegrams with different number combinations: with number one: BOA.DH.ŞFR., 464/36 (7 March 1915); 467/106 (17 April 1915); with number two: BOA.DH.ŞFR., 464/31 (8 March 1915); 654/188 (20 December 1919); with number three: BOA. DH.ŞFR., 461/84 (17 February 1915); 519/24 (9 May 1916); with number four: BOA.DH.ŞFR., 465/69 (17 March 1915); 668/12 (10 October 1917); with number five: BOA.DH.ŞFR., 457/11 (10 January 1915); 486/04 (30 August 1915); with number six: BOA.DH.ŞFR., 464/34 (7 March 1915) and with number nine: BOA.DH.ŞFR., 467/106 (17 April 1915).

30. Even though the labels 6, 7, 8 and 9 were related to different numbering groups within a digit group, one would expect them to be explicitly mentioned in the document as to which digit group they belong. For example, they would have said, 6, 7, 8 or 9 of the five-digit group, etc. However, this was not the case. The simplest answer is that there is no need to mention this specifically because one would readily see whether the ciphered telegram has a four or five-digit group.

31. BOA.DH.ŞFR., 502/80, Cipher cable, dated 25 December 1915, from [Aleppo] Governor Mustafa Abdülhalik to the Interior Ministry.

32. BOA/DH.ŞFR., 497/79 (15 November 1915) and 520/23 (18 May 1916).

33. BOA.DH.ŞFR., 486/139 and 498/62, Cipher cables, dated 2 September and 21 November 1915, from Director of [Tribal and] Immigrant Settlement Şükrü Bey to the Interior Ministry.

34. BOA.DH.ŞFR., 499/87, Cipher cable, dated 2 December 1915, from the President of the Trebizond Canik Commission on the Liquidation of Abandoned Property Nazım Bey to the Interior Ministry.

35. Second Army Commander Ahmet Izzet Pasha's note, in a cable to the interior ministry dated 5 September 1916: "extremely urgent, to be handled personally [by minister]" and "with the province code," informs the ministry that "the Second Army's administration of provisioning matters has reached a worrisome state, and the need was felt for extraordinary measures [to be taken] in order to ensure the [continued] functioning of the whole." (DH.ŞFR., 531/21); The Provincial Governor of Mamuretülaziz, Sabit, sent a cable dated 8 September 1916 with the demand that the currently 150 person-strong cavalry unit in Hozat be allowed to stay in Mazgird (DH. ŞFR., 531/61); and the cable sent by Mustafa Kemal on 7 October 1917 on behalf of the Seventh Army Command, containing the demand that someone new be appointed in place of Reis ül-'Ayn County Executive (*Kaymakam*) Refi Bey (DH.ŞFR., 568/3).

36. BOA.DH.ŞFR., 59/155, Cipher cable, dated 30 December 1915, from the Interior Ministry to the President of the Kayseri Disposal [of Abandoned Property] Commission.

37. BOA.DH.ŞFR., 56/125, Cipher cable, dated 22 September 1915, from the Interior Ministry to the President of the Niğde Commission on Abandoned Property.

38. BOA.DH.ŞFR., 55/185, Cipher cable, dated 26 August 1915, from Interior Minister Talat to all of the provinces.

39. BOA.DH.ŞFR., 472/111. Since the deciphering of this specific cable was done on the same sheet of paper, it is possible to see how the official did the deciphering by dividing the five-digit cipher into four-digit number groups. Whether or not our observation is true can be verified only by the publication of the relevant Encryption Key Registries.

40. Orel and Yuca, *Talat Paşa'ya Atfedilen*, 66.
41. BOA.A.}d, Ministry Registries, 01520.001.
42. BOA.DH.ŞFR., 52/209, Cipher cable, dated 4 May 1915, from the Interior Ministry to the Prosecutor's Office of the Van Court of Appeals.
43. BOA.DH.ŞFR., 48/9, Cipher cable, dated 16 December 1914, from the Interior Ministry to the Provinces of Edirne, Erzurum, Adana, and Aydın, to the Acting Governors of Basra and Baghdad (Vekalet); to the [Provinces of] Beirut, Hijaz, Trebizond, Kastamonu, Mosul, and Van, to the Acting Governor of Yemen, and to the Provincial Districts of Canik, Kale-i Sultaniye (Dardanelles), and Antalya.
44. BOA.DH.ŞFR., 48/195, Cipher cable, dated 29 December 1915, from Interior Minister Talat to the Governor of Baghdad.
45. BOA.DH.ŞFR., 48/268 and 274, Cipher cables, dated 4 January 1915, from the Interior Ministry to the Provincial District of Bolu; and to the Provinces of Ankara and Diyarbekir.
46. BOA.DH.ŞFR., 51/182, Cipher cable, dated 31 March 1915, from the Interior Ministry to the Provinces of Konya and Adana, and to the Provincial District of Antalya.
47. BOA.DH.ŞFR., 51/227, Cipher cable, dated 7 April 1915, from Interior Minister Talat to the Provinces of Sivas, Van, Bitlis and Mamuretülaziz (Elazığ), and to the Provincial District of Kayseri.
48. BOA.DH.ŞFR., 52/24, Cipher cable, dated 17 April 1915, from the Interior Ministry to the Province of Aleppo, and to the Provincial Districts of Urfa and Marash.
49. BOA.DH.ŞFR., 52/140, Cipher cable, dated 28 April 1915, from the Interior Ministry to the Provincial District of Kütahya.
50. BOA.DH.ŞFR., 52/174, Cipher cable, dated 1 May 1915, from the Interior Ministry to the Provinces of Mamuretülaziz (Elazığ) and Hijaz, and to the Provincial District of Kayseri.
51. BOA.DH.ŞFR., 53/125, Cipher cable, dated 26 May 1915, from the Interior Ministry to the Provinces of Van and Bitlis.
52. BOA.DH.ŞFR., 53/210, Cipher cable, dated 2 June 1915, from the Interior Ministry to the Provinces of Diyarbekir, Baghdad, and Basra, and to the Provincial Districts of Siverek and Deyr-i Zor.
53. BOA.DH.ŞFR., 54/357, Cipher cable, dated 8 July 1915, from the Interior Ministry to the Provinces of Ankara and Kastamonu.
54. BOA.DH.ŞFR., 45/214, internal document of Interior Ministry [undated].
55. BOA.BEO, 4461-327029, 13 June 1915.
56. BOA.DH.ŞFR., 47/254, Cipher cable, dated 30 November 1914, from the Interior Ministry to the Province of Hüdavendigar (Bursa).
57. Orel and Yuca, *Talat Paşa'ya Atfedilen*, 76.

58. Orel and Yuca, *Talat Paşa'ya Atfedilen*, 75.
59. Ibid.
60. BOA.DH.ŞFR., 500/53, Cipher cable, dated 7 December 1915, from Civil Service Inspector (*Mülkiye Müfettişi*) Fuat to the Interior Ministry.
61. BOA.DH.ŞFR., 490/96, Cipher cable, dated 25 September 1915, from Director of Immigrant [Resettlement] (*Muhacirin Müdürü*) Şükrü to the Interior Ministry.
62. BOA.DH.ŞFR., 498/62, Cipher cable, dated 21 November 1915, from Director of Immigrant [Resettlement] (*Muhacirin Müdürü*) Şükrü to the Interior Ministry.
63. Just to expel any doubts on the matter, here are a few more: **2 and 3 September 1915** Eskishehir (DH.ŞFR., 486/139 ve 487/14); **26 September 1915** Bursa (490/16); **8 October 1915**, Aleppo (DH.ŞFR., 492/90) and Ankara (DH.ŞFR., 492/97); **2 December 1915** Ordu (DH.ŞFR., 499/87).
64. Şinasi Orel and Süreyya Yuca, *Talat Paşa'ya Atfedilen*, 75.
65. Ibid.
66. Ibid., 66.
67. BOA.DH.ŞFR., 513/73; 514/82 and 103; 515/79.
68. The coded documents in question are between BOA.DH.ŞFR., 513/98 and 514/001.
69. Ibid., 60.
70. For the full document translation and photographic plate, see Aram Andonian, *Medz Vojirě*, 169–170. Orel and Yuca, *Talat Paşa'ya Atfedilen*, 56, 156.
71. BOA.DH.EUM.MH., 136/43, Message, dated 27 August 1916.
72. BOA.DH.EUM.LVZ., 34/116, Message, dated 27 August 1916.
73. BOA.DH.EUM.LVZ., 40/45, Message, dated 6 November 1917.
74. BOA.DH.KMS., 510, Message, dated 29 October 1913, from the Office of the Grand Vizier to the Interior Ministry.
75. BOA.ŞD., 2825-15, Message, dated 29 October 1913, from the Office of the Grand Vizier to the President of the State Council.
76. BOA.DH.KMS., 5-10, Message, dated 24 November 1915, from the Interior Ministry to all administrative units/regions.
77. BOA.A.}d, Ministry Registries, 01520.001.
78. BOA.DH.KMS., 24-2-22.
79. BOA.DH.KMS., 24-2-44.
80. *Minhü* is often used in Ottoman documents meaning "of that [same] month," with the preceding number indicating the date. For the image of the document, see the Armenian version of Naim Efendi's memoir, Aram Andonyan, *Medz Vojiru*, 152; for the text, see: Naim Efendi, *Hatırat*, 06 [06].

81. Regarding Governor Mustafa Abdülhalik's appointment to the office, see BOA.İ.MMS, 200/27, From Interior Ministry to Sublime Porte, Ministry of the Interior, Directorate of Personnel and Service Registers, 3 October 1915; BOA.BEO., 4377-328273-01-01, from Grand Vezier's Chancery Office to the Interior Ministry, 4 October 1915. Regarding the beginning of his duties, see BOA.DH.ŞFR. 496/53, Cable from Director-General of Security İsmail Canpolat to the Interior Ministry, 7 November 1915.

82. Even though he had the photographic image of the document dated 25 October 1915, Andonian did not use it in his book.

83. Aram Andonyan, *Medz Vojiru*, 21.

84. BOA.DH.ŞFR., 62/18, Cipher cable from the Interior Ministry to the Province of Sivas, 1 April 1915.

85. BOA.DH.EUM.2. Şb., 14/58-1, Note from the Foreign Ministry to the Interior Ministry, 1 December 1915.

86. The Rumi was based on the Julian (hence, "Rumi," or "Roman") calendar, but began its dating from 622 CE, like the Muslim Hijri calendar. It was employed, alongside other calendars (Hijri, Mali) for various administrative purposes by the Ottoman government from the Tanzimat Period (1839) until the early years of the Turkish Republic

87. Orel and Yuca, *Talat Paşa'ya Atfedilen*, 12.

88. For Enver's document, see Aram Andonyan, *Medz Vojiru*, 232–233. Andonian incorretly read the year on the document by Enver as 1918. It should be 1915.

89. BOA.İ.MMS, 200/27, Note from Sublime Porte, Ministry of the Interior, Directorate of Personnel and Service Registers, dated: 3 October 1915.

90. If the date written on the 16 September document is accurate, why did Bekir Sami (who was in Aleppo at the time) not respond to it? And did Mustafa Abdülhalik write the date "5 *minhü*" (the fifth of this month) by accident? These questions remain open to speculation.

91. Two examples of the correspondence of the "Acting Governor" (*Vali Vekili*) are BOA.DH.ŞFR., 494/34 and 496/17, Cipher cables from Acting Provincial Governor of Aleppo Kadı Halit to the Interior Ministry, 19 October 1915 and 4 November 1915.

92. The six signatures on the list from Column II of the Interior Ministry's Cipher Office are, in descending order: BOA.DH.ŞFR., 77/042; 79/061; 79/216; 82/221; 84/113; (and especially) 91/221.

93. These two signatures follow the Governor's short note of places to which the information in the cable should be forwarded. See Genelkurmay Başkanlığı, *Arşiv Belgeleriyle Ermeni Faaliyetleri (1914–1918), Cilt VII*, 408 and 523.

94. For the photographic images of the documents that were quoted, see: Aram Andonyan, *Medz Vojirĕ*, 152, 184; 136 and 147–148 (The image for

the last quoted document was not used by Andonian, but a copy is in the author's possession)

95. BOA.DH.ŞFR., 91/221, Cipher cable from Mustafa Abdülhalik to the Provincial District Governor of Batum, 24 September 1918.

96. List of the handwritings and referrals in Volume 7; (1) p. 408 (English translation of the text p. 236); (2) p. 515 (English translation, p. 315) (3), pp. 516–518 (English translation, p. 316); (4) p. 523 (English translation, p. 321); in Volume 8: (5) p. 405 (no English translation of this document); (6) p. 412 (English translation: 268); (7) p. 413 (English translation: 269).

97. Genelkurmay Başkanlığı, *Arşiv Belgeleriyle Ermeni Faaliyetleri (1914–1918), Cilt VII (1914–1915)*, 236.

98. Orel and Yuca, *Talat Paşa'ya Atfedilen...*, Foreword, 12.

99. It is perhaps necessary here to dispel any misunderstanding. There are certainly some very valuable documents that explain the subjecting of the Armenian population to a process of systematic annihilation, and they are an important indicator of a systematic annihilation having taken place. What I am trying to say here is simply that there are a great number of documents similar to these in both style and content in the Ottoman archives.

Subjects and Events Mentioned by Naim Efendi Corroborated in Ottoman Documents

Within the Ottoman documents that Naim hand-copied, he often added information having to do with events mentioned therein that he personally witnessed. One particular characteristic of this information is that it could only have been known by someone who actually worked in the Deportation Office.

Let us here closely examine the information and details provided by Naim in light of the documents that we have discovered in the Ottoman archives. Our purpose here is to show that the things recounted by Naim are completely in line with actual events, of which there are various traces in the Ottoman archives. For this purpose, we have used the copy of his memoirs in our possession. In certain rare cases, we will also turn to the sections published by Andonian which we do not possess.

Certain Armenians Being Sought

In his memoirs, Naim writes that the government (primarily Interior Minister Talat) frequently sought information regarding certain Armenians and their families. These requests concerned persons of whom it had been requested that they return to the places to which they had long before been deported, or others who had received permission to remain in Aleppo. In one example he gives, "Even though a cipher cable arrived from the [Interior] Ministry ordering that the families of **Leon Amiralyan, Toros Tchaghlasyan**, and the **Dishchenkyan, Hazarabedyan**, and

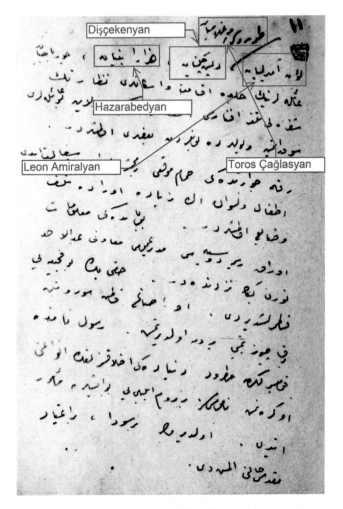

Image 1   Four Armenian names in Naim Efendi's memoir

Chorbajian were to remain and reside in Aleppo, the [governor of the] province deported these families, some of whose members perished on the route"[1] (see Image 1).

As can be understood from Naim's account, Talat had requested via an encrypted cable that the aforementioned persons and families be allowed to remain in Aleppo. The Governor of Aleppo had already deported them, presumably to Deyr-i Zor, and some had not survived the journey. He states that a cable arrived to this effect, and claims that, while he could not recall every detail of the communication, he has repeated the information to the best of his ability. We discovered a Talat Pasha cable in the archives that does indeed correspond to the one mentioned by Naim. The message, dated 14 March 1916, was sent to the Province of Aleppo and contains the interior minister's request that the aforementioned persons not be deported and that they be allowed to remain in Aleppo instead (see Image 2).

> The individuals and families by the names of Marashlı Hazarabedyan Melkon, Amiralyan Leon, Dishçekenyan Oseb, Nishan and Santuh Burunsuzyan, Kotsan, Honan and Varjabedyan who are residing in Aleppo, the individuals by the name of Ayıntablı Hana Kürekchiyan, and Kilisli Tcaglasyan Toros and their families who are also there, should be left in Aleppo [and the situation reported back to me].[2]

A clearer proof of the authenticity of Naim's memoirs one is not likely to find. It goes without saying that only an official actually working in the Office of Deportations could have known that such a telegram regarding the aforementioned persons had arrived and that it listed them by name. Another important point to recall here is that Andonian did not see this information as important, and thus left it out of his published edition.

THE CASE SOGOMON [SOGHOMON] KUYUMJIAN

In his memoirs, Naim mentions an incident involving a certain Sogomon [Soghomon] Kuyumjian Efendi, a relative of Matyos Nalbantian, the Parliamentary Deputy for Kozan. Sogomon Kuyumjian had been deported to the County of Maara (within the Province of Aleppo). Through his interventions with Talat Pasha, Nalbantian had persuaded the interior minister to allow him to come to Aleppo and settle there. According to Naim, Talat's order in this regard was sent to the Deportation Office in Aleppo. As a result, Sogomon came to Aleppo and presented his petition to relocate. But underneath this petition the governor wrote a note that "[the petitioner] must remain in Maara."

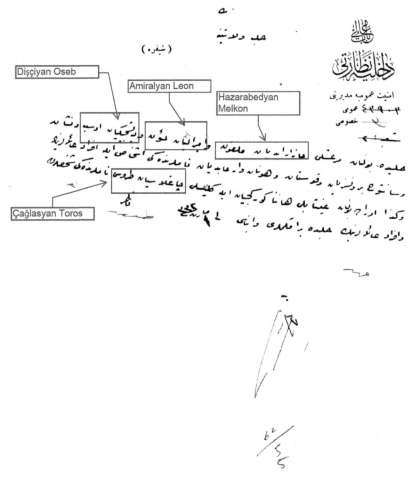

Image 2   Armenian names on Talat's telegram, 14 March 1916

However, "several days later, the order was given for [the camp at] Maara to be emptied out [of Armenians]." Sogomon "appealed again [to be allowed to settle in Aleppo]", but "although his settlement in Aleppo was the result of a[n] [interior] ministry order," Deportation Office Director Abdülahad Nuri Bey did not act on it, stating that "since

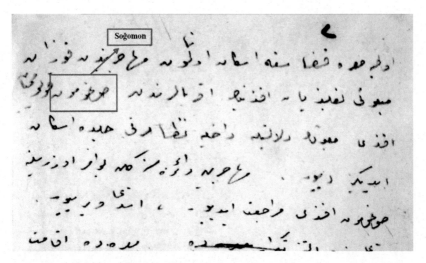

Image 3   Sogomon Kuyumjian in Naim Efendi's memoir

this person has fled from Maara and come here, he keeps pestering the [Immigrant and Refugee Resettlement] Office here and must be subject to the general deportations." The Governor, Mustafa Abdülhalik, accepted Nuri Bey's explanation, and Sogomon was duly deported[3] (see Image 3).

Again, Naim did not provide a single Ottoman document related to Sogomon Kuyumjian. Rather, he tells the story from memory. Nevertheless, we possess a sufficient amount of Ottoman documents from the archive to confirm that the things he wrote on Nalbantian and Kuymjian are accurate.[4] We learn from these documents that Kozan Deputy Nalbantian did not only intervene on behalf of Sogomon Kuyumjian, but also for a great many of his relatives. On 12 October 1915, for instance, a cable was sent to the Province of Aleppo requesting that "it be reported back concerning the return to Kozan of Kigork [Kevork] Nalbantian, the brother of Parliamentary Deputy Nalbantian Efendi."[5] Later on, in a petition submitted on 19 November 1915, Nalbantian listed 21 of his relatives by name and requested that they be allowed to return to their homes and the properties confiscated from their be returned to them"[6] (see Image 4).

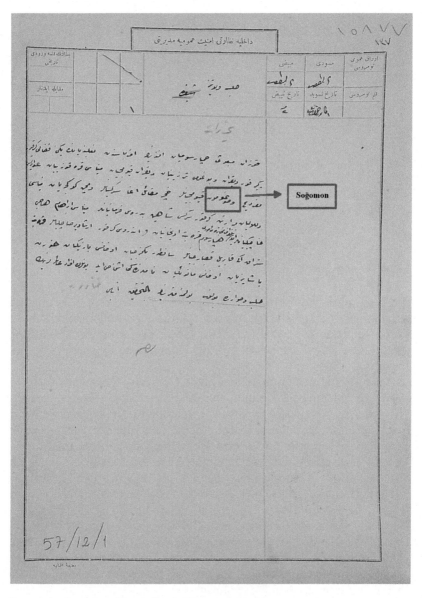

Image 4   Sogomon Kuyumjian in Ottoman documents

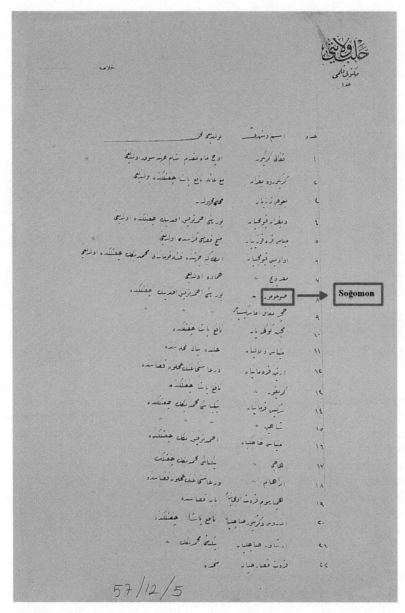

Image 4 (Continued)

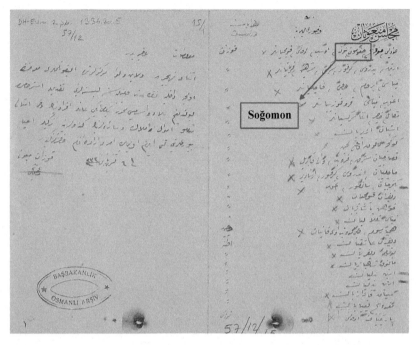

Image 4   (Continued)

On this subject, there is a great deal of correspondence that passed between the various offices of the interior ministry and the governor's office in Aleppo. On 5 December 1915, the interior minister wrote to Aleppo requesting information as to whether or not the persons in question had been deported, and, if they had, to where. On 4 January 1916, another interior ministry cable asked whether Sogomon Kuyumjian and a number of his relatives (who are named) were still in the environs of Aleppo. In the course of the correspondence, it is determined that Sogomon Kuyumjian was then residing outside of Aleppo, and it is claimed that "the ministry has not separately given an order" regarding his staying in Aleppo.[7]

It is once again clear that only an official working at the Deportation Office could have provided the information that Naim did, information that we have shown to be accurate by comparing them with Ottoman documents. We should add that Andonian did not see Sogomon

Kuyumjian's story sufficiently important, and thus it did not appear in the published version.

ARMENIAN PARLIAMENTARY DEPUTIES AND THEIR RELATIVES

The efforts made by the Kozan Deputy Nalbantian to intervene on behalf of his relatives was not exceptional; rather, it is but one of many such instances of which examples could be given. In the copy of the memoirs published by Andonian (but not in the part we have in our possession), Naim claims that all of the Armenian parliamentary deputies intervened on behalf of their relatives, hoping thereby to have them exempted from the deportations, or, if they had already been sent off to Aleppo, to allow them to remain there. However, these efforts did not often meet with success. According to the author, the individual principally responsible for the failure of their efforts was the Governor of the Province of Aleppo, Mustafa Abdülhalik. Naim recounts his attitude toward these interventions: "That man was an enemy of the Armenians, and attempted in the name of Turkishness to annihilate the Armenian nation. The orders he communicated to the General Directorate of Deportees were so severe that it is not explainable. Some Armenian members of the Ottoman parliament, probably through one thousand and one pleadings, obtained permission from the Interior Ministry for their families to stay in Aleppo. The Ministry sent instructions to him about them, but he hid those orders, and sent those families also to the desert. I know of 15–20 families whose residence in Aleppo was ordered, and whom he sent to the desert."[8]

There are dozens of documents in the Ottoman archives that confirm the accuracy of Naim's account. We understand from these that, just as Naim claimed, special orders and instructions went out—whether general or on behalf of certain parliamentary deputies—requesting that the deputies and their families not be deported to Aleppo. The documents also indicate that the question was not limited to Aleppo, which remained as part of a larger, more general problem. For instance, a message was sent on 15 August 1915 to all the provinces where deportations were taking place, including Aleppo, requesting that "Armenian parliamentary deputies and their families not be expelled."[9] Likewise, the archival evidence shows that, despite these clear orders to the contrary, neither the deputies nor their relatives were allowed to remain where they were, but were instead deported.

An example of this is the case Onnik Efendi, the Armenian parliamentary deputy for Izmir, and his relatives. At first, cables were sent to the cities in which the deputy's relatives lived, requesting permission that they not be deported, but instead be allowed to come to Istanbul.[10] Again, despite clear orders to this effect, in cases where some of his relatives had been deported, they were located either en route or in places like Adana (Tarsus),[11] Afyon,[12] Konya,[13] and Aydın,[14] and it was requested that they either be sent back home or be allowed to remain where they currently were.[15] Some of his relatives were sent as far as Aleppo—in spite of orders—and a cable was sent to Aleppo asking that those who were currently there be allowed to return to their homes.[16] However, just as in the cases that Naim recounts, Onnik's relatives, too, were ultimately deported to Deyr-i Zor. In this regard, it is instructive to view the response to two cables that were sent to Aleppo on 5 October and 14 November in regard to one of these, a certain Artakis Arusyan.[17] The Governor, Mustafa Abdülhalik, replied to the second of these as follows: "Before the cable arrived containing the order regarding Artaki Arusyan, the relative of Izmir Deputy Ihsan Onnik, he had been sent off to resettlement in [Deyr-i] Zor."[18]

Another example that can be given is that of the correspondence regarding the relatives of Parliamentary Deputy Hırlakyan of Marash.[19] These communications also support Naim's description of Governor Mustafa Abdülhalik. The first of these messages on the topic was sent by Talat directly to Aleppo on 15 August 1915. In it, the interior minister requests that "Deputy Hırlakyan Efendi and his family not be expelled [from Aleppo]."[20] Talat sent another message on October 24 requesting the same thing for Hırlakyan Efendi's brothers: "Leave... the brothers of Marash Deputy Hırlakyan Efendi...in Aleppo,"[21] and again, it appears that the order was not observed and his siblings were subjected to deportation. After having found signs that Hırlakyan's siblings were in Birejik, on 7 May 1916, he sent a cable to the Provincial District of Urfa requesting that Hırlakyan's brother "Avadis Hırlakyan, along with his children, his wife, his in-laws and other relatives be returned to Aleppo."[22]

Hırlakyan's brother and the latter's family did indeed reach Aleppo, but Mustafa Abdülhalik once again disregarded the order and had them deported. In a message to Abdülhalik's office, dated 18 May 1916, Talat reminded the governor of Aleppo that "[messages] had been written to the Provincial District of Urfa [ordering] the return to Aleppo of Avedis, who is the brother of Hırlakyan, the Deputy for Marash, and his family, who are currently in Birejik," and stated that he had received reports that the politician's relatives "had gone to Aleppo and had once more been deported from there." He then reiterated the earlier order that those of Hırlakyan's relatives "who were to be found there, should return to Marash and those who had been deported should be brought back."[23]

Similar telegrams continued to be sent for Hırlakyan's other requests for some of his relatives. On 14 March 1916, for instance, a cable was sent by Talat Pasha to the Province of Aleppo requesting that "Marash Deputy Hırlakyan Efendi's relatives who were sent from Antep to Aleppo" be returned to Marash.[24] Nevertheless, the relatives in question had been deported to Deyr-i Zor. That very day Interior Minister Talat learned of this state of affairs, and sent a cable to Deyr-i Zor ordering the persons in question to be returned to Aleppo immediately.[25] Fifteen days later (30 March 1916) he sent yet another message to Aleppo requesting that the deputy's relatives who were thought to have arrived there be returned to Marash.[26] Once again, Mustafa Abdülhalik disregarded this order and had these persons deported to Meskene. Still persisting, Talat sent the governor another cable on 29 May stating that he had learned that Hırlakyan's relatives were in Meskene and ordering them to be immediately sent back to Marash.[27]

From another cable, dated 14 June 1916, we learn that the governor had disregarded Talat's last order as well, instead sending off the deputy's relatives to Deyr-i Zor. In it, Talat tersely informs the Aleppo governor that "it is being claimed that the relatives of the Deputy for Marash Hırlakyan Efendi, who were sent off to Meskene, and the need for said persons to be returned to Marash having been repeatedly communicated [to you], have since been sent from Meskene to Deyr-i Zor." He then asks Abdülhalik the reason these persons had been sent there in spite of his personal order to the contrary, and demands that they be immediate returned to Marash: "...once the reasons for these persons' deportation to Deyr-i Zor—against orders [to the contrary] is communicated, [they are to be] returned to Marash."[28] Even so, the inquiries into the fate of Hırlakyan's relatives would continue throughout 1917.[29]

There are other archival documents showing that similar cables were sent out on behalf of the relatives of other Armenian deputies. As a final example, we might give that of the relatives of Artin Boshgezenyan Efendi, the Deputy for Aleppo. In this case, the earliest communication we were able to find is dated 25 September 1915. It is a direct communication from Interior Minister Talat Pasha to the Province of Aleppo and, by extension, to its governor, Mustafa Abdülhalik: "Since it has been learned that the Bedros Ashjian, the father-in-law of Aleppo Deputy Artin Gezenyan Efendi, as well as his brother Mesrob Gezenyan and his nephew Karajian Serkis Agha are currently in Aleppo, the aforementioned persons [should] be allowed to remain there."[30] Talat added the names of some other relatives to the list in his 4 October 1915 communication and again repeated a similar order that "the uncle of Aleppo Deputy Artin Gezenyan Efendi and his brothers be left in Aleppo."[31] Some of these persons were deported nevertheless.

In another cable to the Province of Syria, dated 15 November 1915, Talat states that Artin's brother-in-law and son-in-law were deported along with some other of his relatives, and that they were now "in the County of Selimiye, in the Provincial District of Hama." The interior minister then requests that these persons "be returned to Aleppo along with their families," and asks "to be informed of the results."[32] The order was repeated again in a 4 January 1916 cable to Aleppo: "The deportation of Terzi Dikran, who is the brother of Artin Boshgezenyan Efendi, along with his wife, who are currently residing in Antep, should be cancelled and they are to be settled there."[33]

Talat must not have received a response to this order, since he repeated it in another cable, dated 16 January 1916: "Terzi Dikran Boshgezen, who is the brother of Aleppo Deputy Artin Efendi, should be left in Antep and, if he [has already been] deported, he should be returned to Antep and settled there."[34] Mustafa Abdülhalik finally responded to these orders on 23 January 1916: "Terzi Dikran Boshgezenyan, the brother of Aleppo Deputy Artin Efendi, was not deported and was instead left in Antep."[35] However, we can understand from later documents that, just as Naim claimed, Mustafa Abdülhalik simply ignored the orders that arrived and continued to deport Artin's relatives. For instance, in a cable on 18 December 1916, Talat repeats his earlier order that "Antepli Terzi Dikran Boshgezenyan, the brother of Parliamentary Deputy Artin, along with his uncle Antepli Ohannes Boshgezenyan and his wife Agobjan and family should be left in Antep."[36] He sent another order on 19 February 1917 repeating his earlier one: "in accordance with the cable of 18 December 1916 regarding Parliamentary Deputy Artin Efendi's brother, Terzi Dikran, his uncle, Ohannes, and his wife, Agobjan, and their family, who are currently in Antep, the [order] is to be carried out [as requested]."[37] As the documents show, the governor ignored this order as well.

In reply, Talat sent a cable on 10 March 1917 reminding the governor of each one of the orders that had been previously sent, even giving the dates of the individual messages; after this he states that he had heard that deputy's relatives had been sent to Meskene, despite these repeated orders to the contrary: "It has been learned that Terzi Dikran Boshgezenyan, the brother of Parliamentary Deputy Artin Efendi, along with his uncle Ohannes Boshgezenyan and his wife Agobjan, have been deported from Antep, despite the need for them to remain there having been communicated by telegram on 18 December 1915 and the subject being raised again in a cable dated 19 February 1917, and that they are today situated in Meskene."[38] At this point, Talat was furious and asked what "the reason was for them to have been deported contrary to repeated messages [ordering the opposite]."[39]

What all of these events show us is the following truth: the information presented by Naim in his memoirs is accurate. Again, it is clear that only a person working in the Deportation Office could provide such information.

THE QUESTION OF DEPORTING ORPHANS FROM ALEPPO TO ISTANBUL

Naim mentions in his memoirs an incident concerning Armenian orphans who had been collected in Aleppo.[40] According to him, a group of Armenian children was assembled in Aleppo through the initiative of a "German lady," and it forced "the government to look after these orphans." Neither the governor of Aleppo, nor the director of the Deportation Office, were at all happy with this situation, and they demanded that these orphanages be closed. In the end, the Interior Minister, Talat Pasha, intervened, sending a message ordering the children to be sent to Sivas. However, there was no money for such an operation, and the convoy was never arranged. Ultimately, the children would be sent at a later time to Istanbul. Here are Naim's own words on the events in question:

> At that time there was a German woman, a humanitarian—I think her name was Hoch—who gathered herself and with the help of others one or two hundred innocent infants; she urged the government to care for these orphans. Such compassion angered the provincial governor, and infuriated the Deportation Office. But nobody said anything publicly.
>
> This merciful and compassionate woman showed these children the tender mercies that a mother would show; she wanted them to live.
>
> The government created a ruse in response to this. "These orphans will be brought together in Sivas," they said. "There, a large orphanage will be opened and they will be taken care of." The aim was actually to murder these poor things en route. I was the one who was ordered to send them off and to run the whole thing. The children would arrive in Ereğli by train, accompanied by a special official, and from there they would be sent by wagon to Sivas. I was to be stationed in Ereğli. At that time the allocated funds for the Office of Immigrant [and Refugee Settlement] had been exhausted. New funding was expected but it was delayed, so the whole operation came to naught. Seven or eight months later, these children were somehow sent to Istanbul.[41]

Naim remembered the woman's name correctly. The person in question was Madam Koch, one of the more prominent names among Aleppo's German community. In December 1915, she persuaded Fourth Army Commander Cemal Pasha to open an orphanage that would look after the Armenian children of Aleppo. Beatrice Rohner, a Swiss citizen, was brought in to head it.[42]

Naim also provided Andonian with two other cables on the subject from Talat Pasha. The first of these, dated 28 January 1917, reads:

> It has been learned that the children of [certain] known individuals (*eşhası malume*) have been accepted into the orphanages that have been opened in various places. Since the state cannot imagine anything but harm to come from [allowing] these [children] to live, anyone trying to work toward the provisioning, sustaining of or feeling sorry for [children] such as these, whether out of the inability to grasp the [gravity of the] situation, in the hope of putting their helplessness on display, or of downplaying [the seriousness of the situation], they are ultimately engaged

[in efforts] contrary to the clear wishes of the government. It is hereby communicated that no effort is to be expended either for the acceptance of small children like these into orphanages or for the establishment of other orphanages.[43]

The second telegram, dated 5 February 1917, reads:

While there are thousands of orphans and widows among the refugees and fallen Muslim soldiers in need of protection and support, there is no need to unneccesarily expend resources for some of the abandoned or bereft children of certain known persons who will in the future only create more damage and problems [for the state]. Such persons are to be removed by attaching them to the deportation convoys and those who have been provided for up to now are to be sent to Sivas in accordance with the most recent communication.[44]

We possess a great many documents in the Ottoman archives that would confirm the information provided by Naim. For example, a cable from the Governor of Aleppo, sent to Istanbul on 10 February 1916, complains about the order by Cemal Pasha to have the Armenian children brought into orphanages under the supervision of the Germans.

[Here t]here are as many as 530 children without parents or guardians. The Protestant Armenian children were already provided with a Protestant education, while the others were later entrusted to the German women in accordance with Cemal Pasha's approval. I told Cemal Pasha while in Damascus that I found it utterly unacceptable that there would be two separate institutions here serving as Armenian orphanages and that it was more appropriate for these children to be sent to Istanbul or other areas within Anatolia.[45]

If the Armenian children could not be sent elsewhere, the governor was in favor of the Armenian children being taken to Istanbul, despite the difficulties that he knew it would entail. He made his first suggestion to this effect on 7 December 1915.[46] When he received no reply to this attempt, he sent a second cable on 6 February 1916, stating that "nothing has been ordered in response to my request that the Armenian children who are found here be sent to Istanbul," and repeating his demand that the children in question be sent "to Istanbul or to one of the cities in Anatolia."[47]

Talat Pasha did not agree that the children should be sent off to Istanbul, and the central Anatolian city of Sivas was chosen as a place more appropriate for their "education and assimilation." He requested that the Governor of Aleppo contact Sivas and to have the children sent there at the soonest possible moment.[48] The situation was reported to Sivas on the same day:

> It is not appropriate for the Armenian orphans in Aleppo to remain there, nor that they be sent here (i.e., to Istanbul). The most appropriate site for their education and assimilation is Sivas. Communicate with Aleppo [that] these [children should] be sent there and placed in the various orphanages.[49]

Nevertheless, the monies necessary to transport the children to Sivas never arrived, so that Governor Mustafa Abdülhalik sent a message on 2 April 1916 asking what had happened:

> Although it was established by Your Esteemed Office that these orphans would be transported to Sivas, they have not been sent because the money has yet to arrive from the allocations for refugees and immigrants.[50]

The governor continued in his insistance throughout May that the orphanages be closed, repeating his opinion that he found "the forming of an institution in Aleppo under the administration of the Germans in no way or shape appropriate."[51] In Abdülhalik's view, Beatrice Rohner was prepared to go to the place where the government advised and to establish her orphanage there.[52]

Even when the months came in which allocations were handed out, no monies were forthcoming, and on 13 August 1916, Talat finally inquired as to the amount of money needed for deporting the orphans.[53] At this time, the Province of Sivas demanded the necessary funds to cover the expenses of the children to be sent there.[54]

We can understand from the Aleppo Governor's cable of 1 December 1916 that at that point the Armenian children had still not been sent off; in it, Abdülhalik states that he is still awaiting an order as to where the deportees are to be sent and claims that the number of children (and thus potential deportees) has increased in the meantime:

Although it was thought appropriate that the orphans in the orphanages of Aleppo—a group who now exceed 1,500 in number, they have not been sent off in consideration of the military situation. Since it does not appear devoid of difficulties for these children here and the ones under the administration of the Armenians, please make your wishes known as to where they are to be deported.[55]

The governor made a second, similar attempt on 26 December 1916, informing the interior ministry that some 2500 Armenian orphans had been collected in various orphanages and warning that this number was increasing daily. "If it is necessary for them to be deported to somewhere," he said, anorder should be issued at the soonest possible moment stating the destination.[56] During those months, Talat was indeed engaged in finding a place for these children. On 11 December 1916, he wrote a secret message to the Ministry of Education, asking whether or not a place had been found to resettle the orphaned Armenian children in Aleppo, since it was unacceptable for them to be left there.[57] In its reply a fortnight later, the ministry stated that the children could be distributed to different areas like Bardizak [Bahçecik], Adapazarı and Izmit, and then any remainder could be brought to Istanbul.[58]

Talat reported on 4 January 1917 that it would not be suitable to have the Aleppo orphans brought to Istanbul, and that children from the surrounding provinces must be brought to Istanbul in their place, claiming that it would be more appropriate for the Armenian orphans to be taken to places that will be opened up [i.e., by those children currently in the orphanages being sent to Istanbul].[59] In the end, the children were sent out to various provinces.

Meanwhile, as the result of the Abdülhalik's constant insistance, the orphanage under Madam Rohner's tutelage was closed down in March 1917. Thus, it should not be seen as coincidental that the Talat Pasha cables provided by Naim were from the beginning of 1917, the very same period that the orphanage would be closed. According to German documents, the Armenian orphans were mostly sent to Konya, Izmit, Balıkesir and Adapazarı,[60] and, just as Naim reported, some of them were indeed sent to Istanbul. On 17 July 1917, Cemal Pasha wrote a message to the Logistical Support Headquarters in Aleppo, informing him that close to 1000 orphans would be sent to Istanbul.[61]

It is possible to find in Beatrice Rohner's memoirs a confirmation of Naim's account. In her recollections, Rohner wrote that she met with Cemal Pasha in December 1915 and that she received from him permission to open a dormitory to look after Armenian children. Cemal's only condition was that Rohner limit her work to Aleppo proper and that she not travel outside of the city. Rohner also confirmed Naim's description of the Governor of Aleppo, Mustafa Abdülhalik, and his hostile attitude toward the orphanage: "The governor harbored no sympathy toward us, but he was obliged give us permission to meet our most urgent needs."[62]

Rohner, who, as mentioned above, had to close down her orphanage at the beginning of March 1917, appealed on 8 October 1917 to the Ottoman Interior Ministry (via the German embassy) for permission to leave the country. The ministry, however, had some concerns about Rohner leaving the country. On the same day, Talat wrote to the governors of Aleppo (where Rohner was) and Marash asking their opinions on the matter. The then-governor of Aleppo, Bedri, gave an interesting response on 17 October, one that we can see again confirms Naim's account:

> Rohner, who is also remembered as Beatrice Roza, established many contacts with the Armenians during the time she was here and became known herself as a 'friend of the Armenians.' This person was occupied for a period with the distribution of funds that arrived, by means of the American Consul in Aleppo, from Europe and America [and were meant to be] distributed for Armenian needs. Afterward, when these funds were cut off, she went to Marash and gathered a great deal of information about the events concerning the Armenians. Her traveling to Europe was thus seen as disadvantageous and inadvisable.[63]

In the end, Enver Pasha was forced to step in; he requested that a positive answer be given to the entreaties made by the German Embassy on Rohner's behalf to allow her to travel to the continent, due to the potential negative reaction that might come from Germany and Switzerland if it was not given. Thus, Rohner would end up traveling to Germany by special permission of Enver Pasha on 3 December 1917:

> On the basis of her service as a nurse that she has successfully undertaken as head of the assistance organization in Marash, and in consideration of the

satisfaction that it will produce in [certain] German and Swiss circles, it is seen as politically advantageous to allow the aforementioned person to travel from Istanbul to Germany and to [thereby] curry favor with the German Embassy in Istanbul.[64]

THE KILLING OF ARMENIAN CHILDREN AROUND MESKENE AND RAKKA

Naim provides a cable sent by Talat on 25 December 1915. In it, Talat requests that the children be collected who are of a young enough age that they would not remember the abuses and injustices suffered by their parents, and that the others be included in the deportation convoys and sent off.[65] In addition to the message itself, Naim provides an brief explanation of the cable and the circumstances surrounding it:

> I don't think it is necessary to give a lengthy explanation in this regard; the content of the telegram itself is very clear. Children who couldn't remember the disasters to befall their parents [would be] of two, three, and four years. Which is to say, that all children above four years of age were being sentenced to death. And that was indeed their fate. What happened to the orphans who were put in the orphanage opened up in Meskene? They all died; they were killed."[66]

For the killing of the Armenian orphans in Meskene, Naim holds the Assistant Director of Deportations in Aleppo, Hakkı Bey, responsible. Nor did he limit Hakkı Bey's accountability to these crimes alone; he also deemed him responsible for the fate those Armenian children who perished on the deportation route, whether from Meskene to Rakka, or from Rakka to Deyr-i Zor. As author of the memoirs puts it:

> Hamam, which is in the environs of Rakka, was an inferno of death and debasement. The women and children suffered the greatest from deprivation and loss. The dossier of official papers containing what was known about this situation was in the hands of the Assistant Director-General, Abdülehad Nuri Bey. Hakkı Bey compounded this disaster. He ordered the mass killing of several hundred of the orphans who had survived the deportations. He appointed a dishonorable man from Rumelia by the name of "Resul" and put him in charge of these affairs. This person had accumulated all of the immoral behaviors in the world and had been dismissed from the

police. He developed a love for killing, and it became for him a sacred practice.[67]

Andonian does not include these descriptions by Naim in the published memoirs. Rather, he offers another cable—one that does not appear in the version of the memoirs in our possession, and summarizes the matter in his own words: The telegraphic cable [reads] as follows:

> The cipher telegram from the Interior Ministry to the Province of Aleppo: Without giving rise to suspicion, on the pretext that they will be given nour-ishment by the deportation offices, in an assembled state, destroy the chil-dren of the known individuals (Armenians) gathered by military bases and nourished by command of the Ministry of War, and inform. 7 March [1]916 Interior Minister Talat.

Andonian then adds the following information:

> Shortly thereafter, Hakkı [had] killed the remnants of the last deportation convoy on the route from Meskene to Deyr-i Zor and then assembled all of the orphans and deported them to Deyr-i Zor. There the bloodletting stopped, because there was no one left to be killed. The number of orphans who had been gathered up was more than 300, but of these, approximately 100 persons failed to reach Deyr-i Zor.[68]

There are three significant points worth mentioning here. The first is the opening of an orphanage in Meskene, the second, the fact that Hakkı was the person appointed to Meskene, and that he closed this institution and sent off its inhabitants, along with others, to their deaths. The third is the appointment of the aforementioned Rumelian, Resul, to the task of deportation and killing. All of these facts are confirmed by various Ottoman archival documents and by the memoirs of various Armenians who sur-vived the deportations.

As we previously mentioned about the investigation in summer 1916, Talat was not aware that an orphanage had been opened in Meskene. In a cable to Aleppo dated 4 August 1916, Talat inquired by whose order the orphanage was allowed to open and what office or agency is meeting its expenses.[69] This cable was sent in the middle of July, after the deportations from Meskene had ceased and the provincial governor of Aleppo had complained about the orphanage having been opened up for Armenian children. It was expected of Hakkı, who arrived in Meskene after this date, that he would get the deportations going again and that, after closing the orphanage, he would include the now homeless orphans on the future convoys to Deyr-i Zor.

There is also ample information from these and other documents to show one of Hakkı's functionaries contending with the orphanage and its operators, eventually emptying it out entirely and closing it down. Some of the most important information that we have on this matter comes from the camp commander, Lt. Colonel Galip, who was stationed in Meskene as the Commander of the Office of Logistical Support, and who was the person responsible for opening up the orphanage there in the first place. In the descriptions (provided earlier) in connection to the Ottoman government's investigations on corruption and improprieties, he stated that the order to establish an orphanage was delivered to him in writing by the commander's office on 16 May 1916. The officer set up the orphanage at the beginning of June in compliance with the order and turned its operation over to the civilian administration on 18 August 1916. The person to whom he delivered the keys was Hakkı, the Assistant Director of Deportations.[70] On 1 March 1917, the interior minister sent a cable to the Aleppo Governor's office asking the "location to which the orphan convoy will be sent by Hakkı Bey."[71]

There is much evidence in the memoirs of Armenian survivors who experienced this regarding the deeds of Hakkı.

> When Hakkı Bey assembled the children [living] south of the transit camp of Meskene one last time and sent them off to [Deyr-i] Zor, more than 800 children, the majority of them sickly or disabled, died of exhaustion under these conditions... Eight hundred orphans were sent...in 17 wagons. The were burned alive at the very same moment with the orphans in Deyr-i Zor (the one who sent them off [to perish] was Hakkı Bey).[72]

Some memoirs and recollections of the period also confirm the fact that Hakkı was the one who entrusted the task of having the orphans killed to "a dishonorable man from Rumelia by the name of Resul." Krikor Ankut, for instance, says that Resul was appointed by Hakkı Bey to be his assistant and adds that:

In order to eliminate the last remaining Armenian deportees...between Aleppo and Deyr-i Zor who had managed to survive...Hakkı Bey, along with his assistant, "Rumelian" Resul, evicted all of the deportees along the Euphrates [River] route, starting from Aleppo [and working his way down]. These he sent straight to [Deyr-i] Zor and even further south... Close to 300 young men and boys...surviving in the camp Hamam were sent to the South in a special convoy. Solid reports about them arrived that they had been killed in Rakka, to the South of Sebka. Elsewhere, we learned in no uncertain terms that in the area around Şamiye, 300 children were thrown into a cave opening, gas was poured in and they were burned alive....[73]

In short, Hakkı (to quote Andonian) was "[Doing] those things that Naim Bey and [Meskene Camp Director] Hüseyin Efendi were unable to do; they brought the deportees found along the entire length of the Euphrates down to the slaughterhouse of Deyr-i Zor."[74] On 14 February 1917, the District Governor of Deyr-i Zor reported that "those Armenians who had fled [the deportations or camps] were deported to [Deyr-i] Zor under the supervision of the Assistant Director of Deportations Hakkı Bey."[75]

Hakkı must have carried out his duties with complete success, for Talat sent a message to the Province of Aleppo on 22 February 1917 asking "whether or not Hakkı Bey, the Assistant Director of Deportations, has any physical needs [necessary] for continuing the duties with which he has been entrusted."[76] The reply was given on February 25 by Governor Mustafa Abdülhalik, saying that "there was no need for Hakkı Bey to continue in his duties" and that he had departed "to Istanbul with a convoy of orphans."[77] Perhaps it would serve to add a final note that Hakkı, who had been sent to the region in order not only to restart the deportations and massacres but also to open an investigation of the corruption and improprieties occurring there, had taken ample bribes and "bakhsheesh" from the deportees while there.[78]

THE DEPORTATION OF THE ARMENIAN RAILROAD WORKERS

Naim provided three cables from Talat Pasha concerning the deportation of Armenians working on the Baghdad Railroad line, and also provides a bit supplementary, clarifying information. The first of these is numbered 801 and dated 8 January 1916:

It has been decided that the Armenians employed in all institutions, railroad operation and construction are also to be deported to the areas of resettlement and the instructions on how to carry this out have been sent from the Ministry of War to the army commanders. [Please] report [back] on the results.

To which Naim added:

The majority of employees working both in the [rail] construction and operation companies are Armenians. The government gave an order out of fear that they might somehow commit treason. In response [to this order], the rail commissioner [office of logistic support] was asked for a list of [Armenian employees'] names.[79]

This cable was followed by two others: number 840 (dated 29 January 1916) and number 845, which was sent as a follow-up/addition to 840. The first of these reads:

It was understood that there were some forty to fifty thousand Armenians—the majority of them widowed women and parent-less children—living along the rail lines, from the camps at Intilli and Ayıran all the way to Aleppo. Since the most severe punishment will be incurred by those who have caused such a concentration of poverty and destitution on the army's most important lines of communication and transportation, it is expected that, after informing [and communicating with] the Provincial Governor of Adana, [these destitute Armenians] be quickly deported to the areas of resettlement without passing through Aleppo. The results [of this operation] are to be reported back within one week.[80]

The third of the aforementioned cables, number 845, which was sent as an addendum to the previous one, reads as follows:

Although it was seen as impossible to deport the Armenians left in the camps at Intilli and Ayıran and employed in construction until the work was concluded, it is nevertheless inappropriate to allow their families to remain there; they [families] are instead to be temporarily resettled in the townships and villages surrounding Aleppo and the remaining women and children who have no guardians or family are to be deported per the previous instructions.[81]

According to Naim, the sending of cable number 845 was precipitated by the complaints of the railroad company engineers, who argued that "the removal of Armenian workers meant the halting of construction."[82] But in response to this order, the families of the Armenians working on the rail lines "were brought to Aleppo in convoy after convoy." These people "were [originally] to be resettled in the villages. Their names were recorded, registries were created, and the poor wretches were given cause to hope. But the hope was a vain one... the police expel them from the area; they submit official requests and petitions [to remain], and the[officials act as if] the petitions are being taken seriously... But there is never any need to process the petitions, because within a few days those submitting them find themselves in the jaws of horror and barbarities in Meskene. These poor, bereft women and girls fall victim to the lustful desires of the local population or the gendarmes.."[83]

What can be understood from Naim's account is that the deportation of all Armenians working at the railroad stations or in construction had been planned, but that, due to the warning by the rail company that work would simply grind to a halt without them, some of the workers were allowed to remain, and their families were allowed to be resettled in the area around Aleppo. However, this respite did not last long, and the Commissariate of Military [Rail] Lines first recorded the names of those Armenians working on the rail lines and in construction and deported both them and their families (who had meanwhile been settled near Aleppo), to Deyr-i Zor.

The documents available in the Ottoman archives show that all of the information provided here by Naim is correct. The first thing that should be clarified is that the two bits of information contained in Talat's cable (number 801) are also to be found in the Ottoman documents. The first of these was that there were some 40,000–50,000 widowed women and orphaned children then living along the length of railroad track stretching from Intilli-Ayıran to Aleppo. These figures are also mentioned in two cables dated 6 and 9 November 1915 that were sent by the Provincial Governor of Adana, Hakkı, and the District Governor of Osmaniye, Fethi, respectively.[84] The second item is that, as we shall see, the deportation of Armenians working on the rail lines was carried out at the request of the Ministry of War.

The process of deporting the Armenian railroad workers was a sticky problem, one that followed an uneven course full of ups and downs. At the beginning of the deportation process, the decision was given *not* to deport all such workers,[85] despite the cables by various local officials, warning that the number of Armenians working in railroad construction and operation was too great, that this fact posed a potential threat to security, and that their numbers must absolutely be reduced.[86] Later on, however, a commission was set up to decide exactly which persons needed to be deported and on what grounds.[87] Şükrü Bey, the Director of Deportations in Aleppo, sent a cable from there on 25 September 1915 demanding that "a list of the Armenians, the craftsmen and laborers among the Armenians who are employed in the operation and construction sections of the railroad... be immediately composed... so that those [deemed] necessary to remain and those to be deported could be divided up by the station commanders to the military and civilian rail commissioners," and so that "the hordes of laborers who were still retained by the station directors and construction engineers on some or other pretext, be immediately deported".[88]

The War Ministry was of the opinion that the deportation of those laborers who worked on the rail lines and of their families should be delayed until the aforementioned commission reached a final decision,[89] which in the end turned out to be mid-October. The commission ruled that, generally speaking, all Armenians would be deported, and their places would be taken by Muslim workers, but since there were certain tasks that demanded crucial technical information and skills, the removal and deportation of Armenian workers from these jobs would have to be done gradually and in stages. Thus, the rail company was requested to prepare registries of such workers and tasks, for which purpose the provincial and district governors would be expected to collaborate with the company's representatives.[90]

Cemal Pasha weighed in with the opinion that delaying the deportation of the workers posed a risk to security and urged those responsible for the operations to make haste.[91] War Minister Enver Pasha was of the same mind, and sent a cable to the third Triumvir, Talat, informing him that the places of the Armenian workers were going to be filled by Muslim labor battalions.[92] On 27 October 1915, the Rail Department of the General Headquarters wrote to the Military Commissioner of the Baghdad Railroad requesting that they prepare a list showing the number of Armenian officials and laborers employed in the company operating the Baghdad Railroad. The list in question was finished by December 8th of that year.[93]

One of the most important decisions in this matter was actually taken in Aleppo on 11 November 1915. At a gathering that included Cemal Pasha, Aleppo Governor Mustafa Abdülhalik, Director of Immigrant and Refugee Resettlement, Şükrü Bey, and the Director-General of Security, Ismail Canpolat, who came from Istanbul for this purpose, the decision was taken both that Aleppo would be cleared out of non-local Armenians and that they would follow the army's lead (and orders) in regard to those working on the rail lines.[94]

As of the beginning of December 1915, Cemal Pasha began to deport Armenian workers from the area around Intilli, where they were found in great number,[95] but this provoked a response from the German company operating the line, which claimed that such deportations of Armenian workers would bring rail construction and travel on that line to a halt, a claim that was sufficiently compelling to persuade Cemal Pasha to temporarily halt the operation.[96] But all credit cannot be given to the force of their argument, for the German authorities were also recruited to bring great pressure to bear on the army commander. As a result of this immense pressure, not only were the deportations temporarily abandoned, but some of those Armenians who had already been deported were actually brought back and returned to their positions. On 23 January 1916, Aleppo Governor Mustafa Abdülhalik complained that this situation directly affected the deportation and requested that the War Ministry inform the Germany company in clear and specific language regarding the deportations that it was going to undertake.[97]

Nor was the problem faced by the government in this regard limited the pressures exerted by individual German authorities.[98] Through bribery, a great many Armenians also succeeded in remaining in rail line construction or in operating the stations by falsely presenting themselves as workers.[99] The interior ministry issued an order to the relevant provinces on 16 January 1916, demanding that they prepare a list of this type of missing person who had been thereby exempted from the deportations.[100] Additionally, it was requested that lists be produced containing the names of persons who had again been employed by the request of the railroad company.[101]

As Naim mentioned, the institution responsible for preparing these lists was the Military's Office of Logistical Support. The Aleppo office, for instance, gave the figure of 3134 persons working on rail construction in Aleppo, although only 430 of these were subsequently given permission to work. The interior ministry requested that persons identified on these lists as superfluous be deported.[102] On 17 April 1916, the interior ministry sent another message inquiring as to whether or not the rail line commissioners had yet completed their aforementioned lists.[103] Two days later the reply came from Mustafa Abdülhalik, who informed Talat that only two registries had been prepared of "Armenian employees and craftsmen" in the Intilli region, but "registries of all officials, laborers, and such" were not yet ready.[104]

Meanwhile, the number of Armenians who were gathered around the various rail stations and construction sites was great and growing. Thus, in a 15 February 1916 message to Cemal, Talat informed the Governor of Syria and Fourth Army Commander that "although permission had been given [by Cemal] to the [railroad] company to keep some three hundred craftsmen..." that they might be employed in rail construction in the rail line sites of Ayran, Intilli and Islahiye, "the amount of Armenian laborers [in these areas] was at about 7,000 in number" and asked him whether or not he had also given permission fort his many persons to remain behind.[105] Hakkı, the Provincial Governor of Adana, actually claimed the number to be closer to 10,000 in a cable dated 22 February 1916.[106] Cemal was greatly distressed to learn this about the situation and cabled the interior minister in reply, saying that he "had not been made aware that any Armenians beyond those [whom he had] permitted had been taken into employment in rail construction" and, having now been made aware of these facts, had ordered an immediate investigation be carried out. He also assured Talat that all of those additional Armenians who had been employed would be deported "to decided-upon locations."[107]

Talat immediately shared the Syrian Governor's reply with Adana and Aleppo:

> Fourth Army Commander Cemal Pasha has informed [us] in reply that the number of Armenian laborers who are employed in railroad construction in the areas of Ayran, Antelli and Islahiye and whose numbers have greatly exceeded those permitted, shall all go to certain designated areas.[108]

And yet, the difficulties in deporting Armenian railroad workers, due as it was both to German pressure and the bribery of Ottoman officials, would continue until March 1916, when Cevdet Bey, the Governor of the

Province of Van, was appointed Governor of Adana.[109] Immediately upon assuming his task, the new governor would begin deporting these workers. He sent a report to Istanbul on 18 June, claiming that he had simply ignored the clamor of the German [railroad] company, and had begun deporting the Armenian workers in the environs of Amanos, along with their families. In his words, "after the Armenians who were living along [the area of construction of] the Toros section [of the rail line] and being protected [by the firm] were deported," all of the Armenians in Adana and its environs "would be sent off in a manner that would make it impossible for them to return."[110]

In fact, all of the Armenian workers were not deported—they couldn't be, since many of them possessed skills that made them indispensible, and, as the German company operating the railroad had warned, their departure would bring the operation of the line to a screeching halt. With this situation in mind, "the families of those employed as 'staff'on the railroad [in Aleppo, for instance] would be left in Aleppo," and "the families of those employed as laborers would be treated as the families of military personnel."[111] Thus, the situation and status of the Armenian rail employees would continue to vex the authorities throughout 1917. As Naim stated in his memoirs, "Even though all of the railroad employees were Armenian, and despite the fact that the Armenians were subjected to this much oppression and cruelty, during the entire four or five year general mobilization, these persons never did anything but work in a completely faithful manner; not a single incident was reported on or near the rail lines."[112]

RAIL LINE COMMISSIONER HAYRI BEY

At one point in his memoirs, Naim mentions a government functionary by the name of Hayri Bey, who worked in the Aleppo Railroad Commissariat (*Hat Komiserliği*). His name appears in connection with the deportation of the railway workers:

> The majority of employees working both in the [rail] construction and operation companies are Armenians. The government gave an order out of fear that they might somehow commit treason. In response [to this order], the rail commissioner was asked for a list of [Armenian employees'] names. In this matter, both Hayri Bey, the Commisioner of Rail Lines, and Cemal Pasha showed great humanity.[113]

As to who this Hayri Bey is, we cannot say with great confidence, although there are several important documents in the Ottoman archives mentioning him. From these documents, we learn that Hayri, with the aid of his family, helped to smuggle a large number of Armenian women and girls to Istanbul, thereby saving their lives. So much so that he was investigated for assisting Armenians, although the event that spurred the inquiry was not getting caught in the act, but that Hayri's sister-in-law, furious that his brother Emiri was divorcing her, went to the police and informed them of the family's activities.[114]

From the correspondence, we understand that in March 1916 Hayri Bey had first assisted two Armenian women to escape to Istanbul with the help of his family (his mother, his wife, his brother Emiri's wife and other relatives), and 40 days later he himself took three other Armenian women and brought them to Istanbul. Once in Istanbul, the Armenian girls either went to their relatives there, or were placed in various house by Hayri. Since Hayri was the responsible official in the Aleppo Rail Line Commissariat, Talat intervened directly in the investigations and served as the conduit for correspondence between Enver and others. In his communications to both the Istanbul Police Directorate and the Provincial Governor of Aleppo, Talat claimed that some of the girls whom Hayri and his family had helped to flee to Istanbul were members of the committee.

While there is no testimony by Hayri among the existing documents, we can nevertheless understand from the extracts from his questioning that he claimed never to have smuggled people; rather, he had brought the girls to Istanbul after receiving permission to do so from the Provincial Governor of Aleppo, Mustafa Abdülhalik. The latter, however, replied by telegram to Talat, stating that he had never given Hayri permission for anything. According to the governor, Hayri had dressed these Armenian women who accompanied him to Istanbul in Islamic clothing, and had claimed "when the women's papers were demanded to be checked, that they were his spouse and her relatives and fellow village inhabitants." Since it was possible for Muslims to stroll around freely, these persons were therefore able to board the train without undergoing any sort of inspection whatsoever.[115]

From one of Talat's messages to Enver, it is possible to see just how important he viewed this subject. According to the interior minister, Hayri was the person responsible for the security of the trains. While those who did not have permission to travel were not allowed to do so, Hayri had dressed the Armenian women with a head covering and so allowed them to travel to Istanbul without documents. For this behavior, he was seen as having "abused his position and authority" and needed to be punished, "in order to become a cautionary tale for others."[116]

Some of these women were subsequently caught in Istanbul, but at least one of them was released by the police when Hayri paid her bail. This state of affairs angered Talat greatly. In response, he gave the Police Directorate a clear directive that he wanted all girls who were caught attempting to escape to be subjected to the same treatment as others attempting to evade or flee the deportation convoys and that they he would immediately order them deported.

Although the interior minister's great irritation and deep involvement in the matter seems, at first glance, to be exaggerated, even incomprehensible, the archival documents show us that his underlying fear in all this was of the possibility that the Armenians who came from Syria would, upon reaching in Istanbul, tell others the things that they had seen and experienced. For Talat, every Armenian traveling from Syria to Istanbul was a potential witness to the massacres and other atrocities taking place there. The very presence of such persons threatened to bring to naught all of his efforts to keep the massacres and atrocities hidden. He explained his concerns to Enver in the following lines:

> It is thus of the utmost importance they do *not* travel on the streets of Istanbul, since they are fully aware of what is transpiring in that region and could therefore bear witness to the events occurring [in Syria]. Moreover, because they are women who have been assembled in Aleppo in order to be sent off to the areas of resettlement, they could easily and without any notice come into contact with Armenian revolutionaries, from whom all manner of evil and misfortune could be expected and [c]ould thereby relate all manner of information produced [by revolutionaries] and carry this information the Istanbul Armenians.[117]

For Talat, it was necessary to prevent such an occurrence.

The documents and the information concerning Hayri Bey must be seen as yet another confirmation of the accuracy of Naim's account.

THE AMERICAN CONSULATES AND THE PHOTOGRAPHS
TAKEN ON THE DEPORTATION ROUTES

One of the significant items in Naim's memoirs is the information and documentation sent by foreign observers, above all American and German consular functionaries and missionaries, from the areas through and in which the Armenians deportations took place. As the "senior partner" of the Central Power alliance, and due to the Ottomans' relative military weakness, Germany sent numerous military and civilian personnel to the Ottoman Empire during the First World War, and many were present within the various regions of the empire in which the deportations took place. Even before their entry into the war, however, there were a number neutral American consuls and missionaries laboring in these areas. These persons sent back regular reports to their embassy in Istanbul, recounting recent events and things that they had witnessed. In some cases they even succeeded in sending photographs that they had taken of bodies piled up on the roads. At times these reports also reached the western press, generating stories of how the Armenians were being annihilated on Ottoman soil. In response to the photos, reports and bulletins that were received, both the German and American governments sent diplomatic notes to the Porte via their embassies in Istanbul. The Ottoman regime was greatly upset by this state of affairs, and attempted by various means and initiatives to prevent such reports from reaching Istanbul.[118]

Naim produced two cables of Talat that concern the efforts to limit the activities of the consulates and foreign functionaries in the area, as well as offering his own observations on the matter. The first of these cables is dated 1 December 1915. In it, Talat complains about the American consulates in the provinces collecting information from a great number of different channels and sending it on to their embassy in the capital. After stating that the note of displeasure submitted by the American Embassy had been based on this information, Talat demands that, during the times when the Armenians in areas close to cities, villages or other population centers are deported, special care be shown that there are no events or incidents that would draw attention to the deportations. Thus, those giving such reports to the consulates must be arrested and delivered over to the Courts-Martial.[119]

In the second of Talat's telegrams provided by Naim (dated 24 December 1915), the interior minister gives the following orders:

Since it is being reported that a number of Armenian reporters have been traveling in those parts, photographing and collecting documentation of a number of calamities [occurring there] and then handing them over to the American consul there, harmful persons such as these are to be arrested and liquidated.[120]

Naim added his own commentary in regard to this communication:

Civil servants were nevertheless employed for tasks such as this. There was even a permanent employee around the American Consulate whose job it was to conduct such surveillance. It was reported that one of the writers for the daily Jamanag, or possibly some other paper, was seen there one day. The importance of investigating th[ese incidents] cannot be overemphasized. In the end, they were not apprehended.[121]

American official documents confirm Naim's information. To give just one example, an American report described the government's general policy in Aleppo as follows: "Any attempts to help the refugees are immediately nipped in the bud by the Authorities and spies are continually watching the American consulate."[122]

In the Ottoman archives, there are dozens of documents about denying foreign diplomatic personnel and missionaries the opportunity to come across deported Armenians on their travel routes, forbidding them from taking photographs on the roads, and opening investigations of persons supplying the foreign consulates with photographs or documents dealing with the deportations. On the basis of these documents, it is possible to show that the descriptions in the Talat Pasha cables and the information in Naim's supplementary explanations is accurate.[123]

In some of the messages written to the provinces, the interior ministry—usually in the person of Talat—requested that "Armenian [deportation] convoys not be found" in places where foreigners are traveling or on roads where they are traveling. Among the orders issued are ones preventing the foreign consulates from coming into direct contact with Armenians, the denying of permission for assistance to be directly given to the Armenians, and the hindering of persons attempting to do so.[124]

The provinces were also issued the warning that any Ottoman official either ignoring or neglecting their duties in these matters would face severe punishment: "In response to the communication from the Office of the High Command [in Istanbul], it is being communicated to all provinces that it will be necessary for those officials who allow the secret and direct provision of funds to the Armenians by American or German institutions and without using government officials as interme-diaries or who become aware of this as the result of some report or inquiry [and do nothing about it] to be severely punished."[125] In 1916, in particular, prohibitions were announced not only for consular per-sonnel and missionaries, but for all foreign nationals to circulate freely, especially in Syria.[126]

Jesse Jackson, the American Consul in Aleppo, whose actions prompted the aforementioned Talat telegrams, was one of the most active consuls in regard to this matter. According a report by the Ottoman bureaucrats in charge of censorship, "In the letters that they have sent to America and various other foreign countries, the Armenians who have been transported to Aleppo are using the address of the American Consulate in Aleppo as the address 'for money and letters to be sent'."[127] Aleppo Provinical Governor Bekir Sami and his successor, Mustafa Abdülhalik, constantly voiced their complaints about Jackson. For exam-ple, in a cable dated 5 October 1915, Bekir Sami informed the Ottoman Interior Ministry that "Monsieur Jackson is constantly involving himself in Armenian matters and secretly giving money to citizens of enemy countries, as well as acting as a means through which the Armenians can report and learn about [events in] the eastern provinces."[128] The gover-nor, who accuses the consul of not being a man of character and warns that "one day he will provoke me to [causing] some unpleasant inci-dent," requests that "the consul be removed from here at the soonest possible moment."[129]

Bekir Sami's successor, Mustafa Abdülhalik, was no different in his complaints. In his reply to Talat's 30 October 1916 cable ordering an investigation to be opened into the secret distribution of money to the Armenians, Abdülhalik reports that "it was understood from the investiga-tion that the money was delivered by the American Consul in Aleppo to a part of the Armenians who arrived" in Aleppo. He adds that "a great number of Armenians who received the money admitted that they had received it from the consulate," and Jackson "did not hesitate to say to his face that...he was helping [the Armenians]."[130]

Similar to the manner in which Naim described it, one measure taken by the government against these efforts by the American consulate was to keep a close watch on all of the foreign missions and to attempt to detain or arrest all of the suspicious-looking individuals entering and leaving the consulate. However, these efforts went so far and were so extensive that Consul Jackson felt obliged to inform the American Embassy in Istanbul of the situation.

In response to a subsequent embassy representation before the Porte, Talat felt compelled to send a telegram to Governor Abdülhalik on 8 March 1916 warning him that "the [American] Embassy has reported that its Aleppo Consulate had been placed under surveillance and that those entering and leaving its premises were upset [by the harassment they experienced]," and ordering that the "necessary instructions [be given] that it is inappropriate for the observation [of the consulate] be done in such a way as to give rise to such a public manner that might give cause for complaint."[131] In accordance with the interior minister's wishes, the surveillance of the consulate was no longer to be carried out in such a manner as to open the way to complaints from the consulate.

In his reply of March, Mustafa Abdülhalik informed Talat that "Hundreds of women and men from among the Armenian refugees... gathered before the consulate every day, and money was then given to them." Even the letters that the Armenians wanted to send, whether to the United States or to the other parts of the Ottoman Empire, would be brought to the consulate, rather than entrusting them to Ottoman authorities. According to the governor, the police were not carrying out their task through observation, but by getting to know the masses on the streets and monitoring or following them in accordance with the law. As a result of the controls put in place, certain documents were obtained that were then "submitted to the court-martial." Abdülhalik added that "those persons entering and leaving the consulate who claimed to have been troubled or harassed are Armenians who possess Ottoman citizenship and are understood to have been given money without regard to their rank or station."[132]

As Naim mentioned, these measures were not particularly successful. Despite government efforts, the American—and even more the German consular staff and missionaries in the region—continued to send to their respective embassies in Istanbul their reports and documentation showing that the true purpose of the Ottoman government's deportation efforts was the annihilation of its Armenian population. Some of the most damning evidence sent was the photographs of piles of corpses taken on the deportation routes.

THE PROBLEM OF BODIES REMAINING ON THE ROADS

Some of the most crucial evidence of the Ottoman government's intent to annihilate its Armenian population is the photographs showing the utter despair and desolation of the Armenian deportation convoys and the countless bodies of those who died en route. For this reason, the Ottoman regime saw it as vital to clear the roads of dead bodies and to prevent them from being photographed. Naim offered two cables; one is from Talat dealing with the subject, and the other from Deportation Office in Aleppo, as well as adding his own information and commentary.

The first of these cables dates from 11 January 1916. In it, the interior minister informs the telegram's recipients that "Since foreign [military] officers have seen and photographed the bodies of certain known persons that have accumulated in great numbers all along the routes, you are being exhorted with great urgency that these [corpses] not be left unburied and out in the open." Naim added the following explanatory note:

Some seven or eight hundred Armenians died every day [at this point] from disaster, destitution, and disease. They were buried in the mud, their remains scattered by the carrion fowl [that feasted on them]; it was a state of affairs that seared the human conscience. The German and Austrian officers [serving with the Ottoman forces] would see these sights and send back written reports to their own countries. Talat Pasha heard reports of this and wished to hide his crimes under a shovelful of dirt, to bury them, but even by moving heaven and earth, these bitter calamities could not be hidden from memory or caused to be forgotten.[133]

The second cable from the Aleppo Deportation Office reads as follows:

You are not to allow a single Armenian [to remain] in Bab.
The force and determination that you will show in [undertaking] the deportations can well ensure the results that you have pursued. Only take

care not to leave any bodies on the roads or in open areas. You should inform us about the maximum fee that will be given to the persons you employ for this purpose.

Do not occupy yourself with procuring means of transport; they can go by foot. The table listing those who have died that comes every week is not satisfactory. It is understood from this that these persons are living there quite comfortably.

Deportations are not like going off on a journey. No regard or importance should be given to complaints and cries of agony and distress. The necessary communications have been sent from the provincial government to the office of the county executive. You should invest great effort [in this enterprise].[134]

In his supplementary note to this second telegram, Naim writes:

According to the latest order, all the exiles of Bab would be deported within 24 hours. They would leave in whatever fashion they wished. In any case, this deportation would conclude with their deaths. The winter season, naked from their heads to their toes, being sent out in this state, they fell and died at the side of the roads. From Bab to Meskene, along the length of the road, the fields became filled with the corpses of Armenians. Even a handful of soil did not cover their bodies. Learning that the corpses had been left in the open, the government panicked. Realizing that those corpses had been seen by foreigners, it ordered that they be buried. Spades and hoes were found. Gravediggers were appointed. In this fashion, supposedly the traces of criminal acts would be covered up.[135]

The Ottoman archival documents show that the events mentioned in both the cables and in Naim's annotations are accurate. There are a number of reports in the archives concerning foreigners—and Germans in particular—filming the deportation convoys and bodies strewn along the roads. On 24 January 1916, for instance, Deyr-i Zor District Governor Ali Suat sent a cable to Istanbul stating that "the German officers passing into Iraq are intentionally seeking out the Armenian ill and dead bodies of Armenian and that they were keen on taking photos [of these]."[136] On 30 October 1916, an Ottoman functionary sent a lengthy report on the deportation situation in the areas around Meskene and Deyr-i Zor. It included the notice that, "[w]hile the orphaned refugees were being deported to [Deyr-i] Zor, they were photographed by [some] German officers who were returning from Baghdad."[137]

There are numerous Ottoman archival documents, especially telegrams sent from Istanbul to the provinces, containing orders demanding that the dead bodies strewn along the roads be removed and buried. A significant portion of these were obtained during the pre-trial investigations of the Unionist leaders responsible for the deportations and massacres in 1918 and 1919. Some of these were later used as evidence in the trials themselves. In what was later referred to as the "Main Trial" of members of the Central Committee of the Committee of Union and Progress, and leaders of the so-called "Special Organization" (*Teşkilat-ı Mahsusa*) and government of the period, lengthy excepts from these telegrams were used in the original indictment.

Among these cables, those sent by Talat and Cemal occupy a special place. One sent by Cemal to the provincial governor of Diyarbekir on 14 July 1915 demanded that, "[s]ince the bodies that are strewn toward the south of the Euphrates are probably the corpses of Armenians who were killed during [their] rebel actions; these must be buried in the areas where they are discovered and their remains must not be left out in the open." In reply, the governor states that "[i]t is likely that the bodies strewn about [belonged to persons who] came from Erzurum and Mamuretülaziz (Elazığ). Those killed in rebel actions are either left [to rot] or thrown into deep caves, or usually [are removed] by being burned in the manner done with most."[138]

A similar cable, dated 3 August 1915, was sent by Talat to the Provinces of Diyarbekir and Elazığ and to the Provincial Districts of Urfa and Deyr-i Zor. In it, Talat ordered the local administrations to "have the dead bodies on the roads buried, not by throwing the corpses into ravines or rivers and lakes, and the possessions that they left along the roads."[139] Another cable concerning the subject that was cited in the indictment was from the provincial governor of Mamuretülaziz, Sabit, to the District Governor of Malatya. In the message, dated 2 January 1916, Sabit informs him that he has received a cable from the interior ministry informing him that "if bodies like these are seen within the borders of the counties [of the provincial district], the county official, sub-district official and gendarmerie commanders will be immediately removed from their positions and [delivered over] to the courts."[140]

In the aforementioned indictment, no mention was made of this telegram, which Sabit got from the interior ministry, but this document is available in the Guerguerian archive. In this cable, Sabit quotes from the telegrams that he received on 1 January from Talat. Talat wrote that "reports have arrived claiming that in certain areas bodies have been encountered that were not buried but left out in the open," and he orders that "if there are bodies left uninterred within your province, the need for them to be ordered buried is to be communicated with full force to the necessary parties; should it later be learned that such bodies have been discovered not buried within some or other county," the responsible "civil official is to be removed from their position," and the ministry is to be kept abreast of the situation.[141] The contents of this telegram are nearly identical with those of the 11 January 1916 cable provided by Naim. It is understood that in December and January, the clearing of the roads of these bodies formed one of the most important items on the government's daily agenda.

Yet, despite the series of orders sent to the provinces, the task of clearing away the bodies and hiding them away turned out to be far more difficult than expected. It was not only the empty fields and spaces around the roads that were full of bodies, but the region's waterways, as well, and the Tigris river foremost among them. The number of bodies in the Tigris was so great that many of those tossed in near Diyarbekir actually reached Mosul. German officers and government functionaries travelling in the area in particular passed through the villages that had been used as "fields of death." Holstein, the German Consul in Mosul, for instance, encountered a great number of bodies that "were only half buried." In many places, the corpses appeared not only not to have been buried, but left inside churches or thrown into cisterns. These officials' written reports and photos of such scenes were regularly sent to their embassy in Istanbul. In the diplomatic notes that they had delivered to the Porte, it is clear that these reports and photos from the provinces had had a great effect.[142]

Ottoman government officials eventually concluded that simple prohibitions on photographing these scenes in the provinces was proving insufficient, so they resorted to threatening German civilian and military personnel in the country with arresting them and putting them on trial as war criminals. In this effort, Cemal Pasha would play the leading role. Upon receiving reports that German personnel working on the Baghdad Railroad had been photographing the Armenian deportations, he sent a letter, dated 10 September 1915, to the head of the railway company, informing him that he had heard that "certain Baghdad Railroad employees and engineers "had taken photographs that featured images of the resettlement of Armenians" and gave the order that the photographs that these employees and engineers had taken as well as all copies be promptly handed over to the military police station within 48 hours. Furthermore, the Fourth Army Commander openly threatened the German officials that "those who do not surrender the photographs in their hands will be judged for the crime of taking unauthorized photographs on the field of battle and punished."[143]

THE INVESTIGATION OF SUSPICIOUS ARMENIANS
IN DÖRTYOL AND HADJIN

In his memoirs, Naim mentions many such events as the ones we have examined here. At one point, he mentions investigations, undertaken in the Dörtyol and Hadjin regions, of several Armenians who appeared suspicious and who were thought to have taken photographs along the deportation routes and sent them to Istanbul. This is but one example of such occurrences.

Naim included in his memoirs a cable of Talat's from 25 October 1915, in which the interior minister ordered that "the requested papers and secret correspondence number 1923 and dated 8 October 1915 be collected within one week" and sent to him.[144] Naim does not produce the official document mentioned by Talat, but gives an extensive synopsis from memory:

> In these secret communications, it is stated that some [prominent] Armenians from Dörtyol, Hadjin, and Mersin must be found and rewarded [in order to] persuade them to write out signed statements in their own hand explaining that '[the Dashnaks] have made the preparations and the [necessary] infrastructure is everywhere in place to launch a rebellion during wartime,' and notice should be taken that these persons are in any case very well-known [prominent] individuals.[145]

Naim continues by claiming that a number of investigations were carried out regarding the subject and offers the following additional information:

> In that period, a number of persons were arrested. They were put in prison. I do know that some testimonies were recorded by a committee made up of an officer of the Courts-Martial, someone from the Justice Ministry, and

Eyüb Bey, the Director of the [Office of] Immigrant [and Refugee Resettlement]. These [arrested] persons were even photographed. But I did not manage to learn the final results of this.[146]

There is abundant and rich documentation in the Ottoman archives regarding the investigations that were done concerning Armenian revolutionaries in the areas of Dörtyol and Hadjin. Just as Naim has claimed, the interior ministry ordered reports to be prepared on the activities of persons in these areas suspected of being members of Armenian revolutionary organizations and for the suspects to be photographed and their pictures sent to the capital.[147] For example, in a cable from the interior ministry to the province of Aleppo on 19 March 1916, it is demanded that "photographs of the seizure and arrest of the Armenian bandits in the county of Süleymanlı be sent [back to the capital] along with the ones showing their ongoing crimes in this regard."[148] The government even sent Esat Bey, the Director of the Second Department, to the region in order to personally ensure that these photographs would be collected.[149]

Telegrams were continually sent to Aleppo throughout the spring months, ordering that photos be taken of Armenians considered suspicious in the regions of Adana, Marash, and Aleppo (which included the areas of Dörtyol and Hadjin), and that they be subsequently sent back to the capital. Naim mentions this subject in connection to the cables that arrived at the Deportation Office during the period he worked there (winter 1915 and spring 1916). Apart from the aforementioned 19 March cable, the central government sent a steady stream of others on this subject to Aleppo during this period. To give but three examples, a 3 May 1916 message requests that "information be sent regarding the results of the inquiry and investigation into the Armenian armed gangs;"[150] another sent five days later asks for "photographs to be taken, gathered up and sent together [to the capital] of the captured members of the Armenian armed gangs, those giving them support and housing them, the weapons that were seized, etc.;"[151] and one from 9 May 1916, again asking that "photographs be ordered taken of Armenian armed gangs and sent [back to the capital] along with a detailed report on the results of the broadening of the investigation [into the same]."[152]

What were the results of these investigations? As we have seen above, Naim recounts that some persons were taken into custody and their testimonies recorded, but that he was not able "to learn about the [final] results." If we remember that Naim left his post in the Deportation Office some time during the summer months, his ignorance of the investigation results becomes more understandable, since it was during these months that the central government was itself showing concern as to results of these investigations. On 13 July 1915, Talat sent a cable to Aleppo inquiring as to "when to expect a conclusion of the trials of the heads and leading members of the revolutionary committee who had been delivered over to the court-martial, and of those apprehended individual gang [members] who had surrendered and been deported," and requesting that he be personally informed of "the results of the investigations and trials that have been conducted by the court-martial until now."[153]

In short, what Naim Efendi *does* provide in his memoirs is his recollections of events that he witnessed first-hand, and this information can be confirmed by various Ottoman archival documents.

Notes

1. Naim Efendi, *Hatırat* [11].
2. BOA.DH.ŞFR., 62/5, Cipher cable, dated 14 March 1916, from Talat to the Province of Aleppo. It should be noted that some of the names of the Armenians were probably written incorrectly!
3. Naim Efendi, *Hatırat* [02].
4. BOA.DH.EUM., 2.Şube, 57/12. We have used this document as a general source of the information here. In addition to this document, however, there are upwards of 10 other documents in the archives concerning Nalbantian's attempts to intervene on behalf of his relatives (particularly his brother). For some of these, see BOA.EUM., 2.Şube, 37/01; BOA. DH.ŞFR., 56/366; 57/297; 61/94; 61/282.
5. BOA.DH.ŞFR., 56/366, Cipher cable, dated 12 October 1915, from Interior Minister Talat to the Province of Aleppo.
6. BOA.DH.EUM., 2.Şube, 57/12.
7. Ibid.
8. Aram Andonian, *Medz Vojirĕ*, 31.
9. BOA.DH.ŞFR., 55/19, Cipher cable, dated 15 August 1915, from Interior Minister Talat to the Provinces of Erzurum, Adana, Ankara, Bitlis, Halep, Hüdavendigar (Bursa), Diyarbekir, Sivas, Trebizond, Konya, Mamuretülaziz (Elazığ), and Van; and to the Provincial Districts

of Urfa, Izmit, Canik, Karesi, Karahisar-ı Sahib (Afyon Karahisar), Kayseri, Marash, Niğde, and Eskişehir.

10. BOA.DH.ŞFR., 54-A/339, Cipher cable, dated 9 August 1915, from the Interior Ministry to the Provincial District of Izmit.

11. BOA.DH.ŞFR., 56/291, Cipher cable, dated 5 October 1915, from the Interior Ministry to the Province of Adana.

12. BOA.DH.ŞFR., 56/345, Cipher cable, dated 10 October 1915, from the Interior Ministry to the Provincial District of Karahisar-ı Sahib (For a similar cable to Afyon, see: BOA.DH.ŞFR., 58/151).

13. BOA.DH.ŞFR., 57/29; 57/121 ve 58/4, Cipher cables, dated 16 October & 14 November 1915, from the Interior Ministry to the Province of Konya.

14. BOA.DH.ŞFR., 58/149, Cipher cable, dated 28 October 1915, from the Interior Ministry to the Province of Aydın.

15. BOA.DH.ŞFR., 58/224, Cipher cable, dated 9 December 1915, from Interior Minister Talat to the Province of Konya (For a similar cable on the same subject, see: BOA.DH.ŞFR., 57/136).

16. BOA.DH.ŞFR., 56/301, Cipher cable, dated 5 October 1915, from the Interior Ministry to the Province of Aleppo.

17. BOA.DH.ŞFR., 58/6, Cipher cable, dated 14 November 1915, from the Interior Ministry to the Province of Aleppo.

18. BOA.DH.ŞFR., 499/49, Cipher cable, dated 30 November 1915, from Aleppo Governor Mustafa Abdülhalik to the Interior Ministry.

19. The parliamentary deputy's name appears in many documents and sources as Hıralakyan, but we have used what is the the spelling in the text (i.e., Hırlakyan).

20. BOA.DH.ŞFR., 55/3, Cipher cable, dated 15 August 1915, from Interior Minister Talat to the Province of Aleppo.

21. BOA.DH.ŞFR., 57/103, Cipher cable, dated 24 October 1915, from Interior Minister Talat to the Province of Aleppo.

22. BOA.DH.ŞFR., 63/229, Cipher cable, dated 7 May 1916, from Interior Minister Talat to the Provincial District of Urfa.

23. BOA.DH.ŞFR., 64/61, Cipher cable, dated 18 May 1916, from Interior Minister Talat to the Province of Aleppo.

24. BOA.DH.ŞFR., 62/4, Cipher cable, dated 14 March 1916, from Interior Minister Talat to the Province of Aleppo.

25. BOA.DH.ŞFR., 62/9, Cipher cable, dated 14 March 1916, from Interior Minister Talat to the Provincial District of [Deyr-i] Zor.

26. BOA.DH.ŞFR., 62/177, Cipher cable, dated 30 March 1916, from Interior Minister Talat to the Province of Aleppo.

27. BOA.DH.ŞFR., 64/145, Cipher cable, dated 29 May 1916, from Interior Minister Talat to the Province of Aleppo.
28. BOA.DH.ŞFR., 65/4, Cipher cable, dated 14 June 1916, from Interior Minister Talat to the Province of Aleppo.
29. For some other examples, see: BOA.DH.ŞFR., 74/253; 75/218; 77/140; 78/1, 78/2; 82/138.
30. BOA.DH.ŞFR., 56/162, Cipher cable, dated 25 September 1915, from Interior Minister Talat to the Province of Aleppo.
31. BOA.DH.ŞFR., 56/282, Cipher cable, dated 4 October 1915, from Interior Minister Talat to the Province of Aleppo.
32. BOA.DH.ŞFR., 58/17, Cipher cable, dated 15 November 1915, from Interior Minister Talat to the Province of Syria.
33. BOA.DH.ŞFR., 59/203, Cipher cable, dated 4 January 1916, from Interior Minister Talat to the Province of Aleppo.
34. BOA.DH.ŞFR., 60/38, Cipher cable, dated 16 January 1916, from Interior Minister Talat to the Province of Aleppo.
35. BOA.DH.ŞFR., 506/66, Cipher cable, dated 23 January 1916, from Aleppo Governor Mustafa Abdülhalik to the Interior Ministry.
36. BOA.DH.ŞFR., 71/27, Cipher cable, dated 18 December 1916, from Interior Minister Talat to the Province of Aleppo.
37. BOA.DH.ŞFR., 73/74, Cipher cable, dated 19 February 1917, from Interior Minister Talat to the Province of Aleppo.
38. BOA.DH.ŞFR., 74/92, Cipher cable, dated 10 March 1917, from Interior Minister Talat to the Province of Aleppo.
39. Ibid.
40. Throughout an entire period that begin in May 1915, when the first deportation convoys reached Aleppo, thousands of orphaned Armenian children would remain in Syria, and the question of what to do with them became a serious problem. At first, a great number of orphanages were set up by permission of Cemal Pasha in areas within the control of the Fourth Army, chief among them Aleppo. These orphanages, most of which were attempts by local Armenian institutions and foreign aid organizations, were eventually closed and the children within them sent off to die. For more detailed information on the subject, see Nazan Maksudyan, *Orphans and Destitute Children in the Late Ottoman Empire* (Syracuse: Syracuse University Press, 2014); Khatchig Mouradian, "Genocide and Humanitarian Resistance in Ottoman Syria, 1915–1917" (PhD diss., Clark University, 2016); Vahram L. Shemmassian, "The Reclamation of Captive Armenian Genocide Survivors in Syria and Lebanon at the End of World War I," *Journal of the Society for Armenian Studies*, 15 (2006):

113–140; Shemmassian, "Humanitarian Intervention by the Armenian Prelacy of Aleppo during the First Months of the Genocide," *Journal of the Society for Armenian Studies*, 22 (2013): 127–153.

41. *Hatırat* [32]–[33].
42. Hilmar Kaiser, *At the Crossroads of Der Zor: Death, Survival, and Humanitarian Resistance in Aleppo, 1915–1917* (Princeton and London: Gomidas Institute, 2002), 52–54.
43. *Hatırat* [13]–[14].
44. Ibid., [31], for the original image of this document see Aram Andonian, *Medz Vojïr̃*, 191.
45. BOA.DH.ŞFR., 503/91, Cipher cable, dated 10 February 1916, from [Aleppo] Governor Mustafa Abdülhalik to the Interior Ministry.
46. BOA.DH.ŞFR., 500/75, Cipher cable, dated 7 December 1915, from [Aleppo] Governor Mustafa Abdülhalik to the Interior Ministry.
47. BOA.DH.ŞFR., 508/30, Cipher cable, dated 6 February 1916, from Aleppo Governor Mustafa Abdülhalik to the Interior Ministry.
48. BOA.DH.ŞFR., 61/18, Cipher cable, date 15 February 1916, from Interior Minister Talat to the Province of Aleppo.
49. BOA.DH.ŞFR., 61/20, Cipher cable, date 15 February 1916, from Interior Minister Talat to the Province of Aleppo. The desire to the send Armenian orphans to Istanbul was not an attitude unique to Aleppo. Similar complaints and demands arrived from other provinces, and, like in Aleppo, Talat also rejected requests by other governors to have the Armenian orphans in their jurisdictions sent to Istanbul, ordering them distributed among the neighboring provinces instead. For cables dealing with his rejection of such a request from the Province of Kayseri, see: BOA.DH.SFR., 520/12 (17 May 1916) and 64/82 (20 May 1916).
50. BOA.DH.EUM, 2.şube., 19/43-1, Cipher cable, dated 2 April 1916, from Aleppo Governor Mustafa Abdülhalik to the Interior Ministry.
51. BOA.DH.ŞFR., 520/31, Cipher cable, dated 18 May 1916, from Aleppo Governor Mustafa Abdülhalik to the Interior Ministry.
52. Ibid.
53. BOA.DH.ŞFR., 66/229, Cipher cable, dated 13 August 1916, from Interior Minister Talat to the Province of Aleppo.
54. BOA.DH.ŞFR., 509/104, Cipher cable, dated 17 February 1916, from Sivas Governor Muammer to the Interior Ministry.
55. BOA.DH.ŞFR., 538/114, Cipher cable, dated 1 December 1916, from Aleppo Governor Mustafa Abdülhalik to the Interior Ministry.
56. BOA.DH.ŞFR., 541/45, Cipher cable, dated 26 December 1916, from Aleppo Governor Mustafa Abdülhalik to the Interior Ministry.

57. BOA.MF.MKT. 1221/81, Note, dated 11 December 1916, from Interior Minister Talat to the Ministry of Education.
58. BOA.MF.MKT. 1221/81, Note, dated 25 December 1916, from the Education Ministry to the Interior Ministry.
59. BOA.MF.MKT. 1221/81, Note, dated 4 January 1917, from Interior Minister Talat to the Ministry of Education.
60. DE/PA-AA/R14096, Report, dated 16 March 1917, from German Consul in Aleppo Rössler to Chancellor Bethmann Hollweg; http://www.armenocide.net/armenocide/armgende.nsf/$AllDocs/1917-03-16-DE-001 (Accessed 4 April 2016).
61. Genelkurmay Başkanlığı, *Arşiv Belgeleriyle, Cilt VIII*, 133.
62. Hans Lukas Kieser, *A Question for Belonging: Anatolia Beyond Empire and Nation (19th–21st Centuries)* (Istanbul: ISIS Press, 2007), 224.
63. For the relevant correspondence, see: BOA.DH.EUM., 5.Şb, 50/15.
64. Ibid.
65. The date that is seen on the photographic image of the document reads "2 Kanuni Evvel 1331" (25 December 1915). However, in his memoirs, Naim Efendi gives the date as "12 Kanuni Sani 1332" (25 December 1917).
66. Memoirs, [26]
67. Memoirs, [11].
68. Aram Andonian, *Medz Vojirĕ*, 197.
69. BOA.DH.ŞFR., 66/136, Cipher cable, dated 4 August 1916, from Interior Minister Talat to the Province of Aleppo. "The orphanage established by the commander of the Office of Logistical Support in Meskene was brought into existence by the order of which office? Clearly explain [the identity of] the party that bore the expenses for this orphanage, along with its current extent and level of importance."
70. Genelkurmay Başkanlığı, *Arşiv Belgeleriyle, Cilt VII*, 73–75. In the statements given during the investigations, the times and dates given were "the beginning of June" and "July 3."
71. BOA.DH.ŞFR., 74/15, Cipher cable, dated 1 March 1917, from the Interior Ministry to the Province of Aleppo.
72. Raymond Kévorkian, *Soykırımın İkinci Safhası*, 251. This information was taken from the "secret newspapers" that were used by the Armenians living in the camps during that period to communicate with one another. The persons who survived wrote their recollections on scraps of paper so that others would discover and learn about the things they experienced. The task of communicating in this fashion was largely entrusted to small children, whose movements would not be noticed by guards or others.

73. Raymond Kévorkian, *Soykırımın Ikinci Safhası*, 280, 311.
74. Aram Andonian, *Medz Vojirě*, 109.
75. BOA.DH.ŞFR., 73/8, Cipher cable, dated 14 February 1917, from Interior Minister Talat to the Province of Aleppo.
76. BOA.DH.ŞFR., 73/58, Cipher cable, dated 22 February 1917, from Interior Minister Talat to the Province of Aleppo.
77. BOA.DH.ŞFR., 545/91, Cipher cable, dated 25 February 1917, from Aleppo Governor Mustafa Abdülhalik to the Interior Ministry.
78. Raymond Kévorkian, *Soykırımın Ikinci Safhası*, 280, 311.
79. Memoirs [23].
80. Ibid., [27].
81. Ibid., [28].
82. Aram Andonian, *Medz Vojirě*, 60.
83. Memoirs, [29].
84. BOA.DH.EUM., 2.Şb., 73/61ve BOA.DH.ŞFR., 666/122, Cipher cable, dated 6 November 1915, from Adana Provincial Governor Ismail Hakkı Bey to the Interior Ministry. BOA.DH.EUM., 2.Şb., 73/60-01, Cipher cable, dated 9 November 1915, from Osmaniye District Governor Fethi to the Interior Ministry.
85. For some examples of cables sent to the provinces requesting that the Armenian rail workers not be deported but left in place, see BOA. DH.ŞFR., 55/48, 287, 318; 54-A/307.
86. Three examples of such cables, sent in August and September 1915 are BOA.DH.ŞFR., 482/30; 488/80 and 489/99.
87. BOA.DH.ŞFR., 56/77, Cipher cable, dated 19 September 1915, from the Interior Ministry to the Provinces of Konya, Ankara, Hüdavendigar (Bursa), and Adana; and to the Provincial Districts of Izmit, Karahisar-ı Sahib, Kütahya, Eskishehir, and Niğde.
88. BOA.DH.ŞFR., 490/95, Cipher cable, dated 25 September 1915, from the Director of Immigrant and Refugee Settlement in Aleppo Şükrü Bey to the Interior Ministry.
89. BOA.DH.ŞFR., 56/232, Cipher cable, dated 29 September 1915, from the Interior Ministry to the Province of Aleppo.
90. For more detailed information on the commission's decision, see: Krikor Guerguerian Archive, 07, "02-Andonian Analysis Dossier IX" [.pdf, pp. 117–128].
91. BOA.DH.ŞFR., 492/129 ve 493/62, Cipher cables, dated 9 and 13 October 1915, from Cemal Pasha to the Interior Ministry.
92. BOA.DH.ŞFR., 58/25, Cipher cable, dated 16 November 1915, from the Interior Ministry to the Director of Immigrant and Refugee Settlement [in Aleppo] Şükrü Bey.

93. BOA.DH.EUM.2.ŞB 73/64, Written communication, dated 8 December 1915, from the Military Commissioner of the Baghdad Railroad to the General Directorate of Security in Istanbul.
94. BOA.DH.ŞFR., 479/19, Cipher cable, dated 11 November 1915, from Refugee [and Immigrant Resettlement] Director (*Muhacirin Müdürü*) Şükrü Bey to the Interior Ministry.
95. BOA.DH.ŞFR., 58/223, Cipher cable, dated 9 December 1915, from the Interior Ministry to the Province of Adana.
96. BOA.DH.ŞFR., 501/42, Cipher cable, dated 14 December 1915, from Governor Mustafa Abdülhalik to the Interior Ministry.
97. BOA.DH.ŞFR., 506/64, Cipher cable, dated 23 January 1916, from Governor Mustafa Abdülhalik to the Interior Ministry.
98. For more information on the attempts made by the rail company to block the deportation of Armenians, see: H. Kaiser, "The Baghdad Railway," 67–112.
99. The complete detailed story of this affair is told in the book by Grigoris Balakian, *Armenian Golgotha*, chapters 11–13, 77–95.
100. BOA.DH.ŞFR., 60/45, Cipher cable, dated 16 January 1916, from the Interior Ministry to the Provinces of Aleppo, Adana, Konya, and Ankara; and to the Provincial Districts of Eskishehir and Izmit.
101. BOA.DH.ŞFR., 60/157, Cipher cable, dated 29 January 1916, from the Interior Ministry to the Provinces of Adana and Aleppo.
102. BOA.DH.ŞFR., 61/1, Cipher cable, dated 13 February 1916, from the Interior Ministry to the Provinces of Adana and Aleppo.
103. BOA.DH.ŞFR., 63/23, Cipher cable, dated 17 April 1916, from the Interior Ministry to the Provinces of Ankara, Konya, Hüdavendigar (Bursa), Adana, and Aleppo; and to the Provincial Districts of Izmit, Eskishehir, Karahisar-ı Sahib, Kütahya, and Niğde.
104. BOA.DH.ŞFR., 516/81, Cipher cable, dated 19 April 1916, from Governor Mustafa Abdülhalik to the Interior Ministry.
105. BOA.DH.ŞFR., 61/17, Cipher cable, dated 15 February 1916, from the Interior Ministry to [Fourth Army Commander] Cemal Pasha.
106. BOA.DH.ŞFR., 506/48, Cipher Cable, dated 22 January 1916 from Adana Governor Hakkı to the Interior Ministry.
107. BOA.DH.ŞFR., 510/69, Cipher Cable dated 22 February 1916 from Cemal Pasha to Interior Ministry.
108. BOA.DH.ŞFR., 61/128, Cipher cable, dated 27 February 1916, from the Interior Ministry to the Provinces of Adana and Aleppo.
109. Regarding the date of his appointment, see BOA.MV., 241/287, Draft (*layiha*), dated 9 March 1916. and: BOA.DH.I.MMS. 201/25, Imperial Decree, dated 11 February 1916. In fact, Cevdet arrived in the Aleppo

region long before his actual appointment as governor of the province. In the Armenian version of the Memoirs, Andonian locates him there already in February, [*Medz Vojirĕ*, 52]. An official document from the Ottoman archive confirms this. See, for instance BOA.DH.ŞFR., 61/197, Cipher cable, dated 6 March 1916, from Interior Minister Talat to Van Provincial Governor Cevdet (who is in Aleppo).

110. BOA.DH.ŞFR., 523/54, Cipher cable, dated 18 June 1916, from [Adana] Provincial Governor Cevdet to the Interior Ministry.

111. BOA.DH.ŞFR., 515/88, Cipher cable, dated 31 March 1916, from Governor Mustafa Abdülhalik to Interior Ministry.

112. *Hatırat* [23]–[24].

113. *Hatırat* [23].

114. The information here was taken from: BOA.DH.2.Şube, 29/43.

115. BOA.DH.2.Şb., 30/7, Cipher cable, dated 31 October 1916, from the Provincial Governor of Aleppo to the Interior Ministry.

116. BOA.DH.2.Şube, 29/43.

117. Ibid.

118. As an example, the following document shows the unease (and subsequent correspondence in response) created within the Ottoman regime by a report appearing in a Berlin paper and claiming that more than one million Armenians had been killed, among which were 100,000 Catholics (including four bishops): HR.SYS., 02883/6.

119. Aram Andonian, *Medz Vojirĕ*, 136, 141–143, 146. In the *Memoirs* text in our possession, the telegram is not to be found, but instead the photographic image that appears in Andonian's edition. Naim's name is also mentioned in the cable. We translated the text from the photographic image: "Certain information has been procured by the American consulates in various areas regarding the manner in which known individuals [Armenians] have been deported; we deduced that this procurement is being organized secretly from the memorandum we received from the American Embassy in Istanbul, which was acting on direct orders of its government. Even though we informed them in our response to this memo that the deportations are being carried out in an atmosphere of security and ease, this alone will never be sufficient to convince them. For this reason, during the deportation of people in cities, towns, or in areas close to [population] centers, you must practice caution and avoid drawing attention, in order produce the belief among the foreigners wandering around in those parts that the purpose of the deportations is nothing other than the relocation. To achieve this, the temporary implementation of compassionate treatment is necessary for political reasons, and the usual measures (massacres) known to you should be implemented in the appropriate regions. Those

persons surveilling the area for purposes of observation should be apprehended using other excuses and be delivered by other means to the courts-martial."

120. Memoirs [22]. According to Andonian, the reporter for the Armenian paper *Jamanag* mentioned in the document was Yervant Odian. As for the photographer, it was Matthew Yeretzian (Mateos Yeretsyan), secretary to the Archbishop of Aleppo; finally, the person who delivered these documents and such to Jackson, the American consul, was Aram Gülyan. Aram Andonian, *Medz Vojirě*, 146–147.

121. Memoirs [22].

122. Ara Sarafian (ed.), *United States Official Records on the Armenian Genocide 1915–1917* (London: Gomidas Institute, 2004), 386.

123. For examples, see: BOA/DH.ŞFR., 59/40, 46, 47, 48; 76/42, 43-1, 44, 210.

124. For examples, see: BOA/DH.ŞFR., 60/178, 281; 62/90, 129, 181; 65/25; 69/210; 72/18; 74/66.

125. BOA/DH.ŞFR., 62/210.

126. BOA/DH.ŞFR., 61/32, Cipher cable, dated 13 February 1916, from the Interior Ministry to the Provinces of Aleppo, Adana, Mosul, and Diyarbekir; and to the Provincial Districts of Urfa and [Deyr-i]Zor.

127. BOA/DH.EUM. 2.şb., 73/42, official communique of censor officer Artin to the Department of Censor Inspectorate dated 20 September 1915.

128. BOA/DH.ŞFR., 492/41, Cipher cable, dated 5 October 1915, from Governor Bekir Sami to Interior Ministry.

129. BOA/DH.ŞFR., 492/41.

130. BOA/DH.ŞFR., 508/29, Cipher cable, dated 6 February 1916, From Governor Mustafa Abdülhalik to Interior Ministry.

131. BOA/DH.ŞFR., 61/226, Cipher cable, dated 8 March 1916, from Interior Minister Talat to the Province of Aleppo.

132. BOA.DH.ŞFR., 513/34, Cipher cable, dated 16 March, 1916, from Governor Mustafa Abdülhalik to the Interior Ministry.

133. Memoirs [24].

134. Ibid., [10]. The date of the telegram is given as 2 February 1917, while the emptying out of the camp at Bab actually occurred during January or February 1916. Thus, it must be assumed that the year given is incorrect and should be 1916. Since we don't possess the image of this document (Andonian never published an original image of it), we do not have the opportunity to review and correct the date.

135. Aram Andonian, *Medz Vojirě*, 97–98. These annotations by Naim are not found in the Memoirs in our possession.

136. BOA.DH.ŞFR., 510/95, Cipher cable, dated 24 January 1916, from Deyr-i Zor District Governor [Ali] Suat to the Interior Ministry.

137. DH.EUM. 2.Şb. 74/30-01, Report, dated 30 October 1916, [Author unclear] to the Interior Ministry. From the text of the report it can be understood that the report was penned by an official who was sent to the areas of Meskene, Rakka and Deyr-i Zor in order to solve various problems surrounding the deportations.

138. *Takvim-i Vekayi*, no. 3540, 5 May 1919. The indictment was read at the first session of the trial, on 27 April 1919.

139. Ibid.

140. Ibid.

141. Krikor Guerguerian Archive, 24 Krieger 02, 01 Box V 01, PDF p. 334. Guerguerian took this document from the archives of the Armenian Patriarchate in Jerusalem; it is found in box number M578 within the latter's holdings.

142. Hilmar Kaiser, *The Extermination of Armenians in the Diarbekir Region* (Istanbul: Bilgi University Press, 2014), 189, 348–350.

143. DE/PA-AA/BoKon/170, Appendix 1 to the Report, dated 27 September 1915, from the German Consul in Aleppo Rössler to the German Embassy in Istanbul. http://www.armenocide.net/armenocide/armgende.nsf/$AllDocs-de/1915-09-27-DE-014?OpenDocument (Accessed 13 February 1916).

144. Memoirs [08].

145. Ibid., [08]–[09].

146. Ibid., [09].

147. The request for photographs and other documentation of murders and depredations caused by "Armenian revolutionaries" in Anatolia were an important policy of the government. The Ottoman regime published these images and documents in 1916 in a work known as the "White Book." For a recent republication of this work, see Erdoğan Cengiz (ed.), *Ermeni Komitelerinin Âmâl ve Harekât-ı İhtilâliyesi; İlân-ı Meşrutiyetten Evvel ve Sonra* (Ankara: Başbakanlık Basımevi 1983). For the documentation requested from the regions in question, see BOA.DH.ŞFR., 54-A/213; 55/150; 56/382.

148. BOA.DH.ŞFR., 62/57, Cipher cable, dated 19 March 1916, from the Interior Ministry to the Provincial District of Marash.

149. BOA.DH.ŞFR., 59/127; 63/263, 272, 282 Esat Bey, who would later adopt the surname Uras, would later go on to publish the well-known work *Tarihte Ermeniler ve Ermeni Meselesi* (Ankara: Türkiye Matbaacılık Ve Gazetecilik A.O, 1950). This work would come to represent one of the main sources for supporting information for the Turkish regime's "official version" of the history of this period.

150. BOA.DH.ŞFR., 63/185, Cipher cable, dated 3 May 1916, from the Interior Ministry to the Province of Aleppo.
151. BOA.DH.ŞFR., 63/241, Cipher cable, dated 8 May 1916, from the Interior Ministry to the Province of Aleppo.
152. BOA.DH.ŞFR., 63/248, Cipher cable, dated 9 May 1916, from the Interior Ministry to the Province of Aleppo.
153. BOA.DH.ŞFR., 65/201, Cipher cable, dated 13 July 1916, from the Interior Ministry to the Province of Aleppo.

Appendix A

We do not have a single, complete version of Naim Efendi's collection. What we have is two different texts! One is the original Ottoman-Turkish text that we discovered in the Guerguerian Archive, and the second is the collection of passages published by Aram Andonian. The original Ottoman-Turkish text and passages published by Andonian are the same, but there are major differences, too, because Andonian did not publish several pages of the original Ottoman-Turkish material. In some cases, he considered some pages unimportant and simply omitted them. In other cases, our Ottoman-Turkish text does not include certain pages that Aram Andonian published in his book. We know why these pages are missing in the Ottoman-Turkish text: Andonian had sent them to Istanbul for a trial.

Appendix A.1 is the complete translation of the original Ottoman-Turkish text. Appendix A.2 contains the passages published by Andonian, but are missing in the Ottoman-Turkish original. Of course, there are also several pages that are similar in the Ottoman-Turkish original and in Andonian's Armenian language book. For the overlapping pages, we have used the Ottoman-Turkish original, since Andonian translated the same text into Armenian. By putting these two documents together, we have a complete version of Naim Efendi's text.

© The Author(s) 2018
T. Akçam, *Killing Orders*, Palgrave Studies in the History of Genocide,
https://doi.org/10.1007/978-3-319-69787-1_6

APPENDIX A.1: THE OTTOMAN-TURKISH ORIGINAL OF NAIM EFENDI'S TEXT

(1) [01]

A villager in Bâb took in two children—one, aged ten, the other, aged eight—who were alone, without mother, father, or anyone else in the world.[1] A few days later, this person brought these children to Aleppo in order to get them some clothes. The children were held by the judge (*kadı*), the soldiers and the police headquarters. After the[ir] investigations, it was understood that the children had been from among the [many] orphaned children.

At the bottom of the documents related to the proceedings of the case, Abdülahad Nuri Bey wrote: "Even though it has been understood that these children were without family or guardian, they should be included in the general deportations, since it is possible that their relatives are to be found among the persons sent to [Deyr-i] Zor."

The papers go to the [provincial] governor. The governor says "in accordance with" [the standing regulations and orders]. These two poor little children are rescued by Haçadur [Khatchadour] Efendi, the assistant in the administrative section of the Police Department at that time.

(2) [02]

The Interior Ministry ordered Soğomon [Soghomon] Kuyumcuyan Efendi, a relative of Kozan Deputy Nalbandyan Efendi, who had previously been resettled in the County of Maara, to settle in Aleppo upon Nalbandyan's request. In response to this order, which arrived at the Office of Immigrant [and Refugee Resettlement], Soğomon Efendi applied and submitted an official petition. At the bottom of his petition it was written in that he must be settled in Maara. [His petition to settle in Aleppo was declined.] Several days later, the order was given for [the camp at] Maara to be emptied out [of people]. Soğomon Efendi appealed again. Even though he was supposed to be relocated to Aleppo per the [Interior] Ministry's order, Abdülahad Nuri Bey wrote back, saying that "since this person has fled from Maara and come here, he keeps pestering the [Immigrant and Refugee Resettlement] Office here and must be subject to the general deportations." The governor of the province accepted this. The papers related these proceedings, which showed how he was to be treated in this regard, were in the possession of Soğomon Efendi. In the hands of one of the desitute and unaccompanied women from Diyarbakır a plate was spotted with a number of pictures painted on it showing images of Armenian independence.

(3) [03]

Both the woman and the plate were brought to the [Deportation] Office. Great importance was given to this [plate]. The woman was asked where she purchased the plate. The woman said that this plate had been with her for years, and that she did not know anything regarding its meaning. The woman was then tortured for eight or ten days in a special room within the gendarmerie station. And this poor woman eventually expired there as the result of torture and hunger.

The Police headquarters did not participate in these crimes. Police Chief Fikri Bey showed great patriotism and honor in this affair. A woman by the name of Antepli Sultan opened up and worked in a tailor's shop consisting of six or seven employees. The workers were only widows, women who had lost their husbands and young girls. One of the workers—a girl of fifteen or sixteen years of age—was arrested by the police and told them where she worked. This busybody police officer went and gathered up the girl's co-workers.

(4) [04]

She was sent to the Office of Immigrant [and Refugee Resettlement]. These poor women and girls, who had gathered and begun working with the notion of earning a few kourush each day to get by, were rounded up on the pretext that if they stayed in Aleppo, some others would join them and disrupt the general deportation; they were thus sent off to the camp of Karlık and from there they were deported [further].

This was a very strange occurrence:

A family from Merzifon, which is in the Provincial District of Amasya, converted to Islam in their home town a few days before the deportations were to begin; they also informed the head of the family, who was in Çorum at the time, of their conversion. Upon receiving news of his wife and children's conversion, this man also converted [to Islam there]. But this could not save them from the deportations. He came all the way to Aleppo. Here he made his appeal. After he converted in Çorum and his family in Merzifon, he entreated them to allow his family to return to their place of origin. Permission was asked of [the governments of both] Merzifon and Çorum. Even though it was understood that the man had converted to Islam and taken on the name of Yusuf Ziya, Abdülahad Nuri Bey said "it doesn't matter if or how he converts; since he could not be exempted from deportations,

(5) [05]

he too was subject to the general deportations so that he could be reunited with his family in [Deyr-i] Zor. The provincial governor confirmed this decision.

A priest from Ankara was taken from the place he was staying in Cedîde at eight o'clock in the night by Bâb-ül-Farac Police Superintendent Fevzi Efendi and brought to Karlık,[2] where he was shot and killed. He was buried in the Muslim cemetery in the area near the barracks. The next day information [about the incident] was given to the Office of Immigrant [and Refugee Resettlement].

The orders to kill and despoil the Armenians coming from Sivas, Harput and other such areas was written from here [Aleppo] [and sent] to the office of the County Executive (*Kaymakam*) of Rumkale. The kaymakam formed an armed gang of [local] Kurds and they were then sent to Samsat; the Armenian [deportee] convoys coming [to?] Behisni via the "Adıyaman" route were slaughtered to a man. Some were thrown into the Euphrates river. According to the estimates contained in an official report, some fourteen thousand Armenians were killed by the gang of marauding Kurds in the area of Samsat alone.

(6) [06]

Copy of Interior Ministry cipher cable number 603, dated 18 November, 1915:

"It has been reported that a number of Muslim families have taken in the orphaned children of certain known persons, who were deported from the Provinces of Sivas, Mamuretülaziz, and Diyarbakır, and who perished en route, and have either adopted them or made them into servants. It is being communicated here in the form of a general memorandum that any such children within your province are to be gathered together and sent to the areas of [re-]settlement, and that the necessary discussions be held on this subject in a manner amenable to the population."

Copy of Interior Ministry cipher cable number 502, dated 16 September 1915:

"It is suggested that the treatment, previously communicated as to be carried out in regard to the male population of certain known individuals [Armenians], be expanded to also apply to their women and children and that it be employed by reliable officials."[3]

(7)[07]

Copy of Interior Ministry cipher cable number 537, dated 12 October 1915:

"Reports have been received that some of the local population and government officials have married a number of Armenian women. You are being exhorted with great urgency to vigorously prevent [such marriages] and to have such women deported without any distinction."

Copy of Interior Ministry cipher cable number 544, dated 16 October 1915:

"The purpose of adopting the Provincial District of [Deyr-i] Zor as an area of settlement was explained in the earlier confidential correspondence number 1843, dated 15 September 1915. Since the general crimes and misdeeds carried out by the [local] population against certain known [deported] individuals en route will ensure that the aims pursued by the government are achieved, there is no need to pursue legal investigations in this regard. The necessary message has been communicated to the Provincial Districts of [Deyr-i] Zor and Urfa."

(8)[08]

Copy of Interior Ministry cipher cable number 563, dated 25 October 1915:

"Please organize and send within one week the documents requested in the secret communication number 1923, dated 8 October 1915."

In these secret communications, it is stated that some [prominent] Armenians from Dörtyol, Hadjin, and Mersin must be found and rewarded [in order to] persuade them to write out signed statements in their own hand explaining that "[the Dashnaks] have made the preparations and the [necessary] infrastructure is everywhere in place to launch a rebellion during wartime," and notice should be taken that these persons are in any case very well known [prominent] individuals.

(9) [09]

Although a number of measures were taken in response to this cable, I do not know what they were or who implemented and carried them out.

In that period, a number of persons were arrested. They were put in prison. I do know that some testimonies were recorded by a committee made up of an officer of the Courts-Martial, someone from the Justice Ministry, and Eyüb Bey, the Director of the [Office of] Immigrant [and Refugee Resettlement]. These [arrested] persons were even photographed. But I did not manage to learn the final results of this.

An order was sent from here to the gendarmes that they should look out for those [deportees] who were left without food or water en route.[4]

Copy of secret communication number 344, dated 2 February 1917 and written by the Office of the Assistant Director General of Immigrant [and Refugee Affairs] to the Extraordinary Director of Deportations in Bab, Muharrem Bey:

"I am confident that you will appreciate the confidence that the Governor's office has in you, as well as the importance of the task that has been entrusted to you by the office on the basis of this confidence.

(10) [10]

You are not to allow a single Armenian [to remain] in Bab.

The force and determination that you will show in [undertaking] the deportations can well ensure the results that you have pursued. Only take care not to leave any bodies on the roads or in open areas. You should inform us about the maximum fee that will be given to the persons you employ for this purpose.

Do not occupy yourself with procuring means of transport; they can go by foot. The table listing those who have died that comes every week is not satisfactory. It is understood from this that these persons are living there quite comfortably.

Deportations are not like going off on a journey. No regard or importance should be given to complaints and cries of agony and distress. The necessary communications have been sent from the provincial government to the office of the County Executive. You should invest great effort [in this enterprise]."

(11) [11]

Even though a cipher cable arrived from the [Interior] Ministry ordering that the families of Leon Amiralyan, Toros Çağlasyan [Tchaglassian], Dişçekenyan [Dishchekenian], Hezarebenyan, and Çorbacıyan [Chorbajian] were to remain and resettle in Aleppo, the provinc[ial government] deported these families, some of whose members perished on the route.

Hamam, which is in the environs of Rakka, was an inferno of death and debasement. The women and children suffered the greatest from deprivation and loss. The dossier of official papers containing what was known about this situation was in the hands of the Assistant Director-General Abdülehad Nuri Bey. Hakkı Bey compounded this disaster. He had ordered the mass killing of several hundred of the orphans who had survived the deportations. He appointed a dishonorable man from Rumelia by the name of "Resul" and put him in charge of these affairs. This person had accumulated all of the immoral behaviors in the world and had been dismissed from the police. He developed a love for killing, and it became for him a sacred practice.

(12) [12]

Even so, it must not be forgotten that there were almost no Turks among those who served in this capacity and carried out [these] acts of cruelty and oppression. They consisted of other peoples, such as Rumelians, Circassians, and Chechens.

Four months earlier in Rumkale the following event happened. An honorable and chaste girl from Sivas, by the name of Binnaz, had for three years been resisting her continual violation by government officials and the other [members of the] population. For the sake of her own honor she never implicated anyone. Finally, the newly arrived county executive (*kaymakam*) tried to breach the girl's "fortress of virtue." The girl, who understood that she would not be able to withstand it, fled. She made it

to Behisni. In response, the county executive sent a detachment of eight
soldiers after her. He also wrote a message to his fellow kaymakam in
Behisni, accusing the girl of theft. They carted the poor lass back and
brought her to him.

(1) [13]

Copy of a message written by the Provincial Governor of Aleppo to the
Interior Ministry against Ali Suat Bey, the District Governor of [Deyr-i]
Zor:
It has been understood from the report by Assistant Director-General
of Immigrant [and Refugee Resettlement] Abdülahad Nuri Bey, who
recently went to Ras-ul-Ayn in order to investigate, that the Armenians
who were sent there had been left there until now and already resettled
there, and it has been shown by the District Governor of [Deyr-i] Zor, Ali
Suat Bey, that these persons were intentionally detained there. [There has
been seen a] concentration of thousands of Armenians coming to and
remaining in a small but strategically important county as Ras-ul-Ayn.
There has been a failure to deport them, based on such pretexts as "we
don't have the means." Despite the string of messages repeating that
th[ose who failed to do so] would bear the responsibility [therefore],
these do not appear to have produced any results.
The forementioned's [sense of] ownership and protection extended
over these [hapless Armenians] was surprisingly extensive, so much so
that, according to reports, he [Ali Suat] would personally clean and feed
the children and mourn the calamities that befell their parents. The
Armenians who were sent there attained in this way a different manner of
well-being in their lives, so that they [felt themselves] indebted to Ali Suat
Bey for this turn of events. Since the prolongation of this situation would
necessarily result in a delay in the[ir] deportation from Aleppo, it is in your
excellence's purview to see that that which is necessary be done.
(5 January 1916)
Governor
Mustafa Abdülhalik
Cipher [cable] written by the Interior Ministry and sent to the Office
of the Provincial Governor of Aleppo on 28 January 1917:
It has been learned that the children of [certain] known individuals
(*eşhası malume*) have been accepted into the orphanages that have been
opened in various places. Since the state cannot imagine anything but

harm to come from [allowing] these [children] to live, anyone trying to work toward the provisioning, sustaining of or feeling sorry for [children] such as these, whether out of the inability to grasp the [gravity of the] situation, in the hope of putting their helplessness on display, or of downplaying [the seriousness of the situation], they are ultimately engaged [in efforts]

(2) [14]

Contrary to the clear wishes of the government. It is hereby communicated that no effort is to be expended either for the acceptance of small children like these into orphanages, or for the establishment of other orphanages.
Interior Minister
Talat
Copy of the cipher cable sent by the Interior Ministry to the Office of the Provincial Governor of Aleppo on 14 December 1915:
The most important persons whose extermination should be attempted are the religious clergy. It would be an utmost mistake to give them permission to travel and settle into the hazardous areas like Syria and Jerusalem. The best place of settlement for these individuals, whose character is prone to conspire maliciously against the government, is the place in which they will be exterminated. The carrying out of such treatment toward them is suggested.
Interior Minister
Talat
Copy of the cipher cable from the Interior Ministry to the Office of the Provincial Governor of Aleppo on 4 March 1916:[5]
The need shown by the army commanders for the artisans and craftsmen among [those groups of] certain known individuals to be employed in military service [has been] thought through in detail, since they cannot be allowed to remain in cities, as they are liable to be sent to military areas, and since it is allowed for them to be used on road construction and outside [such areas] so long as their families are not ordered to be included in the general deportations, and since special instructions have been sent by the Interior Ministry to the various army commands in this regard, they are to be treated according to the aforementioned instructions, as [previously] communicated.
Interior Minister

(3) [15]

Copy of the cipher cable sent by the Interior Ministry to the Office of the District Governor of Urfa on 21 September 1915:

There is no need for such an orphanage. Now is not the time for expending one's time [and energy] on the provisioning and preserving of the [orphans'] lives out of some sensitivity [to their plight]. We eagerly await [your] reporting on their deportation.

Interior Minister

Copy of the secret communication written by the Interior Ministry to the Provincial Government of Aleppo on 22 October 1915:

For the Armenians, their rights on Turkish soil, such as the rights to live and work, have been eliminated, and not one is to be left—not even the infant in the cradle; the government accepts all responsibility for this [situation], and effective measures [in line with this order] have already been seen in some provinces. Despite this decision, some persons have, for reasons of secrecy, temporarily been receiving exceptional treatment and are not being sent directly to their [final] places of resettlement; they are instead left free to wander around Aleppo and the government is thus now left facing a second difficulty.

As the result of ignorance, material interests will naturally win out over patriotic sentiment. The people, who will never understand the government's overall policy in this regard, must absolutely be prevented from protecting these persons or saving their lives.

(4) [16]

In regard to the expulsion of these persons, no excuse or exception whatsoever is to be accepted, whether for women, children, or persons who cannot stand or walk. You must not waste time: work with all your soul and being, since the force and speed (*şiddet ve hız*) that will be shown [by you] [and] the elimination [of such persons] by virtue of travel hardships and life-threatening deprivations that has been accomplished in other places through intermediaries will be able to be realized there without [such] intermediaries.

The Ministry of War has issued the general order to the army commanders, [informing them] that Offices of Logistical Support should not interfere in deportation matters. Notify the officials who are engaged in this service that they need not concern themselves with [the question of] responsibility but need to strive to attain the true aim [of the operation].

Please be so kind as to inform by cipher every week on the results of [your] efforts.

Interior Minister

Talat

Copy of the cipher cable from the Interior Ministry to the Office of the Provincial Governor of Aleppo, dated 16 February 1917:

The delegation under the leadership of Mustafa Nail Bey, which was sent to Urfa entrusted with conducting an investigation into the revolutionary ideas and efforts of certain known individuals and with producing the necessary documents, is, after

(5) [17]

having completed its duties, also to investigate [similar incidents] in the areas of Antep and Kilis, which are attached to your province; [please] communicate secretly to the necessary parties the need to facilitate and widen its [i.e., the committee's] efforts.

Interior Minister

Talat

The book about the Armenians which was published later, would be the product of this delegation's completed duties.[6]

Copy of the cipher cable sent by Zeki, the District Governor of [Deyr-i] Zor to the Office of the Provincial Governor of Aleppo, dated 13 August 1916:

I received from the [Interior] Ministry the order, that in the wake of the lightening up of the deportations from Aleppo, the area of settlement of those currently here is to be changed. In light of this fact, please report on how much longer the deportations will continue.

District Governor

Zeki

Copy of the cipher cable written and sent by the Office of the Provincial Governor of Aleppo to the Office of the District Governor of Antep on 24 January 1917.

Do not allow any of the Armenians from the population of Sivas or Mamuretülaziz, who are understood to currently be within your province, to congregate or gather there; rather, handle them within the framework of the familiar and previously communicated guidelines and then report back on the results.

Governor

(6) [18]

This cable was given for those who were killing the Armenians found in those areas. The phrase "[handling them] with familiar and previously communicated guidelines" implies that they were to be killed. Seven days later the following message from the Antep District Governor was received in connection with communication of the head official of the aforementioned county.

24 January 1917
To the Office of the Provincial Governor of Aleppo

From the message of the head official of the aforementioned county it has been understood that certain known persons, who are more than 500 in number (the majority women and children) and who are from those coming from the aforementioned province, are understood to have settled within the province only in Rumkale; they have been sent off (accompanied by Kurdish guards within the framework of the familiar and previously communicated guidelines for dealing with them so that they might not return here again).

What is being said here is that the 500-odd Armenians, mostly women and children, were killed in compliance with orders. From the phrases "in order that they not return again" and "accompanied by Kurdish guards" shows that they were killed.

(7) [19]

Copy of the cipher cable written and sent by the Assistant Director-General of Immigrant [and Refugee Resettlement] to the Director-General of Tribal and Immigrant Resettlement (*İskân-ı Aşâir ve Muhacirîn Müdüriyet-i Umumiyesi*) on 26 February 1916:[7]

With the exception of those who have arrived in Syria as artisans and craftsmen, only one quarter the Armenians who have been deported up to this point may have reached the areas of resettlement; the rest have perished en route from natural causes. The necessary measures are liable to be taken in order to speed up the deportation of those who, for a variety of reasons, have been removed from Aleppo.

What can be understood from this message is the following reality: the orders and wishes of the central government, which is to say of Talat

Pasha, were being carried out: the Armenians were either dying or being killed. Information about this was being provided on an official level.

(1) [20]

Although the intent has long existed to eliminate the [empire's] Armenian subjects, who have for centuries longed to undermine the sound foundations of the state and posed a serious threat for the government, the [suitable] conditions [to do so] did not exist, and it was therefore not possible to realize this sacred aim. Since all obstacles [to this course of action] have now been removed, and the time has come to rescue the homeland from this dangerous element, it is necessary to work, both consciously and with full commitment, and without giving in to feelings of mercy and compassion, to blot out the name "Armenian" in Turkey by putting a complete end to their existence; also great care should be taken that the officials who are to be employed in this enterprise be persons of the greatest honor and decency who will be able to achieve this aim.

Interior Minister

This is a copy of a telegram; it was [found] among the secret papers of the Assistant Director-General. There are no indications as to when it arrived or to whom it was written.

3/691
To the Office of the Provincial Governor of Aleppo

The Armenians of the Eastern Provinces who come into your hands there are to be eliminated by secret measures.

5 December 1915.
Interior Minister
Talat

(2) [21]

Upon the receipt of this message, the investigations are to be immediately carried out by the police department, and [persons] such as these were included under guard in the general deportations, during which each one was ordered eliminated.

To the Office of the Provincial Governor of Aleppo
723

The Armenians who were earlier settled in the area around Aleppo are to be sent to the areas of resettlement without a second's delay [after which please] report on the [outcome of the] operation.
16 December 1915.
Interior Minister
Talat
After Aleppo became an area of resettlement at the beginning of the deportations, a great many deportees were settled in the surrounding villages, and these poor deportees began to work in the areas in which they had been settled with the hope that they had already been spared [the worst]. Upon reception of this telegram, both mounted and foot gendarmes were sent out to the countryside, rousting a thousand-odd persons who were expelled from the[se] villages, of which a great many were liquidated.

(3) [22]

To the Office of the Provincial Governor of Aleppo
745

Since it is being reported that a number of Armenian reporters have been traveling in those parts, photographing and collecting documentation of a number of calamities [occurring there] and then handing them over to the American consul there, harmful persons such as these are to be arrested and liquidated.
24 December 1915
Interior Minister
Talat
Civil servants were nevertheless employed for tasks such as this. There was even a permanent employee around the American Consulate whose job it was to conduct such surveillance.
It was reported that one of the writers for the daily Zhamanag, or possibly some other paper, was seen there one day. The importance of investigating th[ese incidents] cannot be overemphasized. In the end, they were not apprehended.

To the Office of the Provincial Governor of Aleppo
762
C. 15 December 1915

Those Armenians who wish to convert to Islam with the aim of avoiding the general deportations are to be told that they will need to convert within the areas of resettlement.
30 December 1915
Interior Minister
Talat

(4) [23]

In the period when the deportations gained force and when every day reports arrived of thousands dying, some poor souls appealed [to the authorities to convert to Islam], saying "perhaps if we become Muslims we will be saved."
The conversion to Islam of one or two was accepted. When the requests to convert continued, requests were made to the ministry for permission [to allow such conversions]. This [above] reply arrived.

To the Office of the Provincial Governor of Aleppo:
801

It has been decided that the Armenians employed in all institutions, railroad operation and construction are also to be deported to the areas of resettlement and the instructions on how to carry this out have been sent from the Ministry of War to the army commanders. [Please] report [back] on the results.
8 February 1916.
Interior Minister
Talat
The majority of employees working both in the [rail] construction and operation companies are Armenians. The government gave an order out of fear that they might somehow commit treason. In response [to this order], the rail commissioner was asked for a list of [Armenian employees'] names. In this matter, both Hayri Bey, the Commissioner of Rail Lines, and Cemal Pasha showed great humanity. Nevertheless, the injustice of Talat Pasha must be admitted. Even though all of the railroad employees were Armenian,

(5) [24]

and despite the fact that the Armenians were subjected to this much oppression and cruelty, during the entire four or five year general mobilization, these persons never did anything but work in a completely faithful manner; not a single incident was reported on or near the rail lines.

To the Office of the Provincial Governor of Aleppo
809

Since foreign [military] officers have seen and photographed the bodies of certain known persons that have accumulated in great numbers all along the routes, you are being exhorted with great urgency that these [corpses] not be left unburied and out in the open.
11 January 1916
Interior Minister
Talat
Some seven or eight hundred Armenians died every day [at this point] from disaster, destitution, and disease. They were buried in the mud, their remains scattered by the carrion fowl [that feasted on them]; it was a state of affairs that seared the human conscience. The German and Austrian officers [serving with the Ottoman forces] would see these sights and send back written reports to their own countries. Talat Pasha heard reports of this and wished to hide his crimes under a shovelful of dirt, to bury them, but even by moving heaven and earth, these bitter calamities could not be hidden from memory or caused to be forgotten.

(6) [25]

This unconscionable sights tore not only at the heartstrings of Christians, but those of Muslims, too.

To the Office of the Provincial Governor of Aleppo
820

It is being communicated to all parties that the Armenians who subsequently arrive from the North are to be sent directly to the places of resettlement by bypassing and without entering any villages, towns, and cities.
17 January 1917.

Interior Minister

Talat

The aim of this telegram was [to ensure that the Armenian deportees] would remain on the roads and expire there, being unable to endure the hardships of the journey because they would be forcibly subjected to hunger and destitution, whereas, if they were to pass through villages or cities they would be shown a bit of mercy and comfort and thereby secure some assistance.

(7) [26]

To the Office of the Provincial Governor of Aleppo

830

The orphaned children of certain known persons who were not in a state to able to recall the calamities [to befall] their parents are to rounded up and given provisions and the remainder to be attached to and included in the deportation convoys.

(25 January 1917)

Interior Ministry

Talat

I don't think it is necessary to give a lengthy explanation in this regard; the content of the telegram itself is very clear. Children who couldn't remember the disasters to befall their parents [would be] of two, three, and four years. Which is to say, that all children above four years of age were being sentenced to death. And that was indeed their fate. What happened to the orphans who were put in the orphanage opened up in Meskene? They all died; they were killed.

(8) [27]

To the Office of the Provincial Governor of Aleppo

840

It was understood that there were some forty to fifty thousand Armenians— the majority of them widowed women and parent-less children—living along the rail lines, from the camps at Intilli and Ayıran all the way to Aleppo.

Since the most severe punishment will be incurred by those who have caused such a concentration of poverty and destitution on the army's most important lines of communication and transportation, it is expected that, after informing [and communicating with] the Provincial Governor of Adana, [these destitute Armenians] be quickly deported to the areas of resettlement without passing through Aleppo. The results [of this operation] are to be reported back within one week. 29 January 1917.

Interior Minister

Talat

As he himself admits, what else was this group of poor souls—a group consisting mostly women and children without guardians or parents—capable of doing? And they remained there for months. What sort of activities [of these individuals] were witnessed anyway? Can one really be afraid of the presence of a few miserable souls pleading for [someone to show them] the slightest human kindness? No, there was no trace of fear in [Talat and the CUP]; they had no other thought than to besmirch the history of the Turks [in a way that would] taint their honorable future.

(9) [28]

and to struggle to wipe out every trace of the Armenians.

To the Office of the Provincial Governor of Aleppo
845

This is the addendum to telegram number 840, dated 29 January 1917.

Although it was seen as impossible to deport the Armenians left in the camps at Intilli and Ayıran and employed in construction until the work was concluded, it is nevertheless inappropriate to allow their families to remain there; they [families] are instead to be temporarily resettled in the townships and villages surrounding Aleppo and the remaining women and children who have no guardians or family are to be deported per the previous instructions.

(10) [29]

The families of a great many of these persons had been brought to Aleppo in a series of deportation convoys. They were [originally] to be resettled in the villages. Their names were recorded, registries were created, and the poor wretches were given cause to hope. But the hope was a vain one. On one side, the police expel them from the area; they submit official requests and petitions [to remain], and the[officials act as if] the petitions are being taken seriously. They go to a couple different departments, and days pass. But there is never any need to process the petitions, because within a few days those submitting them find themselves in the jaws of horror and barbarities in Meskene. These poor, bereft women and girls fall victim to the lustful desires of the local population or the gendarmes.

Their husbands, their fathers, and their brothers all labor in the service of the military, [they work] together with us for the good of the nation, while here these men's daughters and their brides are defiled and killed.

(11) [30]

After the ministry said "Settle the families of such persons in the area around Aleppo," an order came by telegraph withdrawing that order.

860
To the Office of the Provincial Governor of Aleppo

C. [answer to] 9 February 1917. [Persons] such as these are to be immediately sent off and deported to the areas of resettlement with the assurance that their male relatives will join them [there] later.
15 February 1917.
Interior Minister
Talat
How very strange. There was no need here to ask permission, to wonder whether such families would go or remain, because the [Interior] Ministry had already ordered that such persons were to be resettled in the townships and villages around Aleppo.

Afterward, the ministry's ignorance of their own decision by giving the order to deport them shows that any remaining compassion within the government toward the Armenians

(12) [31]

had disappeared.

To the Office of the Provincial Governor of Aleppo:
853

While there are thousands of orphans and widows among the refugees and fallen Muslim soldiers in need of protection and support, there is no need to unnecessarily expend resources for some of the abandoned or bereft children of certain known persons who will in the future only create more damage and problems [for the state]. Such persons are to be removed by attaching them to the deportation convoys and those who have been provided for up to now are to be sent to Sivas in accordance with the most recent communication.

5 February 1917
Interior Minister
Talat

What an appalling level of cruelty. It looks very much as if they are snatching the last piece of bread from the mouths of a collection of poor innocent souls, whose only crime was to be born Armenian. They are being denied the very right to exist.

(13) [32]

At that time there was a German woman, a humanitarian—I think her name was Hoch—who gathered, herself and with the help of others, one or two hundred innocent infants; she urged the government to care for these orphans. Such compassion angered the provincial governor, and infuriated the Deportation Office. But nobody said anything publicly.

This merciful and compassionate woman showed these children the tender mercies that a mother would show; she wanted them to live.

The government created a ruse in response to this. "These orphans will be brought together in Sivas," they said. "There, a large orphanage will be opened and they will be taken care of." The aim was actually to murder these poor things en route. I was the one who was ordered to send them off and to run the whole thing. The children would arrive in Ereğli by train, accompanied by a special official, and from there they would be sent by wagon to Sivas. I was to be stationed in Ereğli. At that time the allocated funds for the Office of Immigrant [and Refugee Settlement] had been exhausted. New funding was expected

(14) [33]

but it was delayed, so the whole operation came to naught. Seven or eight months later, these children were somehow sent to Istanbul. If there had been even a hint of Muslim religious sentiment in Talat Pasha, the person who gave this order, it was not capable of separating good from evil, and he would not have worked to kill these bereft and parentless souls, poor creatures whose parents were subjected to beatings and oppression and who had become orphans as a result of his orders and his cruelty. How will humanity remember this handful of oppressive tyrants who have tarnished the history of a great nation?

To the Office of the Provincial Governor of Aleppo
745

Even though there is no harm in accepting the telegrams containing the complaints of certain known persons, there is no need to actually [devote time and energy] to [follow up] inquiries and investigations that would simply be a waste of time; [instead,] inform the complainants that they should seek their rights in the new places of resettlement.
22 January 1917.
Interior Minister
Talat

(15) [34]

The reason for this cipher telegram is as follows:
Telegram messages of complaint arrived at the offices of the provincial governor and of the Office of Immigrant [and Refugee Resettlement] from a number of different places. A secret memo was written and sent to the Provincial Governor and Directorate of Post and Telegraphs in Aleppo instructing them not to accept such cables.
It seems that the director-general had written to the Ministry of Posts and Telegraphs, and the ministry had in turn appealed to Talat Pasha. So what would be the great harm in accepting them? State revenues would increase [due to the charges for the telegrams], but no importance was to be given to this, because [at that point] the Armenians had no more rights within this country, even their right to life had been revoked. [In any case,] what possible effect could the complaints of those sentenced to death have? These plaints were like voices from the grave. The government was terrified of these voices, however; it was hard for them to listen to them; they were unable to do so.

(16) [35]

In short, there wasn't a soul who would not weep before these unconscionable crimes.

Translated by Paul Bessemer

APPENDIX A.2: THE PASSAGES OF NAIM EFENDI'S MEMOIRS AS THEY WERE PUBLISHED BY ARAM ANDONIAN

In this section are the missing Ottoman-Turkish original pages of Naim Efendi's memoirs as they were published by Aram Andonian. In order to keep the flow of the text, we kept some passages that we already have in the Ottoman-Turkish original and Aram Andonian's explanatory statements. Naim's text is in normal font; Andonian's explanations are in italic. Words made bold in parentheses are additions to Naim's words by Andonian for explanatory purposes. If not explicitly written otherwise, all the footnotes in the text are from Andonian. Chapter numbers are also taken from Andonian's book, so that the reader can compare these with the Armenian text. We took the liberty of not including some of Andonian's footnotes, because in those he was referring to some other pages in his book, which cannot make any sense here.

Chapter One
Naim Bey's recollections begin during the days of the preparations for the Ras-ul-Ayn massacre. Ras-ul-Ayn is a small station of Chechens established in the ruins of the former empire of Mesopotamia, with barely fifty houses. It used to be one of the unimportant places subject to the government of Zor, but thanks to its being located on the Baghdad railway line, it suddenly attained great importance, and the kaymakam [district governor], who previously was located in the nearby Chechen village of Sefa, was transferred there. During the period recalled by Naim Bey, the kaymakam was Yusuf Ziya Bey, who could not carry out the orders for massacre given to him, and was removed from office.
Now, I will let Naim Bey speak.
I think that the issue of the tragic deportation and murder of the Armenians, which makes the name Turk worthy of the perpetual curse of mankind, does not resemble any of the horrible incidents recorded in

world history until today. No matter which corner of the vast territories of Turkey is searched, no matter what darkest cavity is probed, thousands of the corpses and skeletons of thousands of Armenians slaughtered in the most merciless manner will be found.

I still was not occupied with the work of dispatching deportees; I was the secretary of the Regie in Ras-ul-Ayn. Opposite the village, I saw a caravan of the misfortunate, composed of hundreds of women and children cast about at the edge of the river. Every day, in the morning, coming to the village they begged. Some of them also carried water, and they tried to live on this bit of bread which they succeeded in obtaining.

It was still summer. They were able to take shelter in the rocks and valleys, or in the cracks of a pile of earth. However, when winter came, throughout the profound silence of the night the groans of those dying from the cold and hunger were heard. The Chechen people of the village heard them, but those rattles of agony did not trouble anyone's conscience or soul.

I will never forget that night. I was at the home of the *kaymakam* [county executive—TA]. A storm was wreaking ruin outside. Ten minutes later, we heard the laments and groans of those poor people remaining in fear of the storm. The *kaymakam*, Yusuf Ziya Bey, was a very decent and conscientious man. Together we got up and went to the house of an "agha," and applying to several other places we obtained two or three tents. Those tents were put up through the cooperation of 10–15 gendarmes and the people so that these misfortunate ones would have at least some shelter. Their death was a tragic thing, but it turned into an infinitely more troubling scene when dogs tore apart their corpses.

They were the poor Armenian deportees and remnants of Sivas, Diyarbekir and Kharpert [Harput]. The population of approximately one million of five or six provinces was being deported. By the time they arrived at their place of exile, barely 100–150 women and boys remained out of each caravan, which proved that they were being massacred while being brought.

While Naim Bey was at Ras-ul-Ayn, the deportees in the hundreds of thousands who had been sent out from the surroundings of Constantinople and Cilicia had not yet arrived there. A little later they would accumulate there, some by railway, some on foot, and the order for their mass slaughter soon would arrive.

Nayim Bey continued.

I arrived in Aleppo. Fate arranged it so that I was appointed to office as chief secretary to Abdülahad Nuri Bey, who arrived only three or four days ago as assistant to the general director of deportations.

While I was in Ras-ul-Ayn, though I saw them with my own eyes, I did not understand the goal of those crimes. I was able to understand their nature and spirit afterwards. As I registered the secret cipher writings that arrived, I would shiver. A great nation, with its women and children, was condemned to death. I began to understand that the matter was not a simple drama [but] would turn into a more terrible thing already when the decision of the Council of State that the subdistricts of Maara, Bab and others of Aleppo were delineated as places of residence for the deported Armenians was changed, and orders were given with the meaning that "the place of habitation for the Armenians is the area of the Khabur River" (near Der Zor).

In order to understand this last paragraph of Naim Bey, it is necessary to know that the great multitude from the areas of Constantinople, the Anatolian railway line, and Cilicia previously had succeeded in establishing themselves in Aleppo and towns in the same province such as Ayaz, Kilis, Bab, Maara and Munbuj. I do not know if a decision of the Council of State was really issued on this. But whatever the case may be, those deport-ees who, generally, through large bribes, had succeeded in remaining in the aforementioned places, would quickly be removed and sent down, in part to Ras-ul-Ayn and in part to Der Zor, to be massacred. Truly, there was no definite place of exile for the deportees. They were constantly being pushed from one place to another without any break. It sufficed that they were walking, and through walking, being wiped out.

....

One day, Naim Bey continued, the Ministry of Internal Affairs sent the following cipher telegram:

"The reason for the sending of the known individuals is the securing of the future prosperity of the homeland, because they, wherever they are settled, will not refrain again from their accursed ideas; it is necessary to work so that their numbers decrease as much as possible."[8]

This telegram arrived in November in the year of 1915. Eight days later, without being annotated by the governor-general, it was given to Abdülahad Nuri Bey. That very evening, at 11:30 (Turkish time), Deportees Director Eyub Bey and Gendarmerie Commander Emin Bey rushed to the office to Abdülahad Bey. Nuri Bey immediately communicated to them the telegraph which had been received, and they met for approximately one hour. The topic of their discussion was the method of extermination of the Armenians. Eyub Bey was in favor of overt fearless destruction. However, Abdülahad Nuri Bey, who was a very cunning man, rejected that idea. In his opinion, it was best to subject the Armenian deportees to deprivation and the severity of the winter and kill them in this way, which, in the future, would serve to defend and strengthen the thesis that they died a natural death. By being assembled at one point, 10,000–15,000 Armenian deportees would of course quickly be subject to deprivation, hunger and sickness. Later, when they would suddenly deport them, in order to push them forward, naturally the people would not be able to obtain means of transportation; they would be forced to walk, and they would fall along the lengths of the road. In the end, his idea won.

Until that time, in Aleppo, gendarmes did not interfere in the affairs of the deportees. However the headquarters of the gendarmes began to cooperate with the police headquarters. Quickly, great activity began in Aleppo. The deportees crowded in Katma, in the area of Kilis, and around Aleppo were being sent bit by bit to Akterin and from there to Bab. Truly, it took place the way they thought. The news of hundreds of people dying daily from hunger, cold [and] sickness reached us. Eyub Bey went to Azaz. Upon his return, he came to the headquarters laughing. He related how he burned the tents. Bab was filled. Typhus burned everywhere, it stormed. The *kaymakam*, the officials sending deportees, each day sent reports of deaths. Death did not only strike the Armenians; it also massacred the native people.

One day I said to Abdülahad Nuri Bey:

"Bey Efendi, let us moderate the dispatch of the deportees a little, because death is threatening the whole of Mesopotamia; at this rate, no one will remain on this vast territory besides demons [tev's]. The *kaymakam* of Ras-ul-Ayn is directing plaintive questions about this."

Nuri Bey laughed.

"My son," he said. "In this way we will destroy two injurious elements at the same time. Is it not the Arabs who are dying with the Armenians? Is this bad? The future path of Turkdom is being leveled."

I fell silent. This terrible answer made me shudder.

* * *

What encouraged this man, so that he without fear and boldly could pursue the implementation of such a merciless and devilish plan? Much can be said about this. However, the copy of an order, which was found among the secret papers of the General Directorship of Deportees, alone suffices to explain that fearless boldness with which Nuri Bey carried out the task entrusted to him—the work of the general annihilation of the Armenians. Here is that order.

> "Although the intent has long existed to eliminate the [empire's] Armenian subjects, who have for centuries longed to undermine the sound foundations of the state and posed a serious threat for the government, the [suitable] conditions [to do so] did not exist, and it was therefore not possible to realize this sacred aim. Since all obstacles [to this course of action] have now been removed, and the time has come to rescue the homeland from this dangerous element, it is necessary to work, both consciously and with full commitment, and without giving in to feelings of mercy and compassion, to blot out the name "Armenian" in Turkey by putting a complete end to their existence; also great care should be taken that the officials who are to be employed in this enterprise be persons of the greatest honor and decency who will be able to achieve this aim.
> Interior Minister"

This is the copy of a telegram; it was [found] among the secret papers of the Assistant Director-General. There are no indications as to when it arrived or to whom it was written.

....

Those frightful massacres and events on which Naim Bey's memoirs cast such a horrifying light took place especially after Mustafa Abdülhalik Bey was appointed governor-general of Aleppo.

At first, *continued Naim Bey*, there was a special committee in the General Directorate of Deportees of Aleppo, by means of which the dispatches of deportees took place (to the desert). As long as this work remained in the hands of that committee, the deportees were partially free of robbery and oppression. The government, understanding that the goal it pursued would not be realized in this fashion, made the governor-general (Bekir Sami Bey) resign and sent in his place Mustafa Abdülhalik [Renda] Bey, who had been won over to its goals. That man was an enemy of the Armenians, and attempted in the name of Turkishness to annihilate the Armenian nation. The orders he communicated to the General Directorate of Deportees were so severe that it is not explainable. Some Armenian members of the Ottoman parliament, probably through one thousand and one pleadings, obtained permission from the Interior Ministry for their families to stay in Aleppo. The Ministry sent instructions to him about them, but he hid those orders, and sent those families also to the desert. I know of 15–20 families whose residence in Aleppo was ordered, and whom he sent to the desert.

The government gave Abdülahad Nuri Bey as a coworker to this man, as the assistant Director General of Deportees. Nuri Bey was an extremely bright and by nature cruel man, and especially was filled with hostile feelings against the Armenians. [He was] an embodiment of refined cruelty. The calamity and misery of the Armenians, the reports of deaths following one another, filled him with joy to such an extent that he would become intoxicated to the degree of dancing. Because all this was the result of his commands. He would say, the government does not want them to live. He related that when he was appointed to this position, at the point when he was going to leave for Aleppo, the advisor to the Ministry of Internal Affairs advised him to meet once with Talat Pasha before leaving. Nuri Bey went to the Sublime Porte. There were several guests with the Pasha.

"When will you depart?", he asked.

Later, getting up from his place, he took him near the window and in a low voice, said,

"Of course you know what is the work that you will do. Henceforth I will not see those accursed ones (Armenians) living in Turkey."[9]

Cemal Pasha ordered that five or six Armenian families working in Intilli with their carts go to Damascus. The governor-general communicated this command to Nuri Bey, and added to it the following annotation. "Does the immense government which deports hundreds of thousands of Armenians need the two broken carts of several Armenians that these people, being separated from the general deportation (toward the desert), are sent to Damascus?" He was very nervous and very severe.[10]

Abdülahad Nuri Bey's chief associate was his immediate subordinate, Eyub Bey, at the same time a bloodthirsty and venal man. He always worked to kill, but especially to rob. After leaving the Deportees Directorate, having accumulated great wealth, he undertook transportation and commission work. This man, who became wealthy thanks to the enormous wealth he plundered from the Armenians, never did anything good for any Armenian. Money was his religion and conscience. He did not commit savageries against the Armenians in the name of a national ideal. By largely appropriating the sums allocated for the provisioning and transportation of the deportees for himself, he multiplied the hunger and misery of their entire people.[11]

Behold it is by means of the orders of these people, Aleppo governor-general Mustafa Abdülhalik Bey and assistant to the Deportees Directorate Abdülahad Nuri Bey, that all the work of the dispatch of the deportees began to be realized, and after they began work, the crimes succeeded one another.

A new and dreadful command, which came to Aleppo from the Ministry of Internal Affairs, gave them every liberty about this. And they already did not need this.

This is the copy of the secret communication written by the Interior Ministry to the Provincial Government of Aleppo on 22 October 1915:

For the Armenians, their rights on Turkish soil, such as the rights to live and work, have been eliminated, and not one is to be left—not even the infant in the cradle; the government accepts all responsibility for this and effective measures have already been seen in some provinces. Despite this decision, some persons have, for reasons of secrecy, temporarily been receiving exceptional treatment and are not being sent directly to their [final] places of resettlement; they are instead left free to wander around Aleppo and the government is thus now left facing a second difficulty.

As the result of ignorance, material interests will naturally win out over patriotic sentiment. The people, who will never understand the government's overall policy in this regard, must absolutely be prevented from protecting these persons or saving their lives.

In regard to the expulsion of these persons, no excuse or exception whatsoever is to be accepted, whether for women, children, or persons who cannot stand or walk. You must not waste time: work with all your soul and being, since the force and speed that will be shown [by you] [and] the elimination [of such persons] by virtue of travel hardships and life-threatening deprivations that has been accomplished in other places through intermediaries will be able to be realized there without [such] intermediaries.

The Ministry of War has issued the general order to the army commanders that Offices of Logistical Support should not to interfere in deportation matters. Notify the officials who are engaged in this service that they need not concern themselves with [the question of] responsibility but need to strive to attain the true aim [of the operation]. Please be so kind as to inform by cipher every week on the results of [your] efforts.

Interior Minister

Talat

When this order arrived, the General Directorate of Deportees of Aleppo, directly on command of the governor-general, had the authority to conduct all types of operations.

The purpose of leaving all operations of dispatch of deportees in the hands of one person was for the orders to be given for the carrying out of barbarities to remain secret as much as possible; many people should not know, and the crime is carried out in silence, without giving rise to rumors.

The ill-famed summit called Karlık, twenty minutes distant from Aleppo, was the general collection point for refugees. The deportees were sent from there to the desert. The lives of the Armenians there depended on the caprice of a gendarmerie corporal and a deportation official.

Already, for those who went a step further than Aleppo, no hope for life existed anymore. The entire line beginning at Karlık and extending to Der Zor had turned into a nest of misery, a cemetery. The trustworthy ones of the officials appointed to deport the refugees were ordered not to hold back from all types of savageries which cause death.

The following two telegrams prove this, both of which were sent by Minister of Internal Affairs Talat Bey.

The first telegram:

"To the Aleppo Governor-Generalship,

We hear that a group of officials has been handed over to the court martial, under the accusation of having committed severities and oppression against known persons (**Armenians**). This, no matter how much it is a formality, again may be able to decrease the daring of similar officials. For this reason, I command that such investigations not be allowed.[12]

Minister of Internal Affairs

Talat"

The second telegram:

"To the Aleppo Governor-Generalship,

The consideration of complaints and lawsuits raised by known persons (**Armenians**) about all types of personal matters not only will be the cause of delay of their dispatch (to the desert) but will open the way for operations

which probably in the future can give rise to political inconveniences. For
this reason, those appeals must not be taken into consideration, and instructions to this effect are be given to relevant officials.
   Minister of Internal Affairs
   Talat"

Because sometimes letters of protest addressed to the governor-
generalship and the Directorate of Deportees against various officials
would arrive, another telegram of the minister of internal affairs recommended that this type of protest letter be accepted but not be taken into
consideration. This telegram became the cause of a secret command from
the Aleppo governor-generalship to the postal administration of the same
city, which prohibited the acceptance of such protest letters from Armenian
deportees. It appears that the director of the Aleppo postal administration
asked a question about this to Constantinople, to the Postal Ministry, and
it was upon the request made by the latter that the Ministry of Internal
Affairs had sent that telegram.
   When an unfortunate, whose family and children were slaughtered on
the roads, his daughter taken forcibly from him, [and] his honor stained,
would come to a town and want to reveal his lamentable state by means of
a telegram and seek help, the telegraph officials would reproach him for
wanting to give a telegram written in such a manner.
   But these were henceforth the protests of those condemned to death;
they were like voices emanating from the grave. The government was
afraid of those voices. Listening to them was a torment for it. It did not
want to listen.

Chapter Two
Naim Bey writes:
When the dispatch of deportees was being conducted toward Ras-ul-
Ayn, *kaymakam* Yusuf Ziya Bey informed that henceforth no room
remains to place Armenians in Ras-ul-Ayn, that every day 5–600 deportees die, [and] that they cannot find time to either send the living further
down, nor to bury the dead. Yusuf Ziya Bey begged that the dispatch of
deportees to Ras-ul-Ayn be halted henceforth.
   He was answered in the following manner: Speed up the dispatches; in
that case, those who are not in a condition to leave will fall and die several
hours distant from the city, and the district [kaza] will be freed of both
those who live and the dead.

It is understood from the last reports of the local deportation official and the *kaymakam* that during the course of four months, 13,000–14,000 Armenians died from hunger and sickness.

...At all times order after order would arrive. Abdülahad Nuri Bey would send the most severe orders to the deportation official of Ras-ul-Ayn, but these too would not be carried out.

But it is better that Naim Bey himself relate those incidents.

The orders sent from Aleppo to the deportation official, *he wrote in his memoirs*, were not executed. By troubling Adil Bey, the deportation official, Abdülahad Nuri Bey understood that the one opposing sending the Armenians found there to the desert was the governor of Der Zor himself, Suad Bey.

Nuri Bey, upon returning to Aleppo, reported the truth to Governor-General Abdülhalik Bey, who immediately ordered Ali Suad Bey in a cipher: "Allowing thousands of Armenians in Ras-ul-Ayn is an instance of disagreement with the sacred goal of the government: Expel them from that place!"

Ali Suad Bey replied: "The means of transportation do not exist so that I could deport the people. If the goal being pursued is to kill them, I can neither do it, nor make it done."

Mustafa Abdülhalik Bey sent this telegram to Constantinople, to the Ministry of Internal Affairs, appending to it the following report about Ali Suad Bey.[13]

....

The new kaymakam of Ras-ul-Ayn turned into a wonderful tool in the hands of the hyenas of Aleppo, in front of whom the field remained completely open because they also succeeded in making Ali Suad Bey, the governor of Der Zor, resign. On March 17, Kerim Refi Bey began the deportation. This task was entrusted to the Chechens, at whose head was the director of the town quarter of Ras-ul-Ayn, Arslan Bey, and about whom Naim Bey wrote the following in his memoirs.

A bandit gang was formed from the Chechens of Ras-ul-Ayn, supposedly to keep the deportees of that place free from attack during travel. This bandit group was given arms. These men bearing the name of guardian had the job, however, of robbing [and] killing the deportees on the road.

The order for the tragic event of Ras-ul-Ayn was given directly from Aleppo. This command was given to the chiefs of that bandit group. Several of them came to Aleppo and met with Governor-General Mustafa Abdülhalik Bey.[14] Four or five days after their return, the *kaymakam* of

Ras-ul-Ayn (Kerim Refi Bey) informed through a cipher that they arrived and accepted the instructions.

The massacres practically followed the deportations because they were carried out in places that were quite close, primarily on the shores of Cırcıb and on the road descending towards Shedaddiye. The Armenians, being removed group by group, were killed in the most brutal fashion. Sometimes people from among them succeeded in escaping; they would come to Ras-ul-Ayn—it was not possible to go anywhere else—[and] they would relate the terror. The awful heartrending emotions, the fright to which the poor defenseless people listening to those stories were subjected can only be imagined when they came to remove them with blows of whips, butts of rifles, canes and cudgels, and drive them toward those slaughterhouses.

...

...

Chapter Three

...

The government in the very beginning maintained a very cautious and circumspect conduct in the Armenian deportations. It still did not know what result the war would have. For this reason, it worked to save appearances, to veil the goal of a general massacre hidden under the pretext of deportation. However, when it gained security about victory, it no longer saw the need for this dissimulation, and sent outright orders for general annihilation. This is why the previously given command which permitted Armenian deportees to reside around Aleppo was annulled.[15]

However, as time passed, this severity lessened, and Armenians in large groups, by one thousand and one means, especially through bribery,[16] *established themselves in the towns of Bab, Maara, [and] Munbuj, and in the villages and fields in the areas of the latter. In addition, along the length of the Euphrates line up to Der Zor, the exiles were found in Meskene, Dipsi, Abuharrar, Hamam, Rakka, Sebka, Der Zor, and several other relatively less significant stations. It was this entire people who were going to be expelled, to be driven to Zor, and massacred, during the period that the Yıldırım Army was being organized.*

Naim Bey:

When the order arrived to drive out the Armenians who were previously settled in the villages in the areas around Maara, Bab and Aleppo, *Naim Bey wrote,* orders were given to the *kaymakams* that were merciless to such a degree that it was not possible to suppress tears while reading them.

An order was given from Aleppo to the gendarmes that they work on the roads, leaving them hungry and thirsty, to decrease the numbers of the deportees as much as possible.

On January 20, 1916, Abdülahad Nuri Bey wrote to Muharrem Bey, deportation official of Bab:

The copy of secret communication number 344, dated 2 February 1917 and written by the Office of the Assistant Director General of Immigrant [and Refugee Affairs] to the Extraordinary Director of Deportations in Bab Muharrem Bey:

"I am confident that you will appreciate the confidence that the Governor's office has in you as well as the importance of the task that has been entrusted to you by the office on the basis of this confidence. You are not to allow a single Armenian [to remain] in Bab.

The force and determination that you will show in [undertaking] the deportations can well ensure the results that you have pursued. Only take care not to leave any bodies on the roads or in open areas. You should inform us about the maximum fee that will be given to the persons you employ for this purpose.

Do not occupy yourself with procuring means of transport; they can go by foot. The table listing those who have died that comes every week is not satisfactory. It is understood from this that these persons are living there quite comfortably.

Deportations are not like going off on a journey. No regard or importance should be given to complaints and cries of agony and distress. The necessary communications have been sent from the provincial government to the office of the county executive (*kaymakam*). You should invest great effort [in this enterprise].

Abdullahad Nuri"

This Muharrem Bey was the former police director of Baghdad, and the most bloodthirsty of the officials appointed for the deportation of exiles. The work entrusted to him was very important, and so that he would not act with tolerance as a consequence of greed, they would give him a monthly salary of 150 golds [gold coins]. This man carried out very large deportations. Alone he became the cause for thousands of Armenians to die on the roads in the most merciless fashion.

Abdülahad Nuri Bey gave to this cruel man as a collaborator a mounted gendarmerie captain, who brought with him to Bab the following new instruction.

"The severities carried out while emptying Bab kaza of Armenian exiles shall not be held to accountability.
Abdülahad Nuri"

This captain, taking with him 5–10 gendarmes, did not shirk from committing all sorts of crimes.

According to the latest order, all the exiles of Bab would be deported within 24 hours. They would leave in whatever fashion they wished. In any case, this deportation would conclude with their deaths. The winter season, naked from their heads to their toes, being sent out in this state, they fell and died at the side of the roads. From Bab to Meskene, along the length of the road, the fields became filled with the corpses of Armenians. Even a handful of soil did not cover their bodies. Learning that the corpses had been left in the open, the government panicked. Realizing that those corpses had been seen by foreigners, it ordered that they be buried. Spades and hoes were found. Gravediggers were appointed. In this fashion, supposedly the traces of criminal acts would be covered up.

The numbers of the dead would be communicated to Constantinople every fifteen days by cipher. This also demonstrates that the office of the Assistant of the General Directorate of Deportations was established with a completely criminal intent.

But despite this situation, Abdülahad Nuri Bey was not yet satisfied. The dispatch of the deportees was not being conducted with the speed he demanded.

...

...

They were days of true horror, referring to which Naim Bey wrote:
The government demanded that the life and honor of the Armenians be destroyed. Henceforth the right to live, the right to exist, did not remain for them. Talat Pasha wrote: "Those who want to secure the existence of the Armenians, who for centuries turn into an element of tribulation for Turkey and most recently are attempting to suffocate the entire Ottoman Empire in blood, must be punished as traitors to the homeland on a different pretext and the appropriate officials secretly must be informed."

In this part of his memoirs, Naim Bey has recorded a series of facts which show what type of situation those successive criminal instructions sent by the center [of the government] created for the Armenians. We reproduce only a few of those facts.

At a moment when typhus had become severe, *Naim Bey writes*, the dispatch of deportees in Aleppo intensified to such a degree that the police and gendarmes pulled them out of houses, dragging them this way and that, and tying them tightly with ropes as if they were pigs, they expelled the poor Armenians, with no refuge other than God, who out of fear of death had hidden. One day a poor unfortunate declared in a petition that his entire family in his home, becoming infected with typhus, was thrown into the street, placed in manure carts and sent outside the city to Karlık. The poor man was pleading, crying: he asked to be able to stay in the city at least 10 more days. The misfortunate did not know that he was condemned to death. No one would feel sorry for him. During my period in office, 10,000 petitions were given to our office by Armenian deportees. I did not see even ten of them being considered....

...

...

Someone named Asadur was denounced as suspect. They searched for him for a long time but did not find him. Finally, they arrested his brother, and sending him under guard, they killed the wretch, who was blameless, on the road. Thus, after becoming the witness of thousands of dramas like this in Aleppo, I was sent to Meskene as [a] deportation official. When I was leaving, Eyub Bey called me.

"Naim Bey," he said, "we saw no good from any of the deportation officials sent to Meskene. You found yourself in the matter; you are aware of the orders which came. See that you do not allow these people (the Armenians) to remain alive: if necessary, kill with your own hands. And killing them is a delight."

I went to Meskene. I learned of the crimes committed by a gendarmerie corporal in Abuharrar. I remained two months there. I only carried out a deportation of exiles once. The number of people I sent did not exceed thirty.

When I was still in Aleppo, the following telegram also arrived from Constantinople.

Copy of the cipher cable sent by the Interior Ministry to the Office of the Provincial Governor of Aleppo on 14 December 1915:

The most important persons whose extermination should be attempted are the religious clergy. It would be an utmost mistake to give them permission to travel and settle into the hazardous areas like Syria and Jerusalem.

The best place of settlement for these individuals, whose character is prone to conspire maliciously against the government, is the place in which they will be exterminated.[17] The carrying out of such treatment toward them is suggested.

Interior Minister
Talat

When I had gone to Meskene, the elderly prelate of Nicomedia [Izmit] was there. Retired under a small tent, he would pass the time meditating on his fate. He would tell those who would come to him that this calamity was from God, and he would advise everyone to refrain from committing any sin. It is not clear how this man, who was incapable of causing harm to anyone in the world, came to the attention of the deputy to the director general of deportations.

Eyub Bey sent word that there was a prelate of Nicomedia [Izmit] there; why are you keeping him? Send him; let him die in a corner of the road. I could not say that this should not be, or that I cannot do it. But we did not send him.[18]

One day, they had seized two married priests and sent them to Meskene. The order given about them was very strict. It simply said to kill [them]. I also did not send these two married priests forward; I kept them there. I cannot recall their names, but I think the two are both in Aleppo now.[19]

The station between Meskene and Abuharrar called Dipsi was one of the most important crime scenes. Those condemned to death were killed there and thrown into the river.[20] Meskene was filled with skeletons from one corner to the other; it simply took on the appearance of a field of bones.

Just from Aleppo alone, 200,000 Armenians were sent via Ras-ul-Ayn and Meskene, and of this huge quantity, barely 5000–6000 people managed to remain alive. Children were killed by being thrown into the Euphrates. Women on various roads were savagely and barbarically killed by gendarmes and the people with bayonets or firearms.

Chapter Four/2

After planning and commencing to carry out the massacres, the Turkish government applied all possible measures so that the civilized world would know nothing about the Armenian massacres. And every time that the occasion arose, it refuted with the most impudent lies the news which had spread about those massacres. But the American consuls in particular found the way to send information to their Constantinople embassy, which greatly troubled the

Turkish government.[21] *The following document is one of the evidences of that anxiety, which at the same time can become one of the greatest proofs of the policy of extermination cultivated by the government concerning the Armenians.*

Cipher telegram from the Ministry of Internal Affairs to the Aleppo governor-generalship:

"Certain information has been procured by the American consulates in various areas regarding the manner in which known individuals [Armenians] have been deported; we deduced that this procurement is being organized secretly from the memorandum we received from the American Embassy in Istanbul, which was acting on direct orders of its government. Even though we informed them in our response to this memo that the deportations are being carried out in an atmosphere of security and ease, this alone will never be sufficient to convince them. For this reason, during the deportation of people in cities, towns, or in areas close to [population] centers, you must practice caution and avoid drawing attention, in order to produce the belief among the foreigners wandering around in those parts that the purpose of the deportations is nothing other than the relocation. To achieve this, the temporary implementation of compassionate treatment is necessary for political reasons, and the usual measures (**massacres**) known to you should be implemented in the appropriate regions. Those persons surveilling the area for purposes of observation should be apprehended using other excuses and be delivered by other means to the courts-martial."

Minister of Internal Affairs, Talat, November 18 [December 1], 1915

Annotated Without speaking about the cipher telegram, meet with the police director. Do such investigators truly exist? In accordance with the order of the ministry, in these places let somewhat moderate operations be carried out.

To the Assistant to the Director General (of Deportees)
November 21, [1]915
Governor-General Mustafa Abdülhalik

I was sure of the existence of these kinds of people, and I had begged the police director several times to conduct the necessary follow-up, but it did no good. If the provincial government warns him effectively, perhaps a result will be secured. On this matter, it is for you to command.

21 November 1915

Assistant to the Director General
Abdülahad Nuri
You also were to write to deportation officials.

To the Assistant to the (Deportation) Director General
22 November 1915
Governor-General Mustafa Abdülhalik
Write to Naim Efendi
(Abdülahad Nuri)
It was written—dossier 741-16

The annotations show those operations which were conducted in connection with the cipher telegram.
The reproduction of the following cipher telegram, which relates to this matter, and was sent approximately one month earlier, also is found in Naim Bey's memoirs.

To the Office of the Provincial Governor of Aleppo
745

Since it is being reported that a number of Armenian reporters have been traveling in those parts, photographing and collecting documentation of a number of calamities [occurring there] and then handing them over to the American consul there,[22] harmful persons such as these are to be arrested and liquidated.
    24 December 1915
    Interior Minister
    Talat
    Naim Bey confirms that secret officials were already assigned for such pursuits; spies even were always found all around the American consulate. One day, the editor of Zhamanag, or another newspaper, was seen in Aleppo. His pursuit was given great importance, but in the end, he was not captured.
    ...
    ...

Chapter Four/3
Assistant to the General Director of Deportations in Aleppo, Abdülahad Nuri Bey, communicated information daily to Constantinople concerning all crimes, as was already recommended in several ministerial commands.

APPENDIX A 213

One of Nuri Bey's cipher telegrams notifies about the method with which they worked in Aleppo, and which carried out the desire of the central government in Constantinople.

No. 57
To the General Directorate of Settlement of Tribes and Deportees [Deportation Office—TA]

It is confirmed after investigation that barely ten out of one hundred of the Armenians subject to general deportation have reached their deportation sites, and the others have died on the road due to natural causes, such as hunger [and] sickness. It is notified that it should be attempted to achieve the same result by acting severely toward those who are still alive.

10 January [1]916
Assistant to the General Director
Abdülahad Nuri

...
We also reproduce here a cipher telegram of Abdülahad Nuri Bey which reveals a lot about this.

No. 76
To the General Directorate of Settlement of Tribes and Deportees

Response to the telegram of 3 March 1916
It is understood from the information received that up to the present, 35,000 in the area of Bab and Meskene, 10,000 in Aleppo's deportation site (Karlık), 20,000 in the area around Dipsi, Abuharrar and Hamam, [and] 35,000 in Ras-ul-Ayn, in all 95,000 Armenians, have died of various causes.
7 March [1]916, Assistant to the General Director
(Abdülahad Nuri)
...
Sometimes orders would arrive from Constantinople even about specific people, about whom information had been given to the government. The following cipher telegram of the office of the Assistant of the Aleppo General Directorate of Deportees shows what the instructions were that were given and in what manner they were carried out.

No. 51
To the General Directorate of Settlement of Tribes and Deportees

It was commanded again through the cipher telegram dated 9 September [1]915 and the eminent telegram bearing the date of 20 November [1]915 to arrest the individuals named Hapet Aramian, Garabed Antunian, [and] Arsen Shahbazian.[23] Being understood that they are found in Ras-ul-Ayn, we notify that, in accordance with the ministerial command, the required operation concerning them has been carried out by an official sent from this place, and the ministry has been informed about the occurrence by the governor-generalship [the provincial government].
13 December [1]915, Assistant to the General Director
(Abdülahad Nuri)
...

One of Abdülahad Nuri Bey's cipher telegrams described the method which customarily was employed in order to kill famous Armenians who were exiled individually.

No. 76
To the General Directorate of Settlement of Tribes and Deportees

Response to the telegram of 10 February 1916
It is understood from the report of the Harran (Tell Abiyad) *kaymakamlık* that the aforementioned, being arrested by the Adana police, was brought here under supervision and from here, while being sent to Mardin, was killed by the officials watching over him for attempting to escape.
17 February 1916, Assistant to the Director General
(Abdülahad Nuri)
To which condemned martyr does this cipher telegram refer? Who knows? As for the proposition, "for attempting to escape," it was the usual pretext for murder.
In general, already the people being sent separately under special surveillance were condemned to death. Naim Bey in his memoirs writes about this:
...there was also the issue of being sent under supervision. There was no longer hope and possibility of living any more for those subject to this misfortune. They in general were youth brought in as suspicious. They first would be crammed into a dirty and narrow room in the courtyard of

the (Aleppo) prison. Dogs would not even want to live in that place. After being left half hungry there for 10–15 days, they would be taken out on the road, their hands and arms tied, accompanied by gendarmes. Because the gendarmes had previously received the order to kill them, they were killed on the road in a deserted place. Afterwards, the matter would be reported to the office of the assistant of the general director of deportees in the following manner: "the individuals, sent on the date, arrived at their place of exile." Those about whom the order was given to be sent under supervision were undoubtedly condemned to death.

We already explained that these wretches were initially sent out supposedly to Diyarbekir, and later they began to be sent supposedly to Mardin, as this cipher telegram of Abdülahad Nuri Bey which we reproduced demonstrates.

...

Chapter Four/4
Several weeks before that, there was an attempt to establish an orphanage in Aleppo, and they began to collect orphans from the streets, not because they had pity on them, but because they were becoming the cause of various contagious diseases, especially typhus, spreading through the city as they wandered from street to street.

However the government, which was informed about the matter, fearing that in this manner the orphans would be saved, immediately sent out the following order.

To the Aleppo governor-generalship,

There is no need for that type of orphanage. It is not the moment to waste time by following feelings, feeding them (the orphans) and prolonging their lives. Send them (to the deserts) and give notice.
21 September 1915, Minister of Internal Affairs
Talat
According to this instruction, on November 16, the office of the Assistant of the General Director of Deportees of Aleppo telegraphed Constantinople, to the General Directorate of Settlement of Tribes and Deportees, of which it was one branch:

No. 31
To the General Directorate of Settlement of Tribes and Deportees

There are over 400 boys in the orphanage; they too by accompanying caravans will be sent to their deportation sites.
26 November [1]915
Assistant to the General Director
(Abdülahad Nuri)
...

No. 63
To the General Directorate of Settlement of Tribes and Deportees

By sending the orphans to the determined place at this time when the cold continues with severity,[24] their eternal rest will be secured. Consequently, we request permission for the remittance of the requested credit.
January 28, [1]916
Assistant to the General Director
(Abdülahad Nuri)
...
...
In this way, those orphans were assembled near military bases. As Meskene had also been turned into a military base, they also were assembled there. They gave each one small loaf of bread daily, and sometimes, once or twice a week, hot water which distantly resembled the concept of soup.

However, the central government quickly learned about this, and immediately an order arrived which recommended taking those boys from the hands of the military authorities and destroying them.

Cipher telegraph of the Ministry of Internal Affairs, to the Aleppo governor-generalship,

Without giving rise to suspicion, on the pretext that they will be given nourishment by the deportation offices, in an assembled state, destroy the children of the known individuals (Armenians) gathered by military bases and nourished by command of the Ministry of War, and inform.
7 March [1]916, Minister of Internal Affairs
Talat
...

Chapter Four/5
While the government on the one hand encouraged crimes, on the other hand it continually pushed the officials of the provinces to understand well the essence of the goal pursued and work in every way to implement it with

enthusiasm. That was the best patriotism and at the same time the most beautiful characteristic which they could show in their job.
Here is a telegram which will more than everything else become eloquent about this.

To the Governor-Generalship of Aleppo,

It has previously been communicated that the government, by order of the Cemiyet (the Committee of the Ittihad), had decided to completely annihilate all Armenians living in Turkey. Those who oppose this command and decision cannot remain part of the official structure of the state.[25] Without paying attention to woman, child, [and] incompetent, no matter how tragic the methods of annihilation might be, without listening to feelings of conscience, their existence must be ended.

16 September [1]915
Minister of Internal Affairs
Talat
…

Chapter 4/6
Already a little after the mobilization, a temporary law threatened with the penalty of death all those who would not surrender their weapons. Turk, Armenian, Kurd rushed to bring whatever weapon they had, even knives. The government did not keep the weapons of the Turks and Kurds, but took even the knives of the Armenians.
This took place much earlier than the general deportation of the people. When all the youth, up to 45 years old, were in the armies, when all weapons, down to knives, had been taken, when the entire intellectual and wealthy class was in prisons or in exile, what could the pitiful multitude of the still remaining elderly, women, [and] little ones do, when the government implemented that general deportation, arguing that it fears that the Armenians threaten the line of retreat of the Ottoman armies? Then, how to make this argument fit also the Armenians who are found very distant from the frontiers and in the provinces near Constantinople, who at such a distance represent no threat at all, and who similarly were deported and massacred?
There is a section in Naim Bey's memoirs about this which I reproduce here.
…While this crime (the Armenian deportations) was being carried out, Talat Pasha, on the one hand, was seeking documents proving his innocence; he had appointed officials to organize and put them in order, and

spent money from the state treasury. By having photographs taken of several weapons, rifles, supposedly found in the homes of Armenians, he wanted to exonerate his crime. Alas...if the existence of weapons is a sign of turmoil and rebellion, then all the parts of Turkey must have been furnaces of rebellion. Whichever Turkish village you go to, you will find hundreds of Martinis [and] Mausers. These weapons are not readied in order to raise rebellion [and] turmoil, but out of fear of bandits are kept to defend their property and lives against them. This truth is revealed from this that the government has placed its people in insecurity.

It becomes clear from the meaning of the above telegram that the government recommends that the commission it sent provide false proofs about Armenian culpability. And the volume published by that commission is solely based on this type of evidence.

...

Conclusion

The instructions to leave unpunished and encourage the crimes committed against deportee Armenians "by the Turkish people," which continually came from Constantinople, assuredly did not have the purpose of proving the innocence of the people.

Even those kinds of Muslim elements which had not participated in the massacres carried out in the time of [Sultan Abdül] Hamid II and defended their Armenian neighbors—as in the region of Adiyaman, the Kurds of Kiakhta, the Dersim people, the Turks of Mush, etc.—this time embraced with great enthusiasm the Armenocidal plan. The Ittihad had spread its poison as far as those strata; it had succeeded in kindling in everyone the instinct to massacre and plunder.

The war barely having begun—*Naim Bey writes in his memoirs*—hunger and misery already began to appear in powerless Turkey. It was necessary to trick, to satiate these miserable ones, and the goods and money to be left behind by the Armenians could realize this. In the provinces of Erzerum, Bitlis, Diyarbekir, Mamuretülaziz and Sivas, the massacre of Armenians and the plunder of their goods began. This occupation made the people forget everything. It was also necessary to busy Syria and Mesopotamia. The plains of Mesopotamia, the roads, the deserts of Syria became filled with Armenians. The vast wealth earned by Armenians through centuries of honorable effort was lost in its entire magnificence and greatness. Whatever remained would be lost in those deserts, the people of which quickly understood that those deportee caravans were being sent to them as victims. Initially, they carried out various small attacks. But when they understood this, they completed the task with mass killings. The most heartbreaking of the incidents took place in those deserts.

And it was not only the wealth of the Armenian element, the women, girls [and] children were also seized. How many Turks did not take advantage of that plunder? How many Turkish homes can be shown where a kidnapped Armenian woman, Armenian girl, [or] Armenian boy is not found?

Translated by Aram Arkun

NOTES

1. Translator's note: Throughout this text, Naim Efendi uses the present tense (-iyor). We have changed it to the past tense to make it sound more like his recollections.
2. Cedîde a neighborhood of Aleppo; Karlık an area of settlement close to Aleppo.
3. We would like to make note of the loaded and ominous "bureaucratese" in these cables and its intentional euphemistic obfuscation ("certain known individuals," "treatment," "reliable officials").
4. The meaning here is that the gendarmes should ensure that the deportees were left without food or water en route. TA.
5. The date on the document is 20 February 332; however, there is no such a date in Ottoman calendar. The dates between 16 and 28 February 1332 were taken out from Ottoman calendar to delete the 13 days of difference. The date should be here 1331!
6. The book Naim Efendi refers to is the "White Book," which was published by the Ottoman Government in late 1916 with the title *Ermeni Komitelerinin Âmâl ve Harekât - ı İhtilâliyesi: İlan - ı Meşrutiyetden Evvel ve Sonra*, (Istanbul: Matbaa-i Amire, 1332 [1916]).
7. The date on the document is 26 February 332. There is no such a date in the Ottoman calendar. The dates between 16 and 28 February 1332 were taken out from Ottoman calendar to delete the 13 days of difference. The date should be here 1331.
8. In all ciphered official messages concerning deportations and massacres, as well as related activities, generally the phrase, "known individuals." is used for the Armenians.
9. Ihsan Bey, the former *kaymakam* of Kilis and then Zahle, who at this point was the director of the Special Secretariat of the Ministry of Internal Affairs in Constantinople, confirmed this point in the recollections of Naim Bey. Ihsan Bey made a declaration of similar meaning concerning these words

of Abdülahad Nuri Bey, and his declaration has been reproduced in the indictment of the trial of the Ittihadists in the following fashion: "Ihsan Bey says that when he was *kaymakam* of Kilis, Abdülahad Nuri Bey, who was sent from Constantinople to Aleppo, attempted to persuade him that the goal of the Armenian deportation was annihilation—[saying] that I met with Talat Bey and personally received the order for annihilation, and the salvation of the country is in it" (*Interrogation Documents*, p. 15).

10. Abdülahad Nuri Bey never took bribes. "I like bribes," he customarily said, "but I am afraid to accept them. I am afraid that in place of the money which enters my pocket an Armenian, a single Armenian, will go free."

11. The government, which was very cautious during the days of the beginning of the Armenian deportation, formulated a credit in the name of the deportees in order to veil the true goal of the deportation. The sacrifice did not come from it anyway. As the property and wealth of the deported Armenians had been confiscated, this credit would be taken from the sum that was created from this. But this again was a formal thing, and they gave one [loaf] of bread once a day only in a few places for a very short period of time and then stopped. The Turkish officials supervising the deportation in any case largely usurped the allotted sums.

12. At one of the stations found along the line of the Euphrates, the *müdür* of Abuharrar, Corporal Rahmeddin, who had become a terror for the deportees found there, and who, with the terrible cudgel from which he was inseparable, constantly killed men, was summoned to Aleppo, after numerous protests, for such a nominal trial. However, in accordance with this telegram, he was immediately again sent back to his post without even being examined. On his return, when he passed through Meskene in order to get off at Abuharrar, he shot at the deportees with his revolver, yelling "You protested, and what happened? Behold, I again go to take my office." It is understood of course that after returning, the barbarities of this man, whom the deportees called "Bone breaker," took on even greater dimensions.

13. For the full report that Naim mentions please see Ottoman memoir page [13] [Taner Akçam].

14. In particular, among them was found Arslan Bey's brother, Hüseyin Bey, who after Arslan Bey's death (in the beginning of 1917), succeeded him as the director of the town quarter of Ras-ul-Ayn. The two brothers also played a large role in the massacres of Der Zor. Hüseyin Bey already was continually going to Aleppo in order to sell the objects that he and his brother and their men incessantly stole from the deportees. Neither the sick, nor the elderly, nor the children were spared.

15. It is worth on this occasion to recall that the order for the general deportation of the Armenians was given after Marshal Makensen broke through the Russian front, when henceforth the destruction of Russia and consequently also the final victory appeared assured to the Turkish government.

16. In Aleppo alone, one or two hundred people amassed great wealth by taking bribes or serving as intermediaries for bribes in order to provide temporary residency permits for the Armenian deportees.

17. It is worth recalling together with this telegram that during the massacres in the provinces, the clergy were the ones killed with the most terrible tortures—the prelates, *vartabeds* [celibate Armenian priests with advanced education], married priests, etc. Generally, they broke them into pieces, after tormenting them for days in prisons. They were even going to kill the Patriarch of Constantinople, when he was exiled to Baghdad, in the same fashion, but the fear of accountability of the Ane *kaymakam* saved him.

18. Later, upon the appeal of the Catholicos of Cilicia, Cemal Pasha permitted this clergyman to go to Jerusalem. After this appeal of the Catholicos, several other clergymen also received the same permission.

19. These were Catholic priests deported from Ankara. When the *müdür* of Meskene was fired without a replacement, they took advantage of the prevalent confusion and fled to Aleppo, bribing a gendarmerie commander and other officials.

20. In Dipsi, entire families died from hunger. Later, they no longer brought caravans there, and the caravans would go directly to Abuharrar. Due to the stench of the corpses, it was not possible to stop there. Arab shepherds killed 36 Armenian women there because...they ate the hay of the animals.

21. The late, lamented Dr. Shepherd would relate the following incident. After the Armenian massacres, a group of American young ladies came from Kharpert [Harput] to Aleppo in order to return to America. These young ladies were robbed on the way and experienced great difficulties. The Turkish government subjected them to the strictest searches so that they would not take any picture or writing with them. They even examined the braids of their hair. "What are you looking for," asked one of the maidens. "What you seek is not on us, but in our minds, our eyes, in our hearts. You can only efface them by killing us."

22. It is true that Armenians gave information about the massacres to the American consul, Mr. Jackson. One of those Armenians was an English writing youth, Mr. Aram Giulian, while the photographs were taken by the secretary of the Aleppo Armenian prelacy, Mr. Madteos Yeretsian. Many people, including Armenian priests, were arrested in Aleppo on suspicion of giving information to the American consulate, and disappeared.

23. We were only able to ascertain that of them, Arsen Shahbazian was from Cilicia. It is unknown to us who the other two are and where they were from.

24. Sivas.

25. We read in the indictment published by the current Turkish government against the Ittihad Committee: "According to the investigations conducted, those who did not want to participate in the aforementioned crimes are considered traitors to the homeland."

APPENDIX B: DR. AVEDIS NAKKASHIAN'S LETTER TO ANDONIAN

October 6, 1925
New York

Mr. A. Andonian,

Dear exiled compatriot,

I received your letter dated September 21. Please forgive my late reply; I was in Boston for a few days. I don't know if I will be able to respond to your two questions. It is not easy for any Armenian to determine which is the saddest or the happiest period in his or her public life. Always on a stormy sea and always in a small, old, rickety boat, the one who makes the journey cannot determine which is the saddest and which is the happiest. I started my career in medicine at the end of 1894, at a time when I had no faith in Armenian reform movements. But before working in a safe place, I was in Marash and was an eyewitness to the first massacre. This was a sad period right at the beginning of a life filled with youthful hope for society and for the nation. The fact that I had done work for the governor protected me. He sent me to Aintab accompanied by a police officer. I abandoned my friends to their fate in Marash and its surrounding areas. It was a cause for happiness for me personally. Hiring a Circassian from Aintab under difficult, unfortunate circumstances, I went to Iskenderun, traveling by night with my two brothers but leaving my parents and hundreds of

© The Author(s) 2018   223
T. Akçam, *Killing Orders*, Palgrave Studies in the History of Genocide,
https://doi.org/10.1007/978-3-319-69787-1_7

relatives and friends in Aintab. Aintab was massacred the very same day I arrived in Alexandretta. The struggle in Zeytun and the wider massacres continued at the same time. One day, the governor of Alexandretta issued an order that I was to be exiled. I was able to have myself exiled by boat and reached Mersin. Months passed, and I started working in Adana once again as a surgeon and a doctor. A year later, in 1897, I went to Paris and London. At that time, I met Miss Mellinger—a woman originally from America, who gave lectures and organized fundraisers—as I toured all the English cities associated with "Friends of Armenia." Miss Mellinger and Miss Fraser are two people who have devoted and sacrificed themselves for Armenians like us. Fraser died in Bulgaria. Mellinger married me and, one year later, she died giving birth to a little girl on a trip to Hadjın. While she was alive, she always worked by corresponding with notable individuals and officials in England. She helped to significantly alleviate the grief of the Armenians. Her death was a sad period in my life.

The Turkish constitution was declared. At that time I was in Constantinople, and it was cause for happiness, during which time we shed tears of joy. I thought we too had been liberated, that we too had been given the chance to live as human beings. For me, this happiness lasted only two weeks. When I was talking to the ophthalmologist, Esad Pasha, one of the Young Turk leaders, he said that the reason for the decline of the Ottoman government was the Christian element. "God made trouble for the Sheikh ül-Islam, Zembilli Ali Efendi, because he did not allow Sultan Selim to massacre all the Christians," is what he said. I could predict where the Young Turks were heading and I did not go to Adana. I moved to Constantinople. I waited without anything to do, because my clinic and work were in Adana. I waited for conditions to improve. When every day they used to say that there was a desire in Adana to take up arms and play with guns, I lost hope. I was not someone who believed in guns. I thought they were dangerous. If only I had been wrong. I am not insisting that the massacres resulted from every boy openly carrying a gun in his hand in the streets or from the arms trade in the marketplace, but they laid the groundwork and presented the opportunity. (Exciting Cause) One day at my house in Gedik Pasha, I woke up to the sound of thousands of guns and went outside. At the top of Divan Yolu, I saw a military officer shot and fall to the ground. I ran home. It was a sad moment. I fled to Ay Stefano with my family. The army arrived and we celebrated and rejoiced, but at the same time, we received news that Cilicia had been massacred. My two new houses and shops had been burned. I spent the summer of 1910 in America with the hope of settling there and encouraging Armenians to immigrate by giving them information about the country. I started to write in New York. A few respected Armenians considered my kind of writing detrimental. They worked to persuade me not to write. I said, "I wish this were not the case, but I won't write." In November of the same year, I returned to Adana and had buildings rebuilt. Sitting on Big Island during the Balkan War, I heard cannon fire from Çatalca, always hoping that help would come. The result is clear.

The Great War was upon us. I waited in Constantinople for the side of justice to triumph. This faith prevented me from leaving. I will see it with my own eyes, I said. I was taken to Ayaş during the April 1915 arrests. It was a sad period, but there was always hope and there always is.

My release from the prison in Ayaş was cause for happiness, but it was mixed with some of my saddest memories. I was a soldier for three years in Pera, and my only joy was the Armenian boys.

I finally saw the arrival of the Allied fleet with my own eyes. I was an eyewitness to the arrival of General Sarrail. I went to the prison and stepped inside. I saw with my own eyes people who had committed countless murders and massacres. I spoke to some of them. I saw horrible faces that had the power to have thousands killed with a single word.

It was the same day that I came across the book you wrote. In particular, I read the communiqués between Talat and Abdulahad Nuri. I understood the kind of role that that monster Nuri had played. I had heard about it from others. People who had been in Aleppo trembled as they recalled that crippled devil: how he had the governors of Der Zor and other places replaced, and how he sent people who had found refuge around Aleppo into the hands of their executioners. But the man was not anywhere to be found. His name did not even exist. I searched in the English embassy. I asked Commissaire Reislick/Commander Rusketlick. He replied that he did not know the name. One day, while I was sitting on a boat on the Bosphorus near Pasha Bahçe, a crippled man greeted someone sitting beside me as he passed, and the man stood up to say hello. "Who is this effendi," I asked. "Abdulahad Nuri," he replied. "What is his position?" "I don't know," was the response. I looked for that man every day for the next week—in the Ministry of the Interior, in the Ministry of Foreign Affairs, in other ministries and in police circles. Finally, I asked the leaders of the Seyri Sefain over the phone, and they replied that he was the *tahrirat müdiri* [secretary-clerk].

I met with Mustafa Pasha, from the Comité Resieie [Panel of Judges] and the head of the War Tribunal, and we decided that I would open a case. I petitioned, but there were many difficulties in all regards that made it impossible to reach the War Tribunal. It was four o'clock. I ran alongside Mustafa Pasha and told him that if he was not arrested today, the man would disappear. He gave the order, and two policemen and one officer went by car to get him. I was sitting next to Mustafa Pasha. They brought the monster inside.

I should say that this was the happiest moment of my life. The man—as pale as a corpse—was shaking on his feet. The 60,000 in Katma and the 300,000 women, talented boys, merchants and artisans, all miserable in Der Zor, came to mind. I felt as if all of them were applauding for me from the grave. In my mind, the hundreds of angelic children thrown into the river in Meskene were extending their small hands toward me. "To the gallows," shouted Kürd Mustafa Pasha. "Do you not have a heart? The Holy Book (*Mashafi Sherif*) forbids all the sins you have committed." This stonehearted man, who had made hundreds upon thousands cry, wept before me. How happy was I.

The day of the proceedings arrived. I spoke for more than a half hour. Nuri wept and sobbed. I had the names of around twenty witnesses written, among which was Ihsan Bey, the governor of Kilis. He called Ihsan Bey to Aleppo and asked him why there were still Armenians in Kilis. Ihsan Bey replied that according to the order he was given, families of soldiers, artisans, Protestants and Catholics were exceptions. Abdulahad Nuri replied that "the goal of the deportation is annihilation," and that all of them should be driven out. Ihsan Bey refused, saying that he would only obey the official order. He lost his position.

The proceedings were about to end. I was preparing myself to see him at the end of a rope in Beyazid Meydanı, which Kürd Mustafa Pasha had promised me—a different kind of happiness. One morning, there was a knock at my door, and a priest whom I did not recognize was there. "I am Father Dajad," he said. "My trip was paid for by the Milli [National] government [National government] in Engüri [Ankara] to free Abdulahad Nuri. That beast is the brother of Yusuf Kemal, the head of the Ministry of Foreign Affairs in Engüri [Ankara]. You are about to hang a dog here, and if you do, 2,000–3,000 Armenians will be annihilated there. I beg you, let this man go free."

It was a sad moment. In that instant, all my dreams vanished into thin air. It was not a question of the past anymore; before me were future events. What was one to do? Vengeance and justice were all fine and good, but the lives of a few thousand Armenians were at the heart of the matter. But the series of tragedies did not end there. While we were working to find a solution and organize our efforts, Ferid Pasha's cabinet was dismissed, and a government sympathetic to the nationalists took its place. The war tribunal was replaced. When I was called before the tribunal, the first words I heard were the following: "You are accusing and tormenting an upstanding, honorable official who loyally defends the interests of this country and army." Should I protect myself, Abdulahad or the extremists in Engüri [Ankara] The proceedings were short. "Wait," they said to me, and I was entrusted to a police officer. I waited for an hour. Let's say, if you like, that this was the saddest moment of my life. An hour later, they let me go home. Mustafa Pasha went to prison and barely saved his own skin. Abdulahad was also freed. This was not the end of it. In 1921, I went to Adana for my work and properties. The agreement in Engüri [Ankara] came to light. I was one of the first to flee, leaving behind 50,000 Armenians and knowing full well what kind of fate awaited them. I knew that the Cilicia they had yearned for had been lost.

The final sad period, which I narrowly escaped, was in Balı Keser [Balıkesir]. I went there in the spring of 1922 to work and to see my brother. The Greeks were there. Everything was peaceful. The offensive in Afyon Kara Hisar began. A few days went by. A rumor that the Greek soldiers fled reached me. The same day, I put my brother's wife and one of her children on a train. Some noticed. They thought that I was crazy. If only I had been.... I only told the children of two friends to come with me, and they came. We started our journey at four o'clock and arrived in Bandırma. The same evening, the road closed. The çetes had come and massacred all the Christians. We sailed to Rodosto, barely making it onto the boat. Awake for 36 hours straight, I wandered the shores to find a way, or a boat, because panic had already begun to set in.

Having a visa issued to leave Constantinople for Egypt as a family was also a major achievement. After watching the Arabs demonstrate for a year and a half to bring down the British and after seeing the triumph of Zaghloul's supporters, we arrived in America. Being welcomed there was a happy day for us. I passed an exam and am officially a doctor.

Now, dear Mr. Andonian, you tell me what in this very brief history is sadder and what is happier. I don't know the purpose of this information. A book about the history of Ayaş with photographs will soon be published. I will send you a copy. I had a picture taken for that book. You will find it enclosed. I am working on having the photographer send a few more.

Respectfully,

Nakkashian

Translated by Jennifer Manoukian

APPENDIX C: ARAM ANDONIAN'S LETTER TO MARY TERZIAN

Dr. Mary Terzian
Pension Melrose
12 Clos Belmont
Geneva, Switzerland

July 28, 1937
Paris

Madam,

Forgive me if I am late in responding to your letter of June 14. I needed to look for some old papers and notes that I had put aside many years ago, which took some time.

The original versions of the telegrams reproduced in my book can be found in London at the Armenian Bureau, which Armenian notables from Manchester had tasked with publishing my report in English. I think you have this English version. It is only a summary published under the title *The Memoirs of Naim Bey: Turkish Official Documents relating to the Massacres of Armenians*,[1] with an introduction by Viscount Gladstone. The telegrams are, however, reproduced in their entirety in this summary. I left London before it was published and I was only able to take with me the original versions that had already had their zinc plates prepared. The rest stayed in London to prepare the plates, and I had completely forgotten

© The Author(s) 2018   229
T. Akçam, *Killing Orders*, Palgrave Studies in the History of Genocide,
https://doi.org/10.1007/978-3-319-69787-1_8

about them until the day that Abdulahad Nuri Bey[2]—the former sub-director of deportees in Aleppo, who began as an official in the Department of the Navy in Constantinople—was arrested in the same city upon Dr. A. Nakashian's request. This was in August 1920. The monster—entirely dismayed by his arrest, which could have had fatal consequences for him—was to be tried before the well-known Military Tribunal, presided over by Kurd Mustapha [Kürt Mustafa] Pasha, who had already condemned a few notorious massacrers to death by hanging in Constantinople.

In light of the trial, Dr. Nakashian—through His Eminence, Patriarch Zaven of Constantinople—appealed to Boghos Noubar [Nubar] Pasha, President of the Armenian National Delegation, to ask him to intervene on my behalf, so that I could send the original documents reproduced in my book to the Patriarchate. I received a letter from Boghos Nubar Pasha per-taining to this matter and immediately wrote to the Armenian Bureau in London for them to send all the original versions they had to the Patriarchate, which they did. At the same time, I sent a long essay that Naim Bey had written in pencil concerning Abdulahad Nuri Bey, an incrim-inating document for his sinister superior, as well as a few of the original versions I had at home, in which Abdulahad Nuri bey was mentioned.

The trial, however, did not take place. Abdulahad Nuri's own brother, Youssouf [Yusuf] Kemal bey—Minister of Foreign Affairs of the Government of the Grand National Assembly who was living in Angora [Ankara]—dispatched the Very Reverend Dadjad, the religious leader of the Armenians in Kastamouni [Kastamonu], to Constantinople, threaten-ing that if during the trial his brother was sentenced to be hanged—which was more than likely—he would have all of the Armenians in the regions of Anatolia controlled by the Kemalist government massacred without mercy. The poor Armenian priest—convinced that this was not an empty threat—had gone to Constantinople to implore the Armenian Patriarchate and Dr. Nakashian to withdraw from the trial.

At this time, the Ferid Pasha Cabinet, which was in power in Constantinople and had signed the Treaty of Sèvres, had to resign under the pressure of the Kemalist movement that was spreading in a menacing way, even in Constantinople, where spirits were running high after the publication of the devastating and disastrous provisions in the Treaty signed in Sèvres. A new Cabinet, distinctly aligned with the Kemalist movement, took the reins of the government in Constantinople, and one of its first acts was not only to release Abdulahad Nuri bey, but also to arrest members of the War Council who were going to try that monster, its president, Kurd Mustapha Pasha and Dr. Nakashian. They were brought before a new War Council, and Dr. Nakashian endured all kinds of tribulations before being released.

If this incident interests you, you can ask Dr. Nakashian himself for more details. He has since settled in New York. The most recent address I have for him is 530 W. 166th Street, New York City.

Regarding the documents sent to the Patriarchate, either from London or by me directly—and which were added to the file for the case brought against Abdulahad Nuri—they, of course, stayed there. I never learned what happened to them.

I had stopped thinking about those documents when, in April 1921—if I am not mistaken—I was summoned to Berlin as a witness by the Court of Moabit, where the trial surrounding the assassination of the former Grand Vizier Talaat [Talat] Pasha would take place. A young Armenian, Soghomon Tehlirian, had shot him on Hardenbergerstrasse in Berlin. Tehlirian's lawyers had informed me, at the same time, that it would be very useful if—to corroborate my book, which they planned to use during the trial—I brought them a few of the original versions of the telegrams reproduced in it.

I left for Berlin, therefore, with the documents I had, in particular Behaeddin [Bahaettin] Shakir bey's letters, as well as a few of the deciphered versions of encoded telegrams that bore notes written by the Vali of Aleppo, Mustapha Abdulhalik bey.

Of course, the question of their authenticity was raised in Berlin during our first meetings with Tehlirian's lawyers. On 10 June 1921, I gave them a short memorandum about the provenance of these documents. I am sending you a copy, which you will find enclosed. This memorandum, only having value for one side, could not resolve the issue, and Tehlirian's lawyers—including two of the most noted members of the Berlin Bar, Dr. Von Gordon and Dr. Werthauer, and one of the most eminent jurists in Germany, Prof. Niemayer of the University of Kiel—did everything in their power to convince themselves of the authenticity of the documents before making use of them and presenting them to the Court. To this end, through the intercession of Dr. Lepsius, they had my book and the documents reproduced in it subjected to examination by an official from the Ministry of Foreign Affairs, Mr. W. Rossler, who had been the German consul in Aleppo throughout the war, and, as a result, an eyewitness and credible about the atrocities committed against the Armenians. Mr. W. Rossler—who lived in Eger—warmly welcomed Dr. Lepsius's request and replied with a long report, which concluded that the documents were authentic.

This report was dated 25 April 1921, but it did not reach the lawyers until the 12th or 13th of June, because its author—as an official—considered himself obliged to submit it to his Minister for approval before sending it to Dr. Lepsius. He gave his approval on the condition that the report—intended for the lawyers' edification—remained strictly confidential and not be mentioned before the Court. At the same time, the Minister—wanting to avoid all interference in the trial—had forbidden Consul Rössler from testifying before the Court, which caused quite disparaging, ironic attacks in a good portion of the Berlin press.

The Rössler report entirely convinced the lawyers, who immediately tasked Dr. Paul Pfeffer of Berlin with the German translation of Talaat [Talat] Pasha's dispatches and published them as a four-page pamphlet, which was disseminated and passed on to members of the Court, to the jurors, to the press and to various unofficial individuals. Once the groundwork was laid, the lawyers knew how to use the original versions of several of these documents quite adeptly in court. They played an important role and contributed significantly to the good outcome of the trial. You must know that Tehlirian was acquitted.

It was upon learning of the Rössler report that the great German polemicist, Maximilian Harden—contrary to his no-less-renowned co-religionist, Emile Ludwig (both were Jewish), who was connected to the pro-Turkish cause—devoted an entire issue of his celebrated weekly newspaper "Die Zukunft" to my book (4 June 1921 issue; he received news of it before the lawyers, likely through Dr. Lepsius) and was one of the most ardent defenders of the accused and of Armenians in general during the entire trial.

You will find enclosed a copy of the pamphlet with Dr. Pfeffer's translation. Regarding Mr. Rössler's report, I have a copy, but it was given to me by the late Dr. Lepsius on the condition that I never mention it publicly without receiving written permission from Consul Rössler beforehand.

This report is in German. It contains a significant amount of criticism about the composition of my book, which he considers entirely lacking objectivity. Furthermore, he refutes the majority of the passages concerning the behavior of the Germans in Turkey during the War. Of course, he is right in the majority of the cases he highlights. He only forgot that my book was not a historical work, but was intended to be propaganda and, naturally, cannot be free from the inherent imperfections in these kinds of publications. We must keep in mind that at that time, to get along in Entente counties, saying something disparaging about Germany was unavoidable. Let me add that over the course of the publication of my book, the Armenian Bureau in London and the Armenian National Delegation in Paris—considering the needs of the cause they were defending—behaved a bit too cavalierly with regard to my manuscript.

But Consul Rössler played fair. Although he was quite irritated with me for the accusations I made in my book against the Germans, he had been quite kind in the part of his report that dealt with the documents concerning the massacres. This part of his report is convincing and at the same time instructive in understanding the Armenian tragedy, which he illuminates.

Among the original documents in question, I only found in my papers the letter from Behaeddin Shakir bey dated February 18. His second letter, as well as the original versions of a few telegrams, was added to the file on Tehlirian's trial. They must still be there. After returning to Paris, I made two successive attempts to retrieve them, but without any luck. In September 1921, one of Tehlirian's lawyers, Dr. Werthauer, was passing through Paris with his wife. Having been informed by a friend, I visited them at Hôtel Crillon, where they were staying and, taking advantage of the opportunity, I brought up the question of these documents. Dr. Werthauer promised me that he would take care of it once he returned to Berlin, but I never heard from him.

Furthermore, you asked me why I did not mention Behaeddin Shakir bey's name in my book as a signatory of the two letters to Djemal bey that are reproduced in it when I knew that his name had already been revealed by newspapers in Constantinople.

The answer is very simple. Over the course of the publication of my book, I did not know that those letters were from Behaeddin Shakir bey. As a signature, there was only an illegible paragraph, which, at first glance, seems to be a conventional marking. The issue was revealed to me a few months after the publication of my book in 1921 in Berlin. An Armenian committee that dealt with Tehlirian's defense in that same city had collected a bunch of Armenian newspapers in which there were publications concerning the massacres. Since in Paris, I did not have the chance to see newspapers from Constantinople, I looked through them out of curiosity and all of a sudden came across a translation of one of Behaeddin Shakir bey's letters, signed with his name spelled out. It was a clipping from an old, undated issue of the newspaper "Joghovurti Tzaine," likely published in 1920. Since in my book the letter in question was not signed with a name, I was of course curious to know why Behaeddin Shakir's name was written at the end of the translation. I, therefore, wrote a letter to said Turkish newspaper (likely "Sabah" of the Armenian, Mihran Bey, which had as its editor-in-chief Ali Kemal Bey, known for his anti-Unionist leanings), which had published it with Behaeddin Shakir Bey's signature. Later I learned that the initials at the bottom of the two letters reproduced in my book composed the word "Beha," a nickname given to Behaeddin Shakir by his close friends. You can see very well that the matter is not complicated enough to be of interest.

Another question you asked me. You wanted to know if Djemal Bey, the recipient of the two letters from Behaeddin Shakir, was under orders from Naim Bey. No! I wrote to you at length about this in my first letter. The difference between the two men is enormous. Naim Bey was an entirely insignificant official, whereas Djemal Bey, as the Secretary responsible (Kiatibi Messoul) for the Committee of Union and Progress in Aleppo, was the absolute master throughout the whole province, and higher in rank than the Prefect (Vali) himself, though naturally only for civil administration affairs. He could not intervene in military affairs, but in civil affairs—such as deportations and massacres—every matter was entirely subjected to his authority. Please reread my first letter as well as page 100 of my book.

It seems that, since the Sub-Director of Deportees, Abdulahad Nuri Bey, was entirely devoted to the Committee of Union and Progress and therefore reliable, Djemal Bey had given Behaeddin Shakir Bey's two letters to his Office to be a course of action that, needless to say, he followed to the letter. This explains at the same time how Naim Bey found them and passed them on with the other documents from Abdulahad Nuri Bey's Office where he was the secretary. It was one of the most disorganized Offices, existing in an indescribable kind of disarray with items from its Archives crammed haphazardly into drawers without numbering, without labeling, without any kind of classification system. However, all of the Offices that dealt with deportees in each city or region were in the same state of disorder.

* * *

In a note that I had sent to Tehlirian's lawyers in Berlin, a copy of which you will find enclosed, you will see described a few of the circumstances through which we were able to procure the documents reproduced in my book. This Note is not complete. There were matters that I could not

APPENDIX C: ARAM ANDONIAN'S LETTER TO MARY TERZIAN

divulge in my book or to Tehlirian's lawyers in order not to discredit the man that was Naim Bey, who was not entirely clean. To us, he had become a spy who betrayed his country. And that is all there is to say! He was, furthermore, not well regarded as an official, but they naturally tolerated him without knowing anything about his treason, because he was not an exception among the administrative personnel of the city of Aleppo, which included some real crooks, in comparison to whom Naim Bey could have been considered a saint. He was a drinker and a die-hard gambler, and these were precisely the vices that led him to treason. The truth is that we bought all the documents he procured for us.

But the core of his being was good. First, despite the decline he suffered, he exuded complete trust. We could always rely on him.

I met him in one of the concentration camps for deportees in the Mesopotamian Desert, in Meskene, where they had sent him temporarily to replace the Mudir (Director) Cherkess Hussein Bey, who had been dismissed for not showing any enthusiasm in carrying out the orders that the authorities in Aleppo had continuously given him. By that time, the massacres in Der-Zor had begun, and the sub-director of deportees in Aleppo put pressure on Hussein Bey to evacuate the camp in Meskene by sending the deportees to Der-Zor to be exterminated. But Hussein Bey did not want to be separated from his deportees, at least his wealthy deportees, who paid him handsomely for his goodwill. Naim Bey, while waiting for Hussein Bey to find a way to justify himself, only followed the same path, and that perfectly illustrated this period in which everyone lived with the terror of being driven back to the areas of the massacres where news was becoming more and more terrifying from one day to the next.

It is in these circumstances that Naim Bey suggested to certain wealthy families that they flee to Aleppo, promising to help them in the matter, naturally through money. These families—originally from Konya, Adana, Ak-shehir, etc.—did not have a choice, but did not dare take advantage of Naim Bey's proposition, thinking—quite judiciously, by the way—that fleeing as a group of six, seven or ten people could not go unnoticed on the long route that separated Meskene from Aleppo and could have grave consequences.

Naim Bey then proposed to first send one man to Aleppo to make contact with a certain Arab coach driver he knew. According to him, this driver—whom he called Nakhli—was a reliable man, discreet, very honest and quite capable of transporting these families without exposing them to any danger. Furthermore, being from that area, he could find significant help during the journey from the Arab villagers of the region, who often felt a sense of solidarity.

Since I had close ties to the families in question and knew about their discussions with Naim Bey, these families asked me to assume the role of emissary. I did not have any choice, and it did not take much time for me to accept their proposition and try my luck.

To this end, I had several meetings with Naim Bey, who wanted to give me a recommendation addressed to the aforementioned Nakhli and, one night, I set out for Aleppo. But since I did not yet know Naim Bey's true character well enough—his position as a Turkish official inspired a reasonable sense of mistrust in me—I did not follow the route he had indicated, fearing an ambush. Instead of walking to the right of the route as he had recommended, and which was, in reality, a shortcut, I walked to the left of the route, which was much more difficult and longer, but covered with mounds of sand and lime that allowed me to hide out and sleep during the day, since I could only walk at night. It took me three days and four nights to reach Aleppo with only cakes as hard as rocks and a supply of carob and cucumbers as food, always walking one or two kilometers from the route without losing sight of the telegraph line that extended all along the route and was the only way for me to orient myself on my way to the city.

Sometimes I was accompanied by two or three hyenas, which followed me calmly at night from a good distance, almost as a way to regulate me as they kept a watchful eye out for my fall. At dawn, they hid like I did. I never saw them in the light of day, or at night for that matter. I only saw the sinister gleam of their eyes, which danced in the dark like will-o'-the-wisps. Naim Bey had already warned me about them, recommending that I continue on my route calmly without taking their presence into account and never running away from them, which could prompt them to attack me. The third night had barely fallen before they released me for good to follow the trail of a noisy group of crows that were likely headed to corpses.

Once in Aleppo, I found the driver, Nakhli, very easily. He was truly a kind and reliable man, who did not have any trouble accepting the proposition and who, in several trips, was able to transport 16 families to Aleppo, taking with each one of them—for free—one or two Armenian intellectuals who found themselves in Meskene without any resources, as it was arranged with Naim Bey.

Of course, it was thanks to measures taken by Naim Bey that Nakhli was able to safely transport 16 families and intellectuals, without the matter being divulged. Both were well paid by these families.

Later, a few people from these families were arrested in Aleppo as fugitives from Meskene. I was also arrested, but they immediately released me thanks to a certificate that friends had procured for me. The others were brought face to face with Naim Bey, who had returned to Aleppo, but who swore to the high heavens that he had never seen them in Meskene, which facilitated their release. The driver Nakhli, he too arrested following a denunciation, vigorously denied everything, as Arabs know how to do. They kept him in prison for months, but he did not denounce anyone.

Naim Bey could have taken advantage of this incident to put the families that fled at his mercy through conventional blackmail, but he never bothered them. He certainly thought of these people each time he found himself short on money, which happened often, but on no occasion did he ask them directly. I usually served as the intermediary, and since these people had resources and, moreover, had a keen sense of gratitude to Naim Bey, whom they considered their savior, my intercession was not unsuccessful. Besides, the sums that Naim Bey requested were quite negligible.

It was by taking advantage of this closeness that, little by little, I was able to use it at first to get news about the course of events and about the intentions of the local government, and then to urge him to remove the documents in the files of the Sub-Directorate for Deportees which, at that time, was no longer operating, being that the massacres in Der-Zor had ended months earlier. With the British near Damascus, the fall of Aleppo was imminent. I told Naim Bey that once the British were in Aleppo, he could sell all kinds of documents concerning the massacres at a considerable price to the Armenian authoritative bodies that would be established. At the same time, I encouraged him to write his memoir about Armenian matters.

It is for this reason that he stayed in Aleppo. After the occupation of the city by the British, the Armenians established a National Union that rushed to buy, after numerous examinations, the documents stolen by Naim Bey. Buying them took place under the conditions described in my Memorandum from Berlin on 10 June 1921.

I am writing all of this in strict confidence with my only intention being to satisfy your curiosity. I sketched an entirely different portrait of Naim Bey in my book, and the reestablishment of pure truth, in what concerns him personally, cannot be for nothing. Naim Bey was a completely amoral being. He had vices because of which he was inclined to sell <u>many things</u>, but not <u>everything</u>. The difference is considerable. I have not forgotten that he never lied over the course of the long relationship I had with him. In a word, his character was made up of entirely contradictory elements, both good and bad. You can get a sense from what I have written that we were able to benefit from the first, without being bothered by the second. I think about him constantly and always with a kind of sympathy that time has not been able to lessen. It is because I often stuck my neck out in my relationship with him—a dangerous exercise, but true to my adventurous spirit—and he never betrayed me.

Regarding the exact name of his position, they translated it in the English edition of my book as "Chief Secretary of the Deportations Committee of Aleppo." This is not entirely correct. It should be "Secretary of the Office of the Sub-Directorate for Deportees in Aleppo." Unfortunately, I do not know English and cannot give you the proper version in English. I hope you manage to sort it out on your own.

Please forgive me for the length of this letter. I took advantage of your curiosity to write down a few recollections from those memorable days that time has still not altered.

I wish you luck in your work and hope you will keep me informed about it. I send you my very best regards.

Sincerely yours,
Aram Andonian

Translated by Jennifer Manoukian

NOTES

1. Here Andonian misidentifies the title of the English translation. The correct version is *The Memoirs of Naim Bey: Turkish Official Documents Relating to the Deportation and the Massacres of Armenians.*
2. In this translation, we reproduced Andonian's errors and internal inconsistencies in capitalization and spelling as they appear in the original French.

APPENDIX D: CONSUL W. RÖSSLER'S LETTER TO DR. LEPSIUS

Consul W. Rössler   Eger, 25 April 1921

Dear Dr. Lepsius,

I received the book about the Armenian massacres by Aram Andonian that you were kind enough to send me, and reading it brought back vivid memories of Aleppo. In the following critique, I will first of all express some reservations, and then address the value of the account about Naim Bey and the documents.

The author is, in my view, incapable of being objective; he instead allows himself to be driven by passion, and also writes with a certain bias against Germany, to which we are unfortunately accustomed. At various points in the book, he writes about Germany in the most hateful fashion, while generally suppressing reports of German intervention on behalf of the Armenians. When he cannot avoid acknowledging German intervention, he attempts to minimize its effect through addenda. If the telegram from Enver Pasha on p. 158 is genuine, the German influence of which he speaks is of the greatest importance and was a resounding success. The author ascribes it to Liebknecht and Ledebour. When he recognizes the intervention of the Anatolian and Baghdad railway, he cites only the Swiss. Only on page 51 does he mention the "engineers" in general, but then immediately qualifies the impression by praising a Swiss person. Not a word about the work of Sister Beatrice, Sister Paula Schäfer, about Urfa and Marash! He seeks to attribute the fact that large numbers of Armenians

© The Author(s) 2018
T. Akçam, *Killing Orders*, Palgrave Studies in the History of Genocide,
https://doi.org/10.1007/978-3-319-69787-1_9

were driven to Der-es-Zor to German instigation (p. 56) and claims that the formation of the Yildirim Army was the cause. He forgets that the expulsion to Der-es-Zor occurred in 1915 and 1916, while the Yildirim Army was not formed until summer of 1917. It is possible that the author may have confused this with military wishes that may have been expressed by the Germans in 1915 and 1916, aimed at preventing contamination of the railway by sick expellees—an effort that, as we know, was only partly successful. These wishes were expressed, however, with great consideration for the Armenians and were used in a direct effort to help the Armenians and to keep them 10–20 feet from the railway lines, as in Bab, so as to make it possible for them to be provided food by the railway.

There are occasional mistakes in the dating of the published documents that make the entire document impossible, but they are apparently errors. The document on p. 132 of the book makes sense if it is dated 15 January 1916, but not 15 January 1915. Also, the document on p. 133, No. 853, must be dated 23 January 1916, not 23 January 1915. Similarly, in document no. 762 on p. 148, the error is obvious. There, a telegram from 17 December 1915 is presented as an answer to a telegram from 2 December 1916. On page 72, the text says 20 January 1917, but the telegram says 20 January 1916.

The author does not always clearly understand the relationships among events. Especially in Chapter III (The Der-es-Zor Massacres), the account constantly jumps back and forth, and seems in many places to be dictated solely by the effort to weave all the available documents into the account. (e.g. tel., p. 70, does not fit into the context).

Aside from these issues, I must say that the content of the book, in its details, makes a credible impression, and that the published documents, compared with the course of events, certainly have an internal probability. Many particular events with which I am familiar are portrayed with absolute accuracy; others with which I was not yet familiar provide an explanation for phenomena that I observed but could not explain at the time. This is the case, for example, with the fact that, for a time, large numbers of Armenians returned to Aleppo from Meskene. The explanation is now provided convincingly by the author on page 13 of the book, in that Naim Bey, like Hussein [Hüseyin] Bey, the Mudir [director] of Meskene, did not carry out the terrible orders they were given. I believe that I remember Hussein Bey; in any case, there was a moment in which I was able, through a recommendation to Meskene, to get permission for six expelled Armenians from an American seminary to return to Aleppo.

In his foreword, the author calls the deportation commissariat (sousdirection générale des déportés sise à Alep) the main organization for the deportations. He is right about this. When the Deportation Commissar arrived from Constantinople, I believed for a moment that this involved an effort to organize the provision of deportees with food, or to provide for them a bit at all, and I approached the Deportation Commissar with a request that he release some Armenians who had served the Germans. He refused in the most brusque manner, and told me in an indescribably haughty tone that I will never forget: "Vous ne comprenez pas ce que nous voulons. Nous voulons une Arménie sans Arméniens."[1] Thus he defined his task, as we now see in Andonian's book. I have forgotten this commissar's name, but it must have been Abdul Nuri Bey, if it was not his superior, Shukri Bey, who spent time in Aleppo before him. Nor can I recall the name Naim Bey, which is not surprising, since I had to be very cautious around the deportation authorities and could only intervene through third parties. On the other hand, I recall Eyub Bey very well; he was in charge of the deportations before the arrival of the commissar from Constantinople and was later assigned to him. [a few words missing here-translator] I consider his description in this book wholly accurate.

The authenticity of the telegrams from Constantinople containing the orders from the Ministry of the Interior is of course difficult to determine, since they only contain the handwriting of the telegraph agents or the writers who decoded them. However, I believe I remember the signature of Vali Mustafa Abdul Khalik Bey. In any case, this signature could be examined in Aleppo, and this would be indirect evidence of the authenticity of the telegrams from the Ministry of the Interior. The writer divides the documents (p. 16) into those that Naim Bey saved and those that he reconstructed from memory (transorité au fur et a mesure de ses souvenirs).[2] The possibility may certainly be conceded that Naim Bey retained official documents in his private possession rather than placing them in the files. To my knowledge, the Turks never kept files. In some offices, there were well-kept registries, but it is quite doubtful that a temporary authority such as the Deportation Commissariat would have cared much about keeping files, especially given the nature of its activities. So the documents described as original could very well be genuine. As far as those reconstructed from memory, one would need to know Naim Bey's character in order to judge their degree of reliability. But I did not encounter anything internally improbable among these. Rather, the facts that I know are well explained by the documents. Their wording, too, speaks for their authenticity rather than the opposite.

I cannot judge the authenticity or non-authenticity of the extraordinarily important letter, predating the deportations, from the Young Turk Committee to its representative in Adana, Cemal Bey, on 18 February

1915 (p. 96 of the book), or the other letters from the Young Turk Committee; nor do I see any way of checking their authenticity.

I urge you to ask Sister Beatrice for her comments. She often had direct dealings with the Deportation Commissar. She knows Eyub Bey personally. I cannot say whether she also knows Naim Bey or Abdul Nuri Bey. In any event, her comments would be valuable. Consul Hoffmann, too, currently in the passport division of the Foreign Office, Behrenstr. 21, may be able to give a considered opinion.

Just a few more particulars on the author's attacks on Germany. The photograph on the back of page 56, "God punish England," shows the crew of the cruiser "Emden" at a garden party given to honor the Germans of Aleppo, wearing Arab headscarves, which they were forced to wear in Arabia to protect themselves from the heat after the loss of their own sailors' garb. Also, the Vali of Aleppo presented officers, like the crew, new headscarves at the reception, as well as coats in some cases, which they have on in this photo. It is understandable that members of the German navy, who had suffered so much from the English, would choose a sign with the words "God punish England" to be photographed with. The author places the photograph in an entirely wrong context. Mücke passed through Aleppo in May 1915. This had nothing to do with propaganda among the Arabs inciting war on the English. In fact, the Emden crew was not well disposed towards the Arabs. After all, they had to fight the Arabs and lost three men, as is retold in Mücke's Ayesha. I do not know enough about the propaganda that the author blames on Mrs. Koch. I did not see the Arab brochure calling for holy war, a page from which is photographed by Andonian on page 60. It is possible that this was ineptitude on the German part, and it is also possible that a brochure meant only for North Africa accidentally found its way to Aleppo.

I sincerely thank you for your report on the status of the file publication.

W. Rössler

Translated by Belinda Cooper

Notes

1. You do not understand what we want. We want an Armenia without Armenians.
2. Transitory as his memory grows.

Appendix E: Memorandum to the Lawyers of Soghomon Tehlirian

10 June 1921
Berlin

The documents reproduced in my book, *Documents officiels concernant les massacres arméniens* (Paris, 1920), were in the possession of Naim Bey, who had been the Secretary of the Sub-Directorate for Deportees in Aleppo. The Sub-Directorate—whose central leadership was located in Constantinople, and which had as director-general a young member of the Committee of Union and Progress by the name of Shukri Bey—was responsible for carrying out all of the orders and measures concerning the Armenian deportees, as Aleppo was the central point from which these deportees were led toward the deserts of Syria and Mesopotamia.

Naim Bey was a thoroughly decent, innocuous man, and the Armenians in Aleppo and in other places—even during the war—saw proof countless times of his goodwill and kindness toward them and toward their deported compatriots.

There is no doubt that these documents were removed from the files of the Sub-Directorate for Deportees in Aleppo, since the Prefect (Vali) of Aleppo—after having had deciphered the encoded orders he had received from the Minister of the Interior (Talat Pasha) about the Armenians—relayed the deciphered texts with a note signed and dated in his writing to the Sub-Directorate for Deportees, which was obliged to carry them out and of which Naim Bey was the secretary.

© The Author(s) 2018   243
T. Akçam, *Killing Orders*, Palgrave Studies in the History of Genocide,
https://doi.org/10.1007/978-3-319-69787-1_10

When Naim Bey agreed to give us these documents, the Armenian National Union of Aleppo—which was an official institution—had the writing and signature from the note on the documents in question evaluated. The evaluation lasted an entire week. We had in front of us other documents signed and annotated by the Prefect Moustapha Abdulhalik Bey and we carefully compared them down to the smallest details. In the end, and without any objection, the notes on these documents were identified as the very writing and signature of the Prefect Mustapha Abdulhalik Bey, which did not leave any doubt as to the authenticity of the documents.

After being entirely convinced of the authenticity of these documents—and, moreover, considering that I was quite well-informed about the massacres and about the atrocities that were committed, since I myself had lived two consecutive years in these horrific circumstances—the National Union tasked me with choosing among the documents in Naim Bey's possession those which could establish responsibility for the Armenian massacres in an unmistakable way.

In examining these documents, I saw that almost all of the orders that were to be carried out—either mass massacres or deportations with the goal of annihilation or the killing of small children—came from Talaat Pasha, the Minister of the Interior, later the Grand Vizier. He was the one who incited and reprimanded officials in order to do away with the Armenian people as quickly as possible by annihilating them completely, without even sparing the very young or the very old. He told them, in particular, that this annihilation was settled, that it must be done at any cost and as quickly as possible, without the fear of punishment or repercussions of any kind. This criminal endeavor was declared by Talaat Pasha to be the greatest of patriotic obligations that an official could fulfill.

From these documents, I chose the most important, and I assure you that before I had the written orders before me, I had already seen them carried out or learned that they had been carried out during the infernal period between 1915 and 1916.

In the end, I was tasked by the Armenian National Union of Aleppo to transport these documents to Europe and give them to the Armenian National Delegation around the time of the Peace Conference, as is stated in the laissez-passer—issued by the French military authorities in Aleppo—that I used as a passport.

I completed this mission by including with the documents that Naim Bey had supplied some comments and clarifications in a detailed report that has since been published in London in English, in Paris in French, and in Boston in Armenian.

Aram Andonian

Translated by Jennifer Manoukian

AFTERWORD

There is a Turkish expression that says, "Truths have a bad habit of coming to light eventually" (*Gerçeklerin bir gün açığa çıkmak gibi kötü huyu vardır*). Over the decades, successive Turkish Governments attempted to hide or erase entirely the annihilation of the Armenian people as a historical truth. A variety of strategies has been devised and implemented for this purpose. The central one of these has been the attempt to present an alternative set of "facts" that, arranged accordingly, attempt to present a different reality, namely, that the whole purpose of deportation was to peacefully remove the Armenian population from the war zones and relocate them, rather than their wholesale extermination. Other branches of this strategy have been the efforts to destroy all documentation showing that the Armenians were annihilated as the result of a conscious plan by the Unionist government and the simultaneous attempt to discredit any evidence that has survived.

One of the principal results of this ongoing campaign has been to perpetuate the trauma of Armenian survivors. As if it were not enough that their ancestors were murdered; even those who survived and their descendants are unable to get some closure for their grief and loss, since the crimes that were committed are not even fully acknowledged as such. Instead, they have subsequently found themselves facing the uphill task of "proving" that their people had been murdered; any account they might give is automatically suspect as "a biased and unreliable source" merely since it came from an Armenian.

© The Author(s) 2018   247
T. Akçam, *Killing Orders*, Palgrave Studies in the History of Genocide,
https://doi.org/10.1007/978-3-319-69787-1

There is hope, however. We see that, despite the coordinated attempts of Turkey to silence this history, in recent decades serious scholarly works have successfully shattered the panes of the denialism's glass pavilion and established the annihilation of the Ottoman Armenians as an indisputable historical truth. Nevertheless, the classic Turkish denialism has continued to assert its views on the basis of two important claims, namely, that "There are no original documents that indicate that there was a planned annihilation of Armenians; if they exist, then produce them!" and rejecting existing documentation that would show precisely this as being forgeries produced by the Armenians.

One of the most important pieces of physical evidence manifesting the genocide is a set of documents known as the "Talat Pasha telegrams" and the memoirs of Naim Efendi. The former are Ottoman government telegrams from Talat Pasha ordering or otherwise indicating government plans for the annihilation of the Armenian population. These cables were sold by the Ottoman official Naim Efendi, who worked in the Aleppo Deportation Office, which was responsible for carrying out the orders. But in addition to the documents themselves, Naim also wrote explanatory notes and his recollections of the period dealing with the events. Until recently, this work and the accompanying documents were largely dismissed by both scholarly and popular circles as "unreliable" and, most likely, forged. This rejection was based on the following logic: (1) It was unlikely that there was an individual by the name of Naim Efendi; (2) a non-existent person cannot publish his memoirs; therefore: (3) the cables attributed to Talat Pasha are forgeries. According to the authors Orel and Yuca, the entire work—memoirs, cables, and annotations—are simply a fabrication by the Armenian journalist Aram Andonian.

Until recently, it has been quite difficult to offer a compelling factual argument disputing these three claims. First of all, it had not been possible to present an original Ottoman document confirming the existence of an Ottoman bureaucrat by the name of Naim Efendi. Second, there was not much evidence to corroborate the information Naim offered or any documentary proof of their authenticity, due to the often spotty or incomplete nature of the materials in the Ottoman archives. Third, the locations of the original memoirs of Naim Efendi and the original cables of Talat Pasha were unknown and they were presumed lost.

Thus, the subject was difficult to discuss and, in the absence of compelling evidence to the contrary, the claim of forgery were impossible to refute. Serious scholars of the genocide have thus largely preferred to avoid using or citing either Andonian's published versions of either Naim Efendi's memoirs or the Talat Pasha telegrams, often avoiding the topic altogether. With this study, the long period of silence and avoidance has now come to an end. As we have shown, there was indeed an Ottoman bureaucrat by the name of Naim Efendi; there are authentic memoirs authored by him. Based on corroborating Ottoman documents that have since been discovered, it is easy to demonstrate that the content of the memoirs, the descriptions and claims that are found therein are accurate.

The same is true for Talat Pasha's telegrams; all of the main claims used by denialist historiography to argue the inauthentic nature of telegrams (in particular their discussion of usage of lined papers, Ottoman wartime encryption methods and the signatures on the documents) are simply wrong and the product of arguments that, upon closer inspection, do not hold water. For example, usage of lined papers and the two-digit encryption method used in the telegrams provided by Naim Efendi is not proof of their fabricated nature, but just the opposite: it is a compelling argument for their authenticity, since these papers and method were the methods used by the directors of the Deportation Office where Naim was working.

The truth is very simple: the original coded telegrams that Naim handed over to Andonian are authentic. If, after this, either the Turkish government or its denialist allies wish to claim that these documents are forgeries, they should publish the encryption notebooks containing these keys and prove it on the basis of these notebooks. These notebooks exist, and those with the authority and ability to make them public are the same ones claiming the documents to be false. In fact, it is our assertion and challenge to the Turkish government that the reason for *not* publishing these notebooks is that they confirm the authenticity of these cables. The burden of proof now rests with them.

This work has not only shown that Talat's telegrams are original but also validated the stories of Armenian Genocide survivors that have been passed down for generations, as well as the reports by non-Armenian eyewitnesses. Likewise, the historical truths uncovered by hundreds of academic works on the subject have also been reconfirmed: during the First World War, the Unionist government in the Ottoman Empire pursued a conscious and deliberate policy of annihilation against its Armenian population. "Truths have a bad habit of coming to light eventually."

BIBLIOGRAPHY

ARCHIVAL COLLECTIONS

Bibliothèque Nubar, Fonds Andonian, Matériaux pour l'histoire du génocide: "Déportations et massacres: Zohrab, Vartkès et divers."

BOA.A.}d Ministry Registries (*Sadaret Defteri*).

BOA.BEO. Grand Vezier's Chancery Office (*Babıali Evrak Odası Evrakı*).

BOA.DH.EUM. Interior Ministry Public Security Directorate (*Dahiliye Nezareti Emniyet-i Umumiye Müdürlüğü*).

BOA.DH.EUM. 2. Şube: Second Department of Public Security of the Interior Ministry (*Dahiliye Nezareti Emniyet-i Umumiye İkinci Şube*).

BOA.DH.EUM.MH. (*Dahiliye Nezareti Emniyeti Umumiye Memurin Kalem Evrakı*).

BOA.DH.EUM.LVZ. (*Dahiliye Nezareti Emniyeti Umumiye Levazım Kalemi*).

BOA.DH.EUM.VRK. (*Dahiliye Nezareti Emniyeti Umumiye Evrak Odası Kalemi Evrakı*).

BOA.DH.KMS. (*Dahiliye Nezareti Dahiliye Kalemi Mahsus Evrakı*).

BOA.DH.ŞFR. Cipher Office of the Interior Ministry (*Dahiliye Nezareti Şifre Kalemi*).

BOA.İ.MMS. Directorate of Personnel and Service Registers (*İrada Meclisi Mahsus*).

BOA. MF.MKT. (*Maarif Nezareti Mektubi Kalemi*).

BOA.ŞD. (*Şuray-ı Devlet Evrakı*).

DE/PA-AA German Foreign Ministry Political Archive (*Politisches Archiv des Auswärtigen Amts*).

Krikor Guerguerian Archive.

© The Author(s) 2018
T. Akçam, *Killing Orders*, Palgrave Studies in the History of Genocide,
https://doi.org/10.1007/978-3-319-69787-1

PUBLICATIONS CITED

Alemdar.

"Les explications de Bernard Lewis." *Le Monde* (January 1, 1994).

Joghovurti Tzayn.

Takvim-i Vekayi.

Şurayı Ümmet.

Vakit gazetesi.

Yeni Gazete.

"TBMM Başkani Bülent Arinç, Hazirladiği Kitapla Sözde Ermeni Soykirimi İddialarini Çürüten Amerikali Profesör Lewy'i Makaminda Kabul Etti." Türkiye Büyük Millet Meclisi (November 22, 2005). https://www.tbmm.gov.tr/develop/owa/tbmm_basin_aciklamalari_sd.aciklama?p1=30684

Aghazaryan, M. *Aksoragani Husher* [Memories of the deportations]. Adana: Hay Tzayn Matbaası, 1919.

Akçam, Taner. *İnsan Hakları ve Ermeni Sorunu* [Human Rights and the Armenian Question]. Ankara: İmge Yayınevi, 1999.

———. "The Relationship between Historians and Archival Records: A Critique of Single Source Scholarship on the Armenian Genocide." *Journal of the Society for Armenian Studies,* 19, no. 2 (2010): 43–92.

———. *A Shameful Act: The Armenian Genocide and the Question of Turkish Responsibility.* New York: Metropolitan Books, 2006.

———. *Türk Ulusal Kimliği ve Ermeni Sorunu.* Istanbul: İletişim Yayınları, 1992.

———. *The Young Turks' Crime Against Humanity.* Princeton, NJ: Princeton University Press, 2012.

Akçam, Taner, and Umit Kurt. *Spirit of the Laws: The Plunder of Wealth in the Armenian Genocide.* Translated by Aram Arkun. New York: Berghahn Books, 2015.

Akdağ, Ömer. "Millî Mücadele Şahsiyetlerinden Yusuf Kemal Bey (TENGİRŞENK)," *Atatürk Araştırma Merkezi Dergisi,* XIV, no. 40 (March 1998). http://www.atam.gov.tr/dergi/sayi-40/milli-mucadele-sahsiyetlerinden-yusuf-kemal-bey-tengirsenk

Altınay, Ahmet Refik. *İki Komite İki Kıtal.* Istanbul: Bedir Yayınları, 1999.

Andonian, Aram. *Documents officiels concernant les massacres Arméniens.* Paris: Imprimerie H. Turabian, 1920a.

———. *Medz Vojirĕ* [The great crime]. Boston: Bahag Printing House, 1921.

———. *The Memoirs of Naim Bey, Turkish Official Documents relating to the Deportations and Massacres of Armenians,* compiled by Aram Andonian with an introduction by Viscount Gladstone. London: Hodder and Stoughton, 1920b.

Arendt, Hannah. *Between Past and Future: Eight Exercises in Political Thought.* New York: Penguin Books, 2006.

Ataöv, Türkkaya. *Talat Paşa'ya atfedilen Andonian "Belgeleri" Sahtedir.* Ankara: Siyasal Bilgiler Fakültesi Yayını, 1984.

Balakian, Grigoris. *Armenian Golgotha: A Memoir of the Armenian Genocide, 1915–1918.* Translated by Peter Balakian with Aris Sevag. New York: Alfred A. Knopf, 2009.

Bardakçı, Murat. *Talat Paşa'nın Evrakı Metrukesi.* Istanbul: Everest, 2008.

Baruch, Bernard. *Baruch: The Public Years.* New York: Holt, Rinehart and Winston, 1960.

Boyajian, Dickran H. *Armenia: The Case for a Forgotten Genocide.* Westwood, NJ: Educational Book Crafters, 1972.

Cengiz, Erdoğan, ed. *Ermeni Komitelerinin Âmâl ve Harekât-ı İhtilâliyesi; İlân-ı Meşrutiyetten Evvel ve Sonra.* Ankara: Başbakanlık Basımevi 1983.

Dadrian, Vahakn N. "The Naim-Andonian Documents on the World War I Destruction of Ottoman Armenians: The Anatomy of a Genocide." *International Journal for Middle East Studies* 18, no. 3 (1986): 311–360.

Dadrian, Vahakn N. and Taner Akçam. *Judgment at Istanbul: The Armenian Genocide Trials.* New York and Oxford: Berghahn Books, 2011.

Erden, Ali Fuat. *Birinci Dünya Savaşı'nda Suriye Hatıraları.* Istanbul: TİŞ Bankası Kültür Yayınları, 2006.

Gauin, Maxime. "Aram Andonian's 'Memoirs of Naim Bey' and the Contemporary Attempts to Defend their "Authenticity." *Review of Armenian Studies* 23 (2011): 233–293.

Genelkurmay Başkanlığı. *Arşiv Belgeleriyle Ermeni Faaliyetleri,1914–1918, Vol. 1.* Ankara: Genelkurmay Basımevi, 2005; Vol. VII, 2007.

Gerçek, Burçin. *Akıntıya Karşı: Ermeni Soykırımında Emirlere karşı Gelenler, Kurtaranlar, Direnenler.* Istanbul: İletişim, 2016.

Günday, A. Faik Hurşit. *Hayat ve Hatıralarım,* Volume 1. Istanbul: Çelikcilt Matbaası, 1960.

Gunter, Michael M. "Review of *The Armenian Genocide in Perspective* by Richard Hovannisian; *Britain and the Armenian Question 1915–1923* by Akaby Nassibian." *International Journal of Middle East Studies,* 21, no. 3 (August 1989): 419–422.

———. "Review of *The Armenian Massacres in Ottoman Turkey: A Disputed Genocide* by Guenter Lewy; *Turkey's Kurds: A Theoretical Analysis of the PKK and Abdullah Ocalan* by Ali Kemal Ozcan." *International Journal of Middle East Studies,* 38, no. 4 (2006): 598–601.

Gürün, Kamuran. *The Armenian File: The Myth of Innocence Exposed.* Nicosia, Cyprus: K. Rustem & Brother, 1985.

———. *Ermeni Dosyası.* Ankara: Türk Tarih Kurumu Basımevi, 1983.

Hofmann, Tessa, ed. *Der Völkermord an den Armeniern vor Gericht, Der Prozess Talaat Pascha.* Göttingen: Gesellschaft für bedrohte Völker, 1980.

İzrail, Nesim Ovadya. *1915 Bir Ölüm Yolculuğu Krikor Zohrab.* Istanbul: Pencere Yayınları, 2013.

Kaiser, Hilmar. *At the Crossroads of Der Zor: Death, Survival, and Humanitarian Resistance in Aleppo, 1915–1917.* Princeton and London: Gomidas Institute, 2002.

———. "The Baghdad Railway and the Armenian Genocide, 1915–1916: A Case Study in German Resistance and Complicity." In *Remembrance and Denial: The Case of the Armenian Genocide*, edited by Richard G. Hovannisian, 67–112. Detroit: Wayne State University Press, 1999.

———. *The Extermination of Armenians in the Diarbekir Region*. Istanbul: Bilgi University Press, 2014.

Kasapyan, Apraham. *Kaç Kişisiniz Boğos Efendi, Bir Ermeninin Hatıra Defteri*. Istanbul: Aras Yayıncılık, 2015.

Kazarian, Haigazn K. "The Murder of 6 Armenian Members of the Ottoman Parliament." *Armenian Review* 22 (Winter 1970): 26–33.

Kévorkian, Raymond. *The Armenian Genocide: A Complete History*. London and New York: I.B. Tauris, 2011a.

———. "L'extermination des déportés Arméniens ottomans dans les camps de concentration de Syrie-Mésopotamie, La deuxième phase du génocide (1915–1916)." *Revue d'Histoire Arménienne Contemporaine*, 2 (1996–1998): 1–336. http://www.imprescriptible.fr/rhac/tome2/

———. *Soykırımın İkinci Safhası, Sürgüne Gönderilen Osmanlı Ermenilerinin Suriye-Mezopotamya Toplama Kamplarında İmha Edilmeleri*. Istanbul: Belge Yayınları, 2011b.

Kieser, Hans Lukas. *A Question for Belonging: Anatolia Beyond Empire and Nation (19th–21st Centuries)*. Istanbul: ISIS Press, 2007.

Krieger, E. "Aram Andoniani Hradaragadz Turk Bashdonagan Vaverakreru Vaveraganutyun" [The Truth About the Official Turkish [sic] Documents published by Aram Andonian], Zartonk Gazetesi (publ.), *1915–1965 Hushamadyan Medz Yegherni* [Album of the Great Disaster]. Beirut: Atlas, 1965.

Kuyumjian, Rita Soulahian, ed. *Exile, Trauma and Death: On the Road to Chankiri with Komitas Vartabed*. London: Gomidas Institute and Tekeyan Cultural Association, 2010a.

———, ed. *The Survivor: Biography of Aram Andonian*. London: Gomidas Institute, 2010b.

Lewis, Bernard. *From Babel to Dragomans: Interpreting the Middle East*. New York: Oxford University Press, 2004.

Lewy, Guenter. *The Armenian Massacres in Ottoman Turkey: A Disputed Genocide*. Salt Lake City: University of Utah Press, 2005.

Maksudyan, Nazan. *Orphans and Destitute Children in the Late Ottoman Empire*. Syracuse: Syracuse University Press, 2014.

Mamigonian, Marc. "Academic Denial of the Armenian Genocide in American Scholarship: Denialism as a Manufactured Controversy." *Genocide Studies International* 9, no. 1 (2015): 61–82.

Mango, Andrew. "Turks and Kurds." *Middle Eastern Studies* 30, no. 4 (1994): 975–997.

Menteşe, Halil. *Osmanlı Mebusan Meclisi Reisi Halil Menteşe'nin Anıları.* Istanbul: Hürriyet Vakfı Yayınları, 1986.

Morgenthau, Henry. *Ambassador Morgenthau's Story.* Garden City, New York: Doubleday, Page & Co., 1918.

Mouradian, Khatchig. "Genocide and Humanitarian Resistance in Ottoman Syria, 1915–1917." PhD diss., Clark University, 2016.

Nakkashian, Avedis. *A Man Who Found a Country.* New York: Thomas Y. Crowell Company, 1940. http://avedis.telf.com/

———. *Ayashi Pandu.* Boston: Hairenik, 1925.

———. *Zuart Patmutiwnner.* New York: n.p., 1926.

Nichanian, Marc. "The Truth of the Facts: About the New Revisionism." In *Remembrance and Denial: The Case of the Armenian Genocide,* edited by Richard G. Hovannisian, 249–270. Detroit, MI: Wayne State University Press, 1999.

Orel, Şinasi ve Süreyya Yuca. *Ermenilerce Talat Paşa'ya Atfedilen Telgrafların Gerçek Yüzü.* Ankara: Türk Tarih Kurumu, 1983.

———. *The Talat Pasha Telegrams, Historical Fact or Armenian Fiction?* Nicosia: K. Rustem & Brother, 1986.

Sarafian, Ara, ed. *United States Official Records on the Armenian Genocide 1915–1917.* London: Gomidas Institute, 2004.

———, ed. "What Happened on 24 April 1915?" *The Ayash Prisoners* (April 22, 2013). http://www.gomidas.org/submissions/show/5

Sarınay, Yusuf. "What Happened on April 24, 1915, the Circular of April 24, 1915 and the Arrest of Armenian Committee Members in Istanbul." *International Journal of Turkish Studies,* 14, nos. 1&2 (Fall 2008): 75–101.

Shemmassian, Vahram L. "Humanitarian Intervention by the Armenian Prelacy of Aleppo during the First Months of the Genocide." *Journal of the Society for Armenian Studies* 22 (2013): 127–153.

———. "The Reclamation of Captive Armenian Genocide Survivors in Syria and Lebanon at the End of World War I." *Journal of the Society for Armenian Studies* 15 (2006): 113–140.

Shirinian, George N. "Turks Who Saved Armenians: Righteous Muslims During the Armenian Genocide." *Genocide Studies International* 9, no. 2 (2015): 208–227.

Stone, Norman. "There Is No Armenian Genocide." *The Journal of Turkish Weekly* (October 21, 2006). http://historynewsnetwork.org/article/31085

Toynbee, Arnold and James Bryce. The Treatment of Armenians in the Ottoman Empire, Documents presented to Viscount Grey of Fallodon, Secretary of State for Foreign Affairs *by Viscount Bryce.* Uncensored edition. Princeton and London: Gomidas Institute, 2005.

Trouillot, Michel-Rolph. *Silencing the Past: Power and the Production of History.* Boston: Beacon Press, 1995.

Tunaya, Tarık Zafer. *Türkiye'de Siyasal Partiler Cilt 2, Mütareke Dönemi, 1918–1922.* İstanbul: İletişim, 2015.

Yakupoğlu, Cevdet. "Bir Sürgün Kahramanı Abdülahad Nuri Bey: Hayatı, Eserleri ve Selçuklu-Beylikler Tarihi Üzerine Çalışmaları." *Ankara Üniversitesi Osmanlı Tarihi Araştırma ve Uygulama Merkezi Dergisi* 21 (2007): 169–189.

Yıldız, Gültekin. "Osmanlı Evrakını Önce Yaktılar sonra Depolara Kapattılar." *Derin Tarih* (June 2014): 112–119.

Zürcher, Erik-Jan. *Turkey: A Modern History.* London: I. B. Tauris, 2004.

Index[1]

[1] Note: Page numbers followed by 'n' denote notes.

© The Author(s) 2018
T. Akçam, *Killing Orders*, Palgrave Studies in the History of Genocide,
https://doi.org/10.1007/978-3-319-69787-1

257